MURDER NEVER DIES

CRIME AND CORRUPTION IN THE FRIENDLY CITY

George T. Sidiropolis

Headline Books, Inc.
Terra Alta, WV

Murder Never Dies:
Crime and Corruption in The Friendly City

by George T. Sidiropolis

To order additional copies of this book or for book publishing information, or to contact the author:

Headline Books, Inc.
P.O. Box 52
Terra Alta, WV 26764
www.headlinebooks.com

Tel: 800-570-5951
Email: mybook@headlinebooks.com

ISBN 13: 978-1-88-265863-3

Library of Congress Control Number: 2016939185

PRINTED IN THE UNITED STATES OF AMERICA

I dedicate this work to you, Mom. A lady I will forever cherish, whose peerless love and dedication gave me life which I have not seen again. A special thanks to all those who helped with the exhaustive research in writing this book. My gratitude to the anonymous and exceptional few who shared their personal knowledge and experience that provided me the unique factual narrative that helped produce this extraordinary revelation. Thanks also to my sons, George and David for their tolerance and valued assistance.

"Anyone interested in true crime, American history, or just plain good writing will enjoy Murder Never Dies, a fascinating story presented by the man best qualified to tell it."

—**Jeff Guinn**, New York Times bestselling author of *Manson and Go Down Together: The True Untold Story of Bonnie and Clyde*

"An excellent account that deserves praise. A fascinating expose and engrossing story."

—**William Gaston Caperton III**, Governor of the state of West Virginia, Fellow at Harvard University and President and CEO of the College Board

"This captivating historical work takes the reader back in time to the days when organized crime ruled Wheeling West Virginia. A book you absolutely cannot put down."

—**David Jividen**, Former Assistant U.S. Attorney for the Northern District of West Virginia. Special Federal Prosecutor in both the Western District of Pennsylvania and the Southern District of Ohio, American Board of Criminal Lawyers

INTRODUCTION

This story is intended to disclose the bitter-sweet legend of a wholesome city, surviving amid unbridled corruption and a tolerance for vice and organized crime.

The ruling class of Wheeling, West Virginia, some who enabled and valued this chicanery, often remained willing participants in a bible challenging bacchanalian exercise, the likes of which would have drawn the envy of Roman Emperors.

At the turn of the twentieth century, the United States was producing thirty percent of the world's goods. Wheeling was cited as one of 832 trading centers in the United States and a city that would be involved in one-half of the nation's business. It had one thousand nine-hundred and ninety-two wholesale and retail establishments within its borders and was recognized as the first wholesale distribution point west of the Allegheny Mountains. (Wheeling Workshop of the Central West, dated 1930) The city of Wheeling was a target of opportunity. Within this distinguished metropolis, a wanton sub-culture would soon emerge from beneath the veneer of its Victorian respectability.

In this book I will tell the uncovered story of a remarkable city, inhabited by the best of the best and the worst of the worst; a city that would become nationally recognized as a bread basket of crime and political corruption. Its genesis emerges soon after the arrival of one of the lead characters, an early Greek immigrant who quickly learns and exploits the weakness of democracy and the power of political corruption.

The intrigue begins with the incorrigible, fourteen year old Basil Kokoliades, aka William G. "Big Bill" Lias, embarking on his criminal career, mounted atop a horse-drawn bread wagon, selling hidden pints of his uncle's moonshine. Before the end of his life, he would become a multi-state real estate magnate, the owner of one of the most modern and extravagant racetracks in the country and amass millions from his bootlegging, lottery numbers, horse bookmaking, casino, slot machine and vending operations.

During his meteoric rise to power, this 350 pound anomaly's appetite was accommodated by federal judges, governors, congressmen, a United States Senator and the President of the United States.

This unremitting crime saga ends nearly eighty years later with the demise of Lias' rivaled successor, a contemporary paraplegic monster with a near genius I.Q., whose life as a hoodlum begins with cracking local supermarket safes. Paul Nathaniel Hankish rose to prominence as a nationally recognized organized crime figure, commanding a multi-state, million dollar bookmaking operation and importing kilos of the purest cocaine aboard a submarine from South America.

As I introduce the initial criminal trailblazer, I will offer a foreshadowing of the unrivaled union of extraordinary people in this new frontier. They were an amalgam of good and decent people that made this region a gospel of success. They endured, despite suffering tyranny and heart breaking impediments. It is to these great men and women and to a very special one among them, my blessed Mother, Josephine, to whom I dedicate this book.

ONE

UNCOMMON CRIMINALS

This odyssey will portray the engrossing division of participants from a rich and diverse contributing culture. It was beneath this environment where the ground breaking, turn of the twentieth century immigrant William G. Lias created his initial prey base and mastered his criminal empire. Nearly one half century later came the regrettable surrender of his villainous throne to a modern day, nationally recognized organized crime figure. From the anonymous to the anointed, the contempt for Lias' despised heir apparent, Paul Nathaniel Hankish, was immediate and unrelenting.

The media and law enforcement quickly became aware, that unlike his predecessor, Paul Hankish had a committed affiliation with and was under the control of Mafia leaders from across the country. Wheeling officials and the media feared powerful, out of state criminal influence would take the city to an unbearable level of corruption. Although Lias was well connected to the Cleveland and Detroit Mafia during his rule, he oversaw his interest and territory without outside interference. Lias' self-directing style may best be described as a cross between Machiavelli and the murderous Joseph Stalin. His first choice was to follow Machiavelli's doctrine "benefits should be conferred gradually, and in that way they will taste better." Lias understood that his progressive benevolence would also last longer. He was capable of employing judicious bribery and ingenious political strategy to get most of what he needed, and if that didn't work, he was prone to psychopathic violence.

An example of the praise and the hypocritical adulation that prevailed for Lias came from a well-respected Northern District Federal Judge who offered the following testimony during an FBI interview: "In my opinion, Lias is a better citizen than fifty percent of Wheeling's sanctimonious and sanctified citizens who are cheaters and dishonest in their shady dealings with their fellow man. I have never known Lias to do a dishonest thing" (FBI file-74-401-10/29/47). He cited Lias' criminal trial for violation of the income tax laws for which he was acquitted and stated the decision of the jury was a just one, and if under the evidence and the facts, it would have gone otherwise, he would have set the conviction aside.

He further stated: "While Lias was in the federal penitentiary, he asked the authorities there to permit him to go back to Wheeling under guard in order to file a proper income tax return and that when this was refused, he asked the authorities to bring his books to him in the penitentiary in order that he could make a correct return. My sincere and honest convictions are that Lias in the overall was not doing anything more or less than is allowed by civil authorities who are engaged in the same type of business." Bill Lias was a bold and ambitious criminal with enough charisma and cash to endear himself to everyone from the beat cop to a United States Senator. He was somewhat sophisticated and a peculiarly celebrated and glorified gangster who for nearly one-half of a century, with the exception of his brief periods of incarceration, ruled his criminal empire with impunity. He was, nevertheless, during the overwhelming majority of time haunted by the United States Immigration Service, Federal Bureau of Investigation and the Internal Revenue Service. He was also the object of U.S. Senate and Congressional Investigative hearings and the fervor of syndicated columnists and national newspapers and magazines, including Coronet, Life and Time.

During the meridian of his reign, while resting comfortably in his modest East Wheeling residence, William G. "Big Bill" Lias ranked as one of the richest criminals in the world. Although the Internal Revenue Service conservatively estimated Lias' net worth at $20 million dollars in 1947, it became known it was nearer $30 million. In today's dollars his wealth would have been $327,644 651.16. This lawless fortune was derived from his bootlegging and numbers writing. He had not yet begun his book making, slot machine or vending operations and a variety of other profitable gambling activities including, of course, Zeller's Steakhouse & Casino and Wheeling Downs Racetrack. William G. "Big Bill" Lias had not yet reached the pinnacle of his ambition which would deliver him immense wealth unmatched by major crime figures in the United States.

Although Lias and his ultimate successor were accomplished vice-lords, they distinguished themselves in many ways. Lias, of course, was highly proficient in acquiring the trust and almost blind support of culpable public officials. He also successfully solicited the affection of his prey. He did all he could to not be recognized as a gangster. For the most part, people liked him and, at the very worst, perceived him more as a gambler who neglected to pay his income tax. Mr. Hankish, unlike Lias, was unsociable and recognized as a public threat—an enigmatic, dangerous organized crime figure.

During the accumulating of Lias' crime-laden wealth, amassing during the Great Depression and years following, most inhabitants in the region were suffering in a culture of poverty, and few experienced the luxury of even marginal comfort. The average annual income of an American family in 1932 was less than $1000. Twenty-five percent of families had annual income of less than $600. One half of the population could not afford milk at 14 cents a quart or a loaf of bread selling for 9 cents. President Herbert Hoover declared, "Nobody is actually starving. The Hobos are better fed than they have ever been." There were so many accounts of people starving in New York that the West African Nation of Cameroon sent $3.76 in relief. Nevertheless, the number of dispossessed residents of the Ohio

Valley remained tolerant, exhibiting unshakable optimism. They looked upon Lias more as a congenial phenomenon rather than a threatening criminal.

It was, for millions, a cruel time in America. Any effort to treat the pain of the disadvantaged was either out of reach, unaffordable or denied. Poverty in America was not then measured by statistical calibration, but the reality of whether or not you had food on the table. In his book, *The Other America*, Michael Harrington wrote about the 1930s: "There was no need then to write books about unemployment and poverty. That was the decisive social experience of the entire society." Those who were employed and capable of caring for their families felt rich. Homogenous ethnic neighborhoods were better equipped to cope with the consequences of the humiliation of grinding indigence. For those blessed with hope and understanding, neither cultural nor economic assimilation stayed out of reach. The mistreated were oblivious to derogation and understood the need and means to overcome bigotry, class distinction and intolerance. Determination and moral courage prepared them for struggle and encouraged them to succeed among the people they loved and the land they cherished. Their desire was only to be good Americans.

TWO

MURDER NEVER DIES

If you wanted to meet up with any of the "Old Gang" who were followers or loyalists of the Lias or Hankish factions, you could visit certain bars, bookmakers, pool halls or the racetrack. One early Saturday, during an afternoon matinee card at Wheeling Downs, I ran into Paul Hankish's former driver, a WWII decorated veteran. When Jimmy was discharged from the service, he chose to enlist with the underworld and developed a working relationship with both Lias and Hankish, but ended up wisely choosing sides with Hankish. His wife worked as Hankish's housekeeper. We sat down together, and I ordered drinks and a couple of Club Sandwiches. We exchanged stories and opinions for about five or six races. During the latter part of our conversation, I brought up the 30 year old murder of a Benwood-High Street girl named Joyce Ralbusky. The Ohio Valley General Hospital Pathologists who performed the autopsy confirmed that Ms. Ralbusky, "… [d]ied from a severe blow to the head." Amazingly, the Coroner announced there would be no inquest into the slaying. The Autopsy Report claimed no evidence of rape. The Newspaper, however, disclosed that the report showed evidence of Ms. Ralbusky putting up a fight before she died, and in addition to the laceration of her skull, there was a one inch by three inch abrasion on the upper part of her thigh, along with bruises to her right leg and both shins.

Accused murderer, Walter V. Rogalski went to trial on July 12, 1953 for the slaying of, quoting the newspaper description: "A beautiful 20 year old Stenographer whose semi-nude body was found crumpled in a lifeless heap on the river bank." Ohio County Judge D.A. McKee ruled during pre-trial that the search warrant issued to the city police to search the garage and automobile of alleged murderer Rogalski was invalid because municipal police did not have the authority to serve such a warrant. That meant that the black onyx ring belonging to Ms. Ralbusky found in Rogalski's car could not be submitted as evidence in the murder trial. Also found during the search of Rogalski's car was a button from the murdered woman's dress and her missing ear ring.

On July 19, 1953 Walter Rogalski walked out of the Ohio County Courthouse a free man. A 12 man jury deliberated 65 minutes to find him not guilty. Like the string of Wheeling homicides that preceded this slaying, Joyce Ann Rabulsky's murder remains unsolved.

I commented to Jimmy, "Over the years, I've probably asked a hundred people who murdered Joyce Ralbusky and got 50 different answers. Who do you think killed her?" Jimmy kept his head lowered, munching on the remaining portion of his toasted Club sandwich. He then slowly raised his head, staring at the ceiling while swallowing his last bite and said, "Georgie, I know you're stand-up, and I'm going to tell you who killed that pretty young girl, but remember, 'A murder never dies', so you didn't hear it from me." He leaned forward, and whispered the murderer's name in my ear..

THREE

Garden In The Rain

It's a routine Saturday morning in the Avellino extended family household. Josephine Avellino Gianopolis is devoted to ironing a bundle of freshly laundered clothing. Her precocious ten-year-old son Tommy has his ear pinned to his Hopalong Cassidy radio, only a short distance from the ironing board. He lowers the volume and shouts to his mom, "Hey Mom, what's a Jew?"

Josephine raises her head. Puzzled, she responds, "Honey, what on earth would make you ask me that?" "Well Mom," he says, "I heard you and Aunt Lizzie talking about Jews that lived out the pike, and when you were young, you did their house-cleaning, and they were so rich, they paid you to iron their bed sheets." Sympathetic to Tommy's naiveté, she patiently explains the toils of the Great Depression. "We were so poor, we thought people who had food in their refrigerator were rich. The Jewish family we worked for were very good to us. They lived in a beautiful neighborhood in Wheeling that people called 'out the pike.' They were very nice to me and Aunt Lizzie."

Tommy's curiosity and compulsive interest did not subside. In fact it rose, and he inquired, "Mommy, how can I become a Jew?" Head down and ironing a crease she admonishes, "Tommy, for now you'll have enough trouble just trying to be a good Greek-Italian Catholic."

For the next hour, Tommy continues to deliberate his path to greatness. He is sure his idea is precedent making. He is familiar with a nearby general clothing store located in the bordering town of McMechen, owned by a man he has heard other adults refer to as "Davy the Jew." He has, in fact, on several occasions accompanied his mother to shop at Star Clothing. Tommy decides to undertake a solo ground breaking voyage to Star Clothing and speak privately with the owner about his quest.

Completing his mile and a half bike ride, Tommy arrives at the front door of Star Clothing and enters without ceremony. He attempts to remain out of sight as he mills around the store, occasionally hiding behind stacks of piled clothing. Tommy, intently confident now, awaits the opportunity to approach Mr. Stern who is currently in the process of completing a sale.

David Stern is carefully wrapping a pair of bib overalls in brown paper, earnestly securing the package from a bolt of cord hanging from an overhead steel support. Stern is a handsome 40–something, with graying temples and grieving eyes, set beneath dark brows that rest below his wrinkled forehead. His eyes follow the customer to the door, then vocalizes his gratitude, waving and shouting, "I see you again Mr. Slonaker."

Instantly, Stern's eyes set upon Tommy, and with polite suspicion, he asks, "Now young man, what can I do for you?" Cocksure, Tommy moves forward and asks, "Are you Mr. Davy the Jew?" Stern's expression sobers. Lowering and shaking his head in repulsion, he looked him off and responds, "No, son, I'm really Mr. Stern, Mr. David Stern. Now may I ask, what is your name?" Sensing his faux pas, Tommy ashamedly declares, "My name is Tommy Gianopolis." Stern replies, "Aha! Do you want me to call you Tommy the Greek?" Hoping this is his chance for redemption from his insult, Tommy replies, "If you want to Mr. Stern, that'll be okay with me." With forgiving admonition, Stern gently rests his index finger on the bridge of Tommy's nose and instructs him, "No, that's not okay. You should always address people by their proper name. But now let's just forget about that, did you come here to buy something?" Wincing in apprehension, Tommy says, "No sir, I came here to ask you what I needed to do to become a Jew." Now Stern appears more amused than annoyed. He slaps his forehead, slams his hand on the counter and asserts, "Mr. Gianopolis, I sell clothing; shirts, socks, underwear and once in while a pair of shoes. I'm not in the religious business. Did you see candles or a statue in my window? Go ask your Priest, or go find a Rabbi. Anyway, what makes a good Greek Christian boy like you want to become a Jew?"

Tommy takes a deep breath, folds his arms to demonstrate his resolve and tells him, "Because someday I want to be rich like you." Quickly realizing Tommy's innocence and understanding his misdirected motivation, Stern leans closer and offers his compassionate counsel, "Tommy, let me give you some advice. Making money or becoming rich has nothing to do with where you were born or where you worship. If you want to be different, if you want to give yourself a chance to be successful, you have to outwork and outthink the next guy. Don't depend upon others, if you want to be happy. Only you can make good things happen. I came to America because they said the streets were paved with gold. When I got here, I found out three things: the streets weren't paved with gold; some weren't even paved, and it was up to me to pave my own street. Let me explain it this way; horses eat oats, and the lazy birds wait around for the horses to poop so they can eat. Don't be like a lazy bird. Never be satisfied just to take what nobody else wants. Get a good education, stay out of trouble and remember, don't wait for the horses to poop. Now go home and think about what I just said and come see me when you need some new underwear."

Tommy thanks Stern and races out the door. All the way home he cheers jubilantly aloud, "Horse shit is for the birds."

FOUR

FREEDOM FIFTIES

We continue to hear nostalgic praise for the 1950's, a decade comprised of a population of post WWII golden baby boomers born to the "Greatest Generation" and thriving in a war free, prospering America. It was a time when many Americans held great hope and limitless expectation for a bright and wholesome future. The Korean War had ended; the polio vaccine was discovered; the Great Depression was becoming a distant memory, and racial segregation was declared unconstitutional by the United States Supreme Court. The American Dream was unfolding for many. It appeared that America was on the threshold of becoming a richer, wiser and more tolerant nation. There was, however, much to be done. Far too many remained mired in hidden poverty. Statistics showed fifty percent of low-income families were deficient in one or more nutrients and hundreds of thousands, if not millions, were living in sub-standard conditions. A significant number of Americans were living on farms and unlike urban dwellers, were able to produce their own food. The rural poor who did not live off farming were much worse off. Seventy percent were said to be suffering from deficient diets. One third of America's men over the age of sixty five were still working.[1] There were still miles to go to allow more Americans to at least dream of sharing the prosperity.

Industrial neighborhoods had common fundamental traits. Few workers owned automobiles and needed to reside in near

1   Wikipedia>Wiki>Great Depression

proximity to the mills and factories, allowing them to walk to and from work. Some of the Benwood residents, unable to secure dwellings near their work stations, resided on a brick lined street at the foot of a hill that was overtaken with vegetable gardens. Houses were contiguous, distinguishable only by the color of the Insul brick siding. It was a civil environment; milk and groceries were delivered to your front door which remained unlocked throughout the day and night.

In this particular High Street neighborhood, dominated by first generation Southern Italians, an inherent ethnic myth held many in fear of pending doom. Of all the superstitious and imaginative beliefs emanating from Southern Italy and the Island of Sicily, the most feared and respected was the "Malochia": an anathema, the evil eye cast upon you by an enemy whose power would condemn you to a life of misery or death. This mythical burden haunted the neighborhood. The nominees who held the power to cast the spell, and those select few possessed with the ability to remove it, were naturally held with reverence. Women and children were warned not to cross or disrespect those in possession of the wizardry. Tommy's grandmother carried the superstition even further. She warned him to avoid eye contact with certain people, especially Mary "The Peddler" and "Alibi" Angelo Quattrone. Alibi was a hopeless bachelor, living in a one room addition to his parent's home. He was loathed even by his parents and feared by all those who knew him. The Quattrones were on Tommy's newspaper route, and he always tried to avoid contact with Alibi. One late Saturday afternoon, Tommy was collecting for his paper deliveries. To his dismay, Alibi answered the door. Keeping his head down, Tommy muttered, "Collecting... it's for two weeks... one dollar and twenty cents." Alibi remained silent and motionless for what seemed like an eternity. Then before slamming the door against Tommy's nose, he grunted, "Nobody's home; I don't read the paper."

Tommy recalls his first and final experience with the "Malochia." He and his friends were gathered near the front of his home on High Street shooting marbles. One of their friends ran up and shouted, "Hey guys! Old lady Manso is takin' the evil eye off Joey Zumpano's mom." They all raced up the street to the Manso's house and saw Joey with his family and friends jammed on the front porch. Joey was treating the screen door like the Wailing Wall, on his knees and praying out loud. Tommy snuck to the rear of the house where he witnessed the exorcism through the kitchen window. Mrs. Manso and Mrs. Zumpano were seated at opposite ends of the table, which held a large can of olive oil, two burning candles, lemons and a large clear glass bowl. Mrs. Zumpano had her head draped, reading her rosaries, as Mrs. Manso, dressed in black, was siphoning lemon juice into an eye dropper and slowly releasing drops into the bowl of olive oil. After several minutes, Mrs. Manso jumped to her feet, blessing herself and screaming. She walked over and gently embraced a sobbing, catatonic Mrs. Zumpano. When Tommy returned to the front porch, the crowd was jubilant. It was over; Mrs. Manso had removed the curse.

Rumors spread around High Street that Mary "The Peddler," a door to door apparel vendor, had conferred the curse. Allegedly, Mrs. Zumpano not only failed to pay Mary for the goods she had purchased, but disrespected Mary, warning potential customers that Mary often overcharged and sold a poor quality of fabric.

FIVE

The Iron City

The local steel mill and railroad industry provided more than just a payroll to employees and their families. Houses throughout the city looked like advertisements for Wheeling Steel. Roof drains were modified from three inch galvanized pipe, with similar but smaller versions of the stolen and bartered pipe being converted for use as water lines, hand rails and table legs.

There were abundant degrees of benevolence in the community. High Street youngsters cherished the arrival of Mildred Klienedler, a kindhearted neighbor. A select few awaited Mildred's return following her week-long day shift as a tobacco stripper for Bloch Brothers Tobacco Company in nearby Wheeling. Mildred would share from the bag of pure hardened licorice, hidden in her purse with her chosen neighborhood boys. The licorice was an essential ingredient in manufacturing chewing tobacco products. For the High Street boys, it was a delightful and affordable candy replacement.

Anomalous and dogged determination helped many community residents overcome their recurring struggles. Many families were forced to withstand austere living conditions and too many remained vulnerable to overnight destitution. Self-reliance and persistence overcame their socio-economic challenge. The city ran parallel to the 980 mile long Ohio River, and inhabitants too often suffered the wrath of flooding which would immerse nearly one-third of their residential community. The waterfront, flood-prone homes were the most affordable and were conveniently located within proximity of the industrial base that bordered the river.

Benwood stretched for about three narrow miles along the river, squeezed between a mountain and the rail yards. The infamous "Iron and Steel" industrial bastion served the desirable employment needs for much of the surrounding area on both sides of the river. Benwood was then home to nearly four thousand residents, a majority of whom were first generation Americans of Irish, Polish, Slovakian and Italian descent. Some withstood the trial, while others enjoyed the dubious distinction of living in a community that offered flourishing industry, three churches, eight grocery stores, a druggist and thirty-two saloons.

The Benwood summer evening sky remained a brilliant orange as showers of residue billowed from the sweltering ovens of Wheeling Steel's open-hearth furnaces. Hundreds of steel employees walked to and from work on unforgiving round-the-clock shifts. They toiled with pride and devotion among these raging fires. The blast furnace was surrounded by sweat-blackened men, laboring within feet of thousand degree, glowing red-hot ovens, fueled from stocked piles of coal and coke that made the iron which became steel.

In the northern section of the city, only a few hundred yards from the Benwood-Bessmer open hearth furnaces, families found comfort on the street-lined porches of their iron oxide stained homes. Their faces glowed, and their shadows danced from the luminous cokeovens yielding toxic carbons. Undaunted, these "Harmony Hill" residents assembled nightly on their porch swings and railings with tamburas and cornstalk fiddles to sing a mix of Croatian and Serbian songs. Their harmony brightened the contaminated night sky. Below their homes, iron street car rails glistened beneath the feet of pedestrians who arrived routinely to enjoy their talented performance.

Frank Avellino worked a daily eight-hour swing shift at the coke ovens. He said his co-workers called him 38, which was his badge number and the identity he was given by his supervisor, who said he had difficulty pronouncing his name. Frank spent intervals above the two thousand Celsius degree ovens. He was called a "Hot Baller" or "Lid Man," the most undesirable and dangerous job in the mill. The "Hot Baller" opened the doors allowing the coal to be dumped into these ovens, converting it into coke. Frank had no choice but to provide his own protection in the hell hole. He dressed in multiple layers of protective clothing to diminish the constant burns resulting from flames shooting from the unbearable hot ovens.

Back in South Benwood, walking along the brick and gravel of High Street, you were more likely to be struck by a speeding wheel barrel than an automobile. Just below High Street, the former Pink Elephant tavern, flourishing under new ownership, had been transformed into the Flamingo Grill. It was an early Easter afternoon, and Grandpa Avellino had smoked his last de nobli cigar. He sent Tommy to replenish his supply. The Flamingo was packed with locals still celebrating and dressed in their Easter outfits. Most came directly from church services, and the women, striving to maintain their holiday allure, remained costumed in their bonnets and wilted carnation corsages. They lined the bar, sitting atop worn bar stools. The smoke-discolored, mirrored back bar displayed a limited choice of liquors, cigarettes, beer nuts, Marsh Wheeling stogies and de nobli cigars. At the far end of the bar, a large plastic barrel of loose pretzels competed with a murky jar of pickled pig's feet for sale at twenty-five cents apiece. The noise was deafening; "Easter Parade" blared monotonously from the juke box, with some patrons agonizingly offering the lyrics between their nicotine and alcohol intake. At a table near the far end of the bar, Stella and Stanley Lewandowski, with raised arms holding frosted glasses of draft beer, remained unaware of their surroundings and joyfully entertained themselves toasting and singing, "In heaven there is no beer. That's why we drink it here, and when we're gone from here, our friends will be drinking all the beer La la, la, la, la, la."

A competitive roar to the cheer and music emanates from another corner of the room, angry guttural sounds reverberating off the thinly paneled walls. In the middle of a small circle, two red-faced men are hunched with their heads together, screaming out numbers in Italian. They are playing Mora, a hand game that is said to date back thousands of years to Ancient Rome and Greek times. It is said that it was often played to decide issues, but this group was playing for entertainment. In the game of Mora, all players throw out a single hand showing zero to five fingers, while calling out loud their guesses at what the sum of all fingers showing would be. If one player guesses the sum, he wins the point. The first player to win three points wins the game. Among the circle of participants was Eugene Giampolo, who they called Quattro. He had lost the majority of his index finger from his right hand, leaving him with four discernable fingers. He created and wore a prosthetic extension made from a hollowed out chicken leg, using it only for Mora matches. Tommy, with his handful of cigars, stopped at the door, paused for a break in the match and, with a self-praising taunt as he was running out the door screamed, "Quattro!"

SIX

BENWOOD JUNCTION

For Tommy Gianopolis and his pals, the established sanctuary in the neighborhood was a niche within what was commonly referred to as the Benwood "junction." The junction was a modest wood-framed single story icon that served as the local freight and passenger terminal for the Baltimore and Ohio railroad. Shrouded within the junction walls was the depot office. The office was occupied by the terminal dispatcher whose duties were comparable to a significantly scaled down version of the modern day air traffic controller. The spacious room adjoining the dispatcher's office was an alluring passenger waiting room furnished

15th Sreet Hill and Benwood, B&O Junction

with long oak benches, a coal burning stove and a modern electric water fountain.

Outside the junction, a passageway separated the freight room from the depot office. An underpass provided shelter for passengers and the valet service, which was overseen by a red-capped uniformed attendant. He often commanded a horse-drawn steel wheeled luggage wagon. For some, the trail to the junction led down a steep, roman-bricked hill less than one hundred yards from the front door of their High Street homes. The Benwood junction was part of the industrial base and stood as an operational symbol of the industrial prominence and future of the "Greatest Generation."

Pulverized black soot spewing from the coal-fired locomotives blanketed the bucolic neighborhood. The thunderous tremors from rolling rail cars rattled the foundations of the nearby homes inhabited by the likes of Saporitos, Scarnecchias, Scullys and Krizaneks. Most of the dwellers in the city developed a "Pavlovian " tolerance for the ceaseless rail screeches that filled the night air. The hot molten signal flares deliberately placed along the tracks yielded spirit-like images rising above the rail lines. Dwellers slept comfortably, knowing these sights and sounds provided security for many.

Fifteenth Street hill, which lead down to the junction, was bordered by a captivating saloon/confectionary and the tallest building in the city. It was a three story residential/commercial structure that included five apartments with two shared outhouses. The candy tavern was on the bottom floor. One of the units was a former barber shop, converted into a single unit residential apartment. The lessee was a gentleman they called "Cowboy" Willis. Mr. Willis was separated from his family, lived alone and shared an ice box and outhouse with the tenant living above him. Nearby residents debated the decisive role a shared outhouse played in their ultimate romantic relationship.

Cowboy was a cryptic, but friendly man in his mid-fifties, who was easily persuaded to allow the High Street boys an occasional review of his library of "dirty" magazines. Inside his one room abode was a day bed, a wall mounted sink and bundles of soiled clothing strewn about linoleum flooring. Cowboy Willis found unequaled, but undesirable, fame soon after his death. His daughter Rosie, who lived a short distance away, met a handsome, young unemployed car thief named

the neighboring town of McMechen.
immediately in love, and within a
nter, they sped off to the Marshall
tolen Studebaker to secure a marriage
wed Rosie Willis would now and forever
Manson.

SEVEN

Holiday La Centra

Grandpa Frank carried the myth of warm-blooded Mediterraneans with his propensity for amore. Tommy was eleven years old when he became a willing accomplice to grandpa's incurable adultery. Tommy was ordained to accompany Grandpa on occasional trips intended to make repairs and improvements for neighbors who called upon Frank Avellino's skill as an established all-around home repairman. The majority of his time and craft was applied on the second floor of the Steel Café where Maria Martini and her husband Eugene resided. Frank said he always scheduled the "repairs" when Eugene was hard at work at Wheeling Steel because he did not want to interfere with his rest or relaxation at home. Tommy loved every minute of his duty as a helper for Grandpa, especially in the early mornings when alone, and the Steel Café bar was closed. Having carried Grandpa's tool box to the front door, he said he was always instructed to wait in the downstairs bar for Grandpa to finish his work and at times eat as many as five bags of potato chips. For the longest time Tommy believed the work was becoming too much for his Grandpa. It seemed as though every time he had work, especially at the Martini's, he began hearing an elevated exchange of profane, piercing screams coming from the "workroom." However, Tommy eventually became suspicious of Grandpa's endeavors and said he knew there was Hanky Panky going on when Grandpa Frank quit taking his tool box upstairs. When the job was finished, Grandpa Frank would climb down the stairs and routinely walk behind the bar and pour himself a double header of Four Roses Whiskey. Then, without fail, as he led Tommy out the door he would sing the opening lines from his fight song: "I s my shoes, to buy some booze, nobody knows how dry I a Tommy learned early that silence was golden, or at least a t to all the potato chips you could eat.

As a young boy, Tommy Gianopolis was impresse riding the elevator at department stores in downtown Wh Even more captivating was the ultra-modern and cr escalator at the popular Stone & Thomas department However, all took a back seat to sliding down the polished chrome hand rail leading to the basement of Murphy's Five & Ten store. Downtown Wheeling was a hopeful place, exciting and robust year around, and like every other city in America, the Christmas season brought out the best: uniformed, white-gloved policemen directing traffic, and bleary eyed Salvation Army volunteers ringing bells in concert with the sounds of caroling flowing from the store fronts. Smartly dressed people were four deep across the sidewalks. Throngs of exuberant shoppers had children in tow while lugging bulging shopping bags. The bus stops were crowded, and taxi cabs jammed the safe streets in a priceless, genuine moment. This was a resplendent time in America. It was an age when people were receptive, respectful of one another and fueled with optimism. Hopes and dreams were always present and abundant.

The joy and exultation of Christmas was for many an incomparable moment. The Avellino's Christmas tradition was tempered by competing ethnic customs, but nevertheless, it delivered unmitigated joy. Mother Josephine used her culinary skills to overcome the ethnic divide of her Greek-Italian-American offspring. She prepared baked goods and arranged meals that crossed Mediterranean borders into America. Josephine offered her children a range of Christmas day delights from stuffed grape leaves and cheese-filled ravioli to candy

AMC -
FLIGHT NO.
DATE
SEAT NO.
AGENT NO.
CASH COLLECTED
FROM
TO

canes, popcorn balls, kourambiathes and pizzelles.

The Avellino Christmas tree was purposely ordered and delivered late. It was routinely purchased from a local Italian grocer who Grandma Avellino scornfully referred to as "mano il nero" (Black Hand). Vincenzo Sciappa seemed to have thoroughly convinced Grandpa Avellino that his best buy was a near-Christmas, discounted short-needle pine tree. He convinced him, year after year that this tree, unlike the ones in the past, would last well into the New Year. The Avellino tree arrived a day or two before Christmas, and the Gianopolis children would reluctantly prepare themselves for the unavoidable inaugural display reserved for Grandpa Frank. Impatiently, but ceremoniously, he retrieved and employed his custom made tree stand. His invention was composed of a modified, galvanized Wheeling Steel wash basin, sand bags and a wooden tripod that he angrily anchored to the wooden floor.

Christmas Eve brought the habitual Avellino dinner to the elongated, custom designed table constructed to accommodate the dozen or so invitees. Yards of checkered red and white oil cloth covered the iron-pipe legged table that displayed the annual Christmas Eve La Centra. Generously exhibited in the center of the table was a mound of freshly homemade bread, surrounded by an overabundance of Neapolitan and Sicilian entrees and bottles of homemade wine. The intentional meatless Christmas Eve culinary exhibit ranged from balls of provolone cheese, deep fried smelts, baked cod fish, spaghetti aglio e olio with fried zucchini cakes to an appetizer of stuffed hot peppers in olive oil with garlic and anchovies that would sear the intestines of an alligator. Immediately following an expressive ingestion of this ceremonial meal, the Gianopolis children escaped to the living room where Josephine would serve them ribbon candy and cookies as they prepared to decorate the tree. Within minutes, bubble lights, angel hair and lead filled icicles were hanging from the weakened limbs, covering the voids from vanishing pine needles. Their Tannenbaum, as well as other holiday décor was held in reserved contempt by their agnostic Grandpa Frank, who most likely shared his holiday spirit with his homemade wine that apparently induced equal or greater images and inspiration than the celebration of the birth of Christ.

Frankie Gianopolis and his sister Barbara continued to assist their weary mother, struggling to complete decorating the tree. They were working on the last string of lights while Frankie and Tommy were busy connecting wire hangers to the remaining glass ornaments. Out in the kitchen, aunts and uncles rejoiced, helping Grandma and Grandpa Avellino continue the celebration. The scent of fish and garlic was now dwarfed by the odor of smoldering cigars. The smoke rose against the kitchen wall displaying a complimentary funeral home calendar, hanging beneath a portrait of Jesus, alongside a print of President Franklin Delano Roosevelt. Out on the front porch, several spare pieces of cod fish hung from a frozen clothes line. A steel cage holding empty Cloverdale milk bottles rested near the front door. Back inside, the tree decoration was complete. Frankie appeared to have redirected his interest. He was lying on the white cotton cloth under the tree, holding the baby Jesus in his crib. His eyes riveted skyward as he called out, "Mom, is Jesse James in Heaven?" Josephine smiled and offered him comforting assurance of God's forgiveness, "I think so honey." Frankie followed up incredulously, "Does he give God a hard time?" Josephine again tried to reassure him, telling Frankie that everybody behaves when they get to Heaven. It was only an hour later, Tommy now dressed and prepared to accompany friends to midnight mass, when one of his friends arrived early at the door with sad news.

EIGHT

The Hobo & Mrs. Kitchen

This Christmas was about to become a bitter-sweet experience for the High Street boys. They would share in the solemn mourning of a friend's loss, but learn the value of friendship, and begin to develop their passion for fairness and equality.

Tommy left the house with his friend, meeting up with the others at the foot of the hill near the junction. There they assembled with their grieving pal, Mike Kitchen, who had lost his grandmother. She was his sole guardian and only known living relative. The Kitchens lived in a one room house with a dirt floor that was covered with old newspapers. The only electricity in the home came from a single light bulb dangling from an exposed truss ceiling. Patches of cardboard and soiled rags served to help cover and insulate the otherwise bare interior walls. A few scorched pots and pans hung above a rusting pot-bellied wood burning stove. The only interior plumbing was a cold water line that led into a free standing metal tub, serving as a wash basin and sink. Many in the community shared a degree of misfortune, but none lived close to the misery of Mike and his grandmother.

Mrs. Kitchen adopted Mike at birth, and from that day forward, this widowed grandmother and her grandchild endured unthinkable hardship. They were among the many victims of hidden and ignored abject poverty in America. They suffered in a nation that in most cases ignored entirely its responsibility to care for its helpless and deserving. Pride and beauty often mask the tragedy of poverty, thus allowing the unfortunate to suffer within an indifferent society. This homogenous community understood the pain of their underprivileged, but lacked the means and resources for rescue.

Soon to arrive at the dispatcher's office within the junction would be their friend, Andy Malchano. Always vigilant, Andy remained militant as he transmitted and received Morse code messages over the telegraph wire machine atop his desk. This form of communication served as the verifiable source and means to receive and transmit traffic orders and information to railroad engineers traveling over miles of interstate track. Andy had become a cherished friend and mentor to the High Street boys. He became their exemplar of strength and direction for vision and character building. His interest and caring helped shape their destiny. Tommy recalled once asking Andy if he believed in God. Andy quoted Camus, "I would rather live my life as if there is a God and find out there isn't, than live my life as if there isn't and die to find out there is." From that moment on, Tommy said he never stopped believing. Andy began working for the B&O railroad a few months after his discharge from the Marine Corps. The High Street boys spent countless hours with Andy and reveled in his Marine war stories. On many occasions they were graced with his charity, and none surpassed his offers of Baby Ruth candy bars and Nehi root beer soda pop.

One of the most exciting events that occurred at the Benwood junction took place on September 12, 1952: the sudden appearance of a passenger car pulled by a relentless whistle and steam blowing locomotive. It slowed as it approached the east side of the junction, allowing the quickly gathered crowd to witness a smiling, hand waving General Dwight D. Eisenhower and his wife Mamie. They were in route to Wheeling where they would meet up with Ike's chosen vice-presidential nominee, Richard M. Nixon. Soon afterward, Nixon appeared on national television and delivered his controversial "Checkers" speech.[2] Later that day, the Eisenhowers and Nixon made a grand appearance before a crowd of jubilant supporters at Wheeling Island stadium. Only a decade earlier, during a much less celebrated time, local residents gathered by the hundreds at the Benwood junction and watched proudly, as their fathers, brothers, sons and spouses boarded troop trains heading off to World War II.

Richard M. Nixon and wife arriving at Wheeling (Ohio County) airport greeted by First Lady, Mamie Eisenhower

Ohio Valley residents were oppressed in a "Dickens" duality environment fostered by the ruling class. A glaring example of the challenge to their moral strength offered by a community leader was illustrated in the following newspaper editorial headlined: "HOW TO LOSE FRIENDS":

---

2   Nixon had been accused of improprieties relating to his campaign fund. He went on national television to defend himself and in doing so, said he intended to keep his one gift, a black and white dog whose name was Checkers.

The controversy stirred up by an alleged Southern scheme to settle a Negro family in the Washington neighborhood where Vice-President Nixon resides should serve as a timely warning to Negroes against the folly of lending themselves to maneuvers of this character. A property owner who has no personal aversion to a particular race may object to a family settling near him for the very practical reason that he knows the value of his property would decline. This is a point which is to be suspected, too many Negroes to overlook. They confuse equality under the law with social acceptance. The first thing is something we must earn, the hard way, often at a very heavy price. It is a matter of evolution. So when Negroes either voluntarily or at the urging of others who are using them as pawns, force themselves upon neighborhoods where they are not wanted or press for such ill-advised law as the one now pending in New York City which would deny landlords the right to choose their own tenants, they are in danger or alienating the support law. Thus they damage their own cause by trying to force that which can only come with time in the orderly process of social programs. Austin V. Wood, Editor, *Wheeling News Register*

The boys anxiously awaited Andy's arrival for his late night shift at the depot. They maintained a safe distance from the unfriendly dispatcher on duty who objected to their presence. The railroad property was sovereign territory, and mid-level management behaved cult-like in their dogmatic protection of their work domain. The B&O commissioned their own police force and employed men who were disparagingly, but in most cases accurately, referred to as B&O "Bulls." The title was bestowed upon them because of their power and reputation for hard-charging and brutal enforcement tactics. Among the Bulls' arsenal was a baseball bat-sized nightstick. This weapon was used too often with savored discrimination and impunity. They often assaulted trespassers and suspected violators. Fortunately, only a few of the Bulls exercised sadistic delight in pummeling these vagabonds. As the boys waited for Andy, they witnessed a long-stepping, imperious Bull passing below them. He pointed his flashlight toward the base of the concrete steps leading up from the junction. He then paused, his light fixed and bellowed, "Hey, get your soon dead ass outta here." Peering over the railing, the boys were unable to identify the object of his rage. Then as the Bull moved closer to his interest, his voice deepened, "Come on…get movin' before I put you in

The Baltimore Lunch at 15th Street Hill. Also the residence of "Cowboy" Willis (bottom right of building)

a deep sleep." It was a hobo, and after several vicious and ugly blows from the Bull's nightstick, the hobo raised his arm in an act of surrender and began crawling away and up the snow covered steps leading to his safety and freedom. Then the Bull raised his head and tilted his cap, giving the boys a forbidding stare he shouted, "You all get your green asses home to bed and wait for Santa Claus."

The boys grew up understanding and tolerating the presence and plight of hobos. They were common visitors and flourished during the post-World War II era. There were thousands of nomadic, destitute men who hopped trains and rode boxcars aimlessly around the country. They were, for the most part, looked upon with curiosity rather than fear or disdain. The underprivileged seldom fear or hold the needy in contempt.

As the hobo reached street level, he collapsed into a sitting position, slumped and leaning against the iron railing at the top of the stairs. The Bull had departed swiftly, so the boys moved closer to the hobo. His face was nearly covered with frozen blood. A golf ball size lump protruded from his lacerated skull, which was covered by a soiled head rag drooping beneath his brow. His shoddy yellowed beard concealed most of his defiled neck scarf. He was carrying his life possessions in a pouch tied to a stick now lightly resting on his shoulder. Tommy and his pals gazed in astonishment as the hobo sat in helpless torment. Within minutes, the hobo blinked, gave a strained reassuring grin and muttered, "I could have kicked his ass sitting down, but I'm way too tired." He then raised his arm, summoning the boys closer and asked, "You boys get me somewhere that's dry, and you guys can split the candy in my bundle." Tommy and his crew gently slid him across the frozen street and carried him into the "coal room" of the Baltimore Lunch. The Baltimore Lunch was a combination speakeasy/diner not affiliated with the railroad, but whose name and reputation caused it to become an alluring water hole for many local and out of town railroaders. It was owned and operated by Frank Slemaki and his sister, Annie. They were hard-nosed, first generation Czechoslovakians. They sold everything from marshmallow ice cream cones to beer and moonshine. They were also masterful in catering to the passions and idiosyncrasies of the lonely rail men.

The sidewalk level, hinged trap door opening to the basement of the Baltimore Lunch led to a room where a coal fired furnace kept it warm enough to keep the water pipes from freezing. Rumor had it that Frank kept it unlocked to attract and accommodate those rail men who were willing to swap coal lanterns and other hijacked goods for booze. As the boys endeavored to comfort the hobo, it became apparent that his condition was rapidly worsening. Mike Kitchen, the eldest of the group leaned close to him and asked, "Are you goinna be okay?" The hobo bemoaned and softly lamented, "I think I'm about finished, thanks for letting me warm up. Now you all better get home before Santa comes." The boys stepped outside and paced around a telephone pole, glancing skyward at the glittering snowflakes dancing around the street light. Mike, however, remained slumped against the pole. Stoic, but obviously defeated by his loss, he remained for the moment listless with an empty look of mortal grief.

Their mentor Andy was scheduled to work the midnight Christmas-Eve shift, and as the hour approached, they moved closer to the junction. It became more and more apparent to them that they were obligated to do more for the hobo, realizing that he was in immediate need of medical attention. They decided to take him to what was known as the B&O hospital, which was an infirmary owned by the railroad and located in proximity of the junction. When Andy arrived, Tommy volunteered to seek Andy's help and permission to transport the hobo to the infirmary. Tommy arrived and explained to Andy what had occurred and explained their fear the hobo wouldn't live without medical attention. Empathizing, Andy shook his head in disgust, but then dismissively informed Tommy that any nurse on duty at the infirmary was obligated only to treat B&O employees and passengers. Tommy, bewildered and confused, stood frozen for a moment, then realizing the need to respect Andy's firm denial, thanked him and left the office. Before stepping outside, he heard Andy shout "Okay, show me where this guy is, but the best I can do is take a look at him." Leaving the office unattended would not be a dereliction of duty for Andy since no traffic was scheduled until late in the morning.

The boys were huddled around the hobo and were thrilled to see Andy. The first words from Andy's mouth were, "Mike, I'm sorry to hear you lost your grandmother. If there's anything I can do to help you, just let me know. I don't mean tomorrow, I mean forever." It was the first and the last time Mike smiled that morning. Andy instructed the boys to bring the hobo closer to the light, where he began to examine the now unconscious victim. Andy loosened the hobo's scarf, and the tarnished silver chain hanging around the hobo's neck became visible and immediately drew Andy's attention. He began carefully examining the chain and its attachments. He then asked the boys to transport the hobo to the infirmary and remain with him until the nurse arrived. Andy returned to the office to phone the on-call nurse. Arriving moments later, she unlocked the door and commanded, "The two biggest of you bring him inside and put him on the table. One of you others go down and tell Andy I'm here." Tommy raced down to the junction where he found Andy mulling over the hobo's chain and tags. After being informed that the nurse had arrived, Andy offered a gratuitous smile and then decorously raised the chain and tags and asked, "Tommy do you know what these are?" Tommy told him that he thought they were "dog tags," and that his uncle Rocco had his hanging from the crucifix in his bedroom. "Well that's exactly what they are. They're notched 'dog tags,' and they bear his name and serial number. This hobo is a man, an Army veteran, and that's why I bent the rules and asked the nurse to come and take care of this soldier." Andy went on to explain that the I.D. tags were hung around the neck of every soldier, and one of the tags was always connected to the longest chain and the other hooked to the smaller one. "If someone found a dead soldier, he kept the long chain and gave the shorter one to the commanding officer. I don't think this man ever stopped fighting the war." Then in a solemn tone he said, "This might just be a hobo to some people, but he's not a bum. He's an American war veteran who served his country and deserves to be treated humanely and with respect."

During the entire time, Tommy stood before Andy, poised and deferential with the hobo's bundle stick flung over his shoulder. Andy's mood lightened, he smiled and said, "Tommy, if your teeth weren't so white, you might pass for a hobo." Tommy quickly explained that the hobo promised they could split the candy in the bundle, but was waiting for the hobo's permission to open it. Then the phone rang; it was the nurse calling, and it became immediately apparent from Andy's expression that the news wasn't good. His voice mellowed as he thanked the nurse for coming out on Christmas Eve. His eyes followed the receiver as he gently hung up the phone. He gazed intently, then whispered, "He faded away." The ambulance arrived to take the body to the local mortuary, where he would remain while police attempted to locate his next of kin. Information from his Army separation papers (DD-214) disclosed his last known address as St. Louis, Missouri. There was no action or interest in the cause of death by law enforcement. The police spent their time unsuccessfully attempting to locate a relative.

Soon after Christmas, the hobo was placed in a pine box supplied by the county and prepared to be taken to the Poor Farm Cemetery for burial among paupers and dead prisoners. Here was this lost and lonely, murdered American veteran, about to be buried anonymously in an unmarked grave, indistinguishable from the convicts surrounding him.

The boys had gathered in Andy's office after the ambulance departed. Mike Kitchen asked, "Andy, what was the hobo's name?" Andy pushed his chair back away from his desk, picked up the "dog tags" and said in a broad, respectful tone, "Nevada Jones." Ironically, they would soon learn that Mrs. Kitchen was also destined for the Poor Farm Cemetery. She and Nevada Jones would be arriving for internment the same day. When Andy learned of this, he chose to intervene and salvage some dignity for these deserving providers. He influenced county officials to have Mrs. Kitchen and Nevada Jones buried alongside one another. He told Mike that Mr. Jones would forever keep his grandmother company and watch over her. Mrs. Kitchen and Nevada Jones, strangers in life, would now remain together forever in symbol and spirit.

The morning after Christmas, the boys assembled at the top of the junction waiting for Andy to drive them to the cemetery for the burial services. Upon arrival at the Poor Farm site, they were met by a State Penitentiary guard and four prison trustees. The trustees had shoveled a coal-cindered path from the graveled road leading up the cemetery hill to the grave site. There, two freshly dug graves awaited the arrival of Kitchen and Jones. The boys stood in solemn respect on that bitterly cold morning. They were several feet from the graves and watched tearfully as the trustees removed the pine coffins from the hearse. Mike Kitchen, in his tattered coat and scuffed clod hoppers, enduring this Sisyphean moment, moved a step closer to his grandma's grave. The soldier went down first, and the boys followed Andy's salute. Mrs. Kitchen was lowered, her coffin too on the tenuous balance of ropes holding the ends of the coffin.

The boys found six cellophane wrapped candy canes in the hobo's bundle and agreed to give them to Mike. The remainder of the bundle contained two empty Heinz baked bean cans, a crumpled paper bag, a few walnuts, a bottle of Mercurochrome, a box of wooden matches and a Purple Heart medal, wrapped in a red handkerchief. Nevada Jones was laid to rest with dignity, valor and his Badge of Military Merit.

Until his marriage Mike Kitchen lived with a number of different families in Benwood. They fed, clothed and cared for him, each enjoying his company and rewarded by his ultimate happiness and success. The High Street boys descended from mediocrity and fell short of becoming Phi Beta Kappas or Rhodes Scholars, but became glaring examples of the Greek aphorism, "Character is Destiny." Each of them found the benefit of being Boy and Explorer Scouts. They played organized Little League, Pony and Legion baseball and were high school athletes. They played, slept and hunted in the woods and swam and fished in the river and creeks. They loved God, their parents, Mickey Mantle and Superman. They were like most of America.

Mike went on to become an active civic leader, an all-sports coach, and he served with distinction as an elected member of the county school board. He and his wife raised five children. The remaining High Street boys excelled as well. All received college degrees; they distinguished themselves as a secondary school principle, mall developer, an insurance executive and a senior aide to the Governor of the state of West Virginia.

NINE

CRIMINAL PIONEER

North Benwood bordered the city of Wheeling and stood within a short distance from downtown Wheeling, a city with a national reputation for joy and relative prosperity. Neighboring steel, mine workers, and railroad men from both sides of the Ohio river eagerly contributed to Wheeling's elation and robust economy. They were the purveyors and recipients of the exclusive joy the city offered.

At the turn of the twentieth century, nearly twenty million immigrants arrived in America. Among the soon to be immigrated was a portly nine-year old, disembarking from his week long journey aboard the Greek Liner, Patrias. This magnificent vessel had just delivered the young Spartan to a country where he would find a city that would become his kingdom. Unlike most of these new Americans who were preparing for the unknown sacrifice and toil that awaited them in this new land of opportunity, this stout, overdressed young man was overcome with tenacious ambition, already challenging his mother's directives. Mrs. Antoinette Kokoliades was overwhelmed, struggling to control her trepidation and her animated son, Basil.

It was an early autumn day in 1909. Railroads had replaced wagon trails, and electricity was finding its way into homes and businesses. The city that awaited them was Wheeling, West Virginia. A single horse drawn carriage trudged along a busy cobblestone street. The coach passed by the German Bank building, which was home to the Grand Opera House, resting on the corner of 12th and Market streets. This opulent icon played host to renowned entertainers appearing before Wheeling's privileged. Seventy six million Americans now occupied the forty eight states of the union. The average worker's wage was $12.98 for a 59 hour work week. Women were being arrested for smoking in public, and the life expectancy of a black man was thirty-two years.

Departing the ferry and arriving on Ellis Island, the puzzled and frightened immigrants checked their luggage and assembled in seemingly endless, disorganized lines as they obediently proceeded to the Great Hall to begin the inspection process. Thousands with numbered white identification tags pinned to their clothing were directed to climb a massive metal staircase to the first in a series of registration rooms, where a fleet of doctors awaited them to conduct an examination for signs of infectious disease, disabilities and obvious signs of illness before allowing them to proceed. Following the examination, Antoinette and Basil returned to the clerk's station and were nearing the end of their four hour ordeal. When she identified her nationality, she was assigned an inspector fluent in her language who asked a series of twenty nine mandatory questions pertaining to her finances, occupation, marital status and destination.

Upon approval, the inspector handed Antoinette the processed papers. Relieved, she embraced Basil and rejoiced, "Basil, you will soon be an American living in the greatest country on earth." They moved quickly to the baggage room to secure their luggage and then boarded a barge to the New York City train station. Ultimately they would complete their journey aboard a Baltimore & Ohio passenger train headed to Wheeling, West Virginia.

It was daybreak, and the Kokoliades family got their first sight of Wheeling. A thriving and promising destination and a welcome reassurance compared to their first American encounter. The active rail yards were filled with passenger, freight and coal cars. On the busy streets a few of the nearly two hundred thousand Model T touring automobiles produced that year were competing with horse drawn ice wagons and the few remaining cable cars.

Luggage in custody, Antoinette anxiously awaited the arrival of her brother-in-law, Louis, who had been in America for several years and enjoyed a rapid assimilation, realizing marginal success as an independent businessman. Louis was now one of one hundred and thirty thousand Greeks living in America, and one of the fifty percent of West Virginia Greek immigrants residing in Wheeling. Louis arrived, respectfully removed his hat and offered Antoinette a gentle welcome embrace. He bestowed a warm welcome in their native tongue. He then stepped back, feinted and taunted Basil with a frolicking suspicious glance, then pulled a handful of candy from his pocket. They set off in Louis' bread wagon for their new home in Alley C., Center Wheeling.

TEN

BEARDLESS & BEERLESS
MOUNTAINEERS

The year is now 1912, and while the first street cars were lining the hills of San Francisco, back in Wheeling, Basil was comfortably mounted atop his Uncle's horse-drawn bread wagon. By reputation and girth, he was becoming known as

1912 postcard, Market House, Wheeling, WV

"Big" Bill and soon would morph into William G. "Big Bill" Lias. The rapidly maturing twelve-year old was confident and in full command, guiding his horse out of the Center Wheeling Outdoor Market to deliver his Uncle's fresh baked goods. A few short blocks north of the Center Wheeling Market was the 10th Street Market House built in 1822 at a cost of $690. This was once the location of the Town Hall and the Mayor's office. At the belfry end of the Market, slaves were bought and sold.

Meanwhile, as millions of working class Americans struggled and suffered from the growing disparity of wealth, the gap between the rich and the poor widened, as it continues today. Then, it was John D. Rockefeller, Andrew Carnegie, J. P. Morgan and the Vanderbilts, the defiant vanguards of Capitalism, who continued exploiting the masses and growing their power and wealth through monopolistic practices. Today the country is ruled by cloak and dagger avant-gardes who engage third world labor and off shore corporations providing them tax loophole savings in billions of dollars. Although America was at the absolute mercy of early twentieth century monopolistic tycoons, none of them were as ruthless and unprincipled as modern day corporate hedge fund moguls.

The elite Eastern establishment arrogantly expected order and refinement from reservations of impoverished and exploited Americans. Too much of the country was struggling and enmeshed in abject poverty with sub-standard living conditions. Wheeling was no exception to the inequality, particularly for the recent foreign born. The art and luxury of Western civilization was reserved for and practiced by the select few. The elite dined on eight course dinners served on imported china, while thousands of West Virginians lived in desolate labor camps, enslaved by coal barons who operated their mines with machine guns.

In southern West Virginia, Mary Harris (Mother Jones), the daughter of a Roman Catholic tenant farmer from the north side of Cork City, Ireland, was terrorizing black-hearted coal operators. A prominent American labor icon, she took up the fight and marched for the safety and rights of suffering miners, living in destitute mining camps throughout West Virginia and the Appalachian coal fields. She was cherished for organizing the brave wives and children of striking workers across America.

1912 was a leap year, and just days before the Presidential election, a quarter of the front page of the Wheeling newspaper portrayed a dismal, satirical cartoon, depicting the gloom across America. The syndicated caricature showed a weary, gaunt, scarfed lady returning from the market carrying an empty food basket. A sign in the foreground illustrated an inventory of the rising and unaffordable cost of food under the current administration. It read in part: "PORK, CHEESE, SUGAR AND COFFEE HAS DOUBLED...VITAL REASONS WHY

YOUR VOTE SHOULD BE FOR WILSON." This would be the first forty-eight state election, with Arizona and New Mexico having joined the union earlier that year. West Virginia held eight electoral votes. Woodrow Wilson carried forty states to win the election over his nearest opponent Taft, a Republican who won two states, and Teddy Roosevelt, who ran on the Progressive "Bull Moose" third party ticket, won the remaining states. Also somewhat formidable in the election that year was Eugene Debs, running on the Social ticket. A powerful labor leader, Debs received just under a million poplar votes.

Fifty-eight percent of the eligible voters participated in the 1912 election. In the preceding general election of 1908, the turnout was 67.5 percent, still the highest percentage of eligible voter turnout. Presidential candidate Eugene Debs was convicted in a 1918 federal court for "disloyal conduct" and obstruction to recruiting under the Sedition Act.[3] He served a portion of his time at the West Virginia State Penitentiary in Moundsville, West Virginia before being transported to a federal prison in Atlanta. The State Penitentiary was also used at the time to house federal prisoners. Former West Virginia Warden Oral Skeen said that Debs practiced what he preached and shared all the presents he received from friends with other inmates.

Years later, up north, the powerful Mafia chieftain, Frank Costello, agreed to a rare interview with a New York news reporter, who asked him about his choice of lifestyles and ascendance in organized crime. Costello told him that in his boyhood, he lived in Harlem, and now he and Mrs. Costello had a seven room apartment at Central Park West and owned a country estate for week-ends in upscale Sands Point, Long Island. He spoke about his childhood and growing up in a

3   The Sedition Act extended the Espionage Act of 1917 to cover a broad range of offenses, notably speech and the expression of opinion that cast the government or the war effort in a negative light or interfered with the sale of government bonds. It forbade the use of "disloyal, profane, or scurrilous or abusive language" about the United States government, its flag, or its armed forces or that caused others to view the American government or its institutions with contempt. Those convicted under the act generally received sentences of imprisonment for 5 to 20 years.

ghetto. "I have done some wrong things. If I had gone to Yale or Princeton, things might have been different, but I quit school early, and times were tough. Tough times make monkeys eat red pepper." Although the tough times did force many Americans to eat proverbial "red pepper," the escalating cost of food also contributed to a change in their diets and behavior.

Inside this same issue of the *Wheeling News Register*, the Archbishop of Ireland took out the following full page ad: "The great cause of poverty is drink….When I hear of a family broke up, I ask the cause…Drink…When I go to the gallows and ask the victim the cause…The answer is drink. Then I ask myself in wonderment, why do no men put a stop to this thing?" Unfortunately, the Bishop's call for the enactment of prohibition provided neither an attractive alternative choice of nutrition, nor a return to sobriety. This 1912 leap year became a peculiar and memorable hallmark. Albert Berry made the first parachute jump from an airplane, the Titanic sank, Fenway and Tiger stadiums opened, and sodomy was legalized in France.

The "Friendly" City of Wheeling, perceived as a showpiece for Victorian splendor and values, would soon face the risk of pejorative, lasting recognition as "Little Chicago." Perhaps overstated, nevertheless, the City's allure for uncontrollable crime, passion and conspicuous consumption would grow exponentially. Then, on June 30, 1914, life would change forever for many of the saints and sinners of the Mountain State, but for no one more than the now anglicized William G. "Big Bill" Lias.

In the recent general election, West Virginia voters, by a majority of 92,342, approved Prohibition. They banned the sale of beer, wine and liquor. This action, of course, preceded the National Prohibition Act which went into effect October 28, 1919. Prohibition in West Virginia remained in effect until its repeal on February 28, 1935. Years prior to this 1935 tri-state repeal, legislation was passed to allow limited sale of medicinal liquor in drug stores. The West Virginia Prohibition Act went into effect in 1914, giving wild and wonderful Mountaineers a head start on National Prohibition. What followed were years of almost exclusive production, retailing and consumption of an array of too often toxic libations, ranging from bathtub gin (made from a mixture of industrial alcohol, ethanol and juniper) to moonshine, containing as much as 75% pure alcohol.

ELEVEN

DANIEL BOOZE

As you might expect, the privileged were liberated from the risk and insult of imbibing the toxic, inebriating substitutes. They procured their pleasure in refined and expensive Canadian liquors transported and sold by the imaginative hooch colonizer, "Big Bill" Lias. This aspiring entrepreneur could never have imagined that the on-

James T. "Blackie" Lacavoli, Cleveland Mafia Leader testifying before U.S. Senate Crime Commission. A 40 year protégé of "Big Bill"

set of National Prohibition would send him on his way to unimaginable wealth. He began selling pints of moonshine from the back of his Uncle's bakery wagon and quickly excelled in the quality of his inventory and marketing skills.

He left for Detroit in 1918 where he learned to refine his bootlegging skills, while working with the infamous "Purple Gang." This mob alliance opened the door for his future bootlegging activity. In time, Lias would develop a lifelong criminal relationship with James T. "Blackie" Licavoli, another successful bootlegger, who eventually ruled as a boss for the Cleveland mafia for fifty years. It was a result of this relationship with Lacavoli that enabled Lias to become an enduring and respected criminal power.

The trade was flourishing throughout West Virginia before the arrival of National Prohibition, but Lias took it to another level when he partnered early with George Seibert, the wealthy, Wheeling WASP who popularized and protected their business with his intrinsic prestige and cooperation from law enforcement. Seibert and Lias soon became the architects and engineers of the Wheeling bootlegging trade. They modified trucks and passenger cars with false floorboards and hidden compartments. They also purchased a fuel tanker to transport hundreds of gallons of liquor from Canada to Wheeling. They were selling thousands of bottles of Canadian whiskey for $8.00 a bottle. Their clients ranged from hole in the wall speakeasy operators to the private homes of the affluent and their watering holes. In addition, smuggled bottles of these bribes were routinely delivered to the residences and offices of City, County and State officials. These generous, customary offerings transformed into cases adorned with bows of red ribbons at Christmas.

In 1916, the state of Michigan also approved prohibition, thus making the bordering state of Ohio a destination for smugglers and bootleggers who could easily travel to Canada to buy premium liquor. The following article was published in the *Detroit News* circa 1921. "The fervor pod for prohibition was sweeping the country and in 1917 the 18th Amendment was passed and by January of 1919 it had become ratified by three-fourths of the states. The Volstead Act (National Prohibition Act) provided the federal vehicle for enforcement and prohibition took effect January 16, 1920. Although individual provinces including Ontario had outlawed the retail sale of liquor, the government of Canada approved licensed distilleries of which there were forty-five in Ontario alone, allowing manufacturing, distribution and exporting of liquor." A news account written by Jenny Nolan aptly described the trade: "Michigan law and judges were lenient, fines for first offense was twenty dollars. The Ohio to Michigan roads were a stream of traffic. The Detroit River was less than a mile across in some places and stretched 28 miles long with thousands of hiding places, and was said to be responsible for carrying seventy five percent of the liquor imported to the United States." Nolan further revealed that illegal liquor revenue was second only to the automobile industry, and in 1929 placed the annual revenue from bootlegging at two hundred and fifty million dollars.

TWELVE

PUT ME IN COACH

Lias faced his first federal conviction on charges of bootlegging in early 1926. His self-sacrificing conviction allowed his partner to avoid prosecution. He served less than a year and was paroled from the Federal Road Camp at Alderson, West Virginia on November 24, 1926. Immediately upon release, he returned to Wheeling, where he remained until December when he was granted leave by the Department of Justice to move to Pittsburgh. He resided in Pittsburgh for nearly a year, and according to FBI accounts was engaged in the buying and selling of second-hand furniture. Lias used this trade to help launder the thousands he had saved from the bootlegging trade. He soon became disgusted with this masquerade and moved on to huckstering produce, remaining under the watchful eye of federal parole authorities. Federal records indicate that he was earning between sixty and sixty-five dollars per-week. Lias stayed on the "lam" under FBI scrutiny, while quietly sitting on thousands of dollars he had saved from his bootlegging days.

The following was taken from an interview conducted by Special Agents of the FBI:

During this time, Lias was interviewed by federal authorities regarding fines and assessments levied against him for previous crimes. He explained, "I had some money at the time I was sentenced in 1926, but ran out of this money. I paid part of my fine and that of my friends which amounted to over five thousand dollars. Also, I paid a considerable amount of money to my three lawyers. I am not now in a position to pay the $5500 I owe, but at the time of my examination for parole, I told the federal parole board about my situation, and my commitment papers to Atlanta stated that I was not to be held for this fine. I am asking you to dismiss this fine so I can be able to start anew and earn an honest living and become a law-abiding citizen.

The federal authorities did not pursue the fine, and Bill and his new wife, Gladys Bradley, moved back to Wheeling where he purchased their new home at 1912 Washington Avenue. Upon Bill's return to his home turf, he immediately surrendered his pledge to become a law-abiding citizen and began planning and renewing his underworld career.

Soon Lias would face his first lengthy experience behind bars, and it would occur shortly following his marriage to Ms. Bradley. Bill met Gladys during one of his many trips to the Big Apple. She was a young, voguish, Jewish girl from Brooklyn, who Bill described to others as "my first lover." He said of her: "I think she liked my bankroll more than me, but she always wanted things to be her way." Gladys relished the underworld glamour and adored the prominence she inherited as the bride of "Big Bill" Lias. She quickly adapted to the sinful ambitions awaiting her and proudly wore the crown of "Queen" of the Wheeling syndicate.

A few years before the repeal of Prohibition and at the beginning of the Great Depression, Lias, now thirty years of age, maintained his bootlegging trade, but began a "numbers" operation that would quickly cover a three state area. He recruited two cousins from Detroit and convinced his longtime friend, George Seibert, to join him in the illegal lottery operation.

Back home, Bill's new bride, Gladys was in full swing, enjoying her migration to Wheeling and relishing the tangible benefits of her marriage. However, her imaginative zeal caused concern that would curtail her creative ambition and strain her union with the Greek Czar. Gladys was tormented by what she described as "so many dumb hillbillies making so much easy money." The big city girl could not resist the temptation for seizing the opportunity to take Wheeling prostitution and her pocketbook to another level, which she believed would deliver a greater stream of revenue and broaden her spouse's political protection. She received Bill's reluctant permission to open what she termed "an upscale, cosmopolitan whorehouse" to compete in "a city full of second class whores and tobacco chewing johns." She convinced her new husband that a sophisticated brothel with "top of the line" working girls would not only draw high-paying customers, but attract his high-powered friends. Reluctant, because he refused to have any direct interest in prostitution, Lias nonetheless felt obliged to finance her venture.

Lias maintained full control of the "Red Light" district in Wheeling by paying authorities the necessary protection money to keep them open. He also financed the venereal disease clinic that routinely examined the prostitutes, which kept the customers safe. He undertook this responsibility only because the "Tenderloin" district was an alluring destination for his gamblers. Bill told friends, "If a good customer is short on cash, I pay for his dinner and get him laid. If he's a winner, he's on his own, and this city will give him all he can afford. I don't want to lose a customer. If they're laughing when they leave town, they'll be smiling on their way back."

Johnny Mathews, a long-time Wheeling syndicate operative, said that when word got out of Gladys' expectant new role as "Madam Lias," the police chief and city manager were terrified. They both served as "back stage" managers of Wheeling's prostitution operations and successfully avoided overwhelming condemnation from ministerial groups and the media opposed to the open city. Although the morally elite were not eager to condone prostitution, they painfully accepted the fact that it served a dual purpose: offered a measure of public health control and treated the uncontrollable passion of those deprived sexual predators whose indiscriminate craving might otherwise pose a public threat. Subsequently, mutually agreed upon and staged periodic raids were conducted with affordable fines that lessened the pressure and call for closing of the houses of ill repute. Following soapbox arrests and a mandatory twenty four hour detainment, the "working girls" were permitted to return to their craft the following day. During this brief interruption, the brothel lights stayed on, and the "bullpen girls" were called into action as replacements.

The terrified Wheeling Police Chief met with Bill to discuss the impending doom expected to result from his wife's grandiose plan. "Bill, we don't need this heat and neither do you. Besides, every time one of these johns or pimps get out of line, upsets or insults your wife, we will be dispatching an ambulance or a hearse," the chief said to Lias. Lias agreed to delay Gladys's ambitious venture, and the idea died quickly after a call went out to Pittsburgh's "Big John" LaRocca, boss of the Western Pennsylvania Mafia. LaRocca maintained a relationship with Lias and enjoyed routine voluntary gifts of cash from him. In fact, according to Johnny Mathews, what apparently sealed the deal was LaRocca sharing some undisclosed, derogatory information about Gladys's unsavory background that "Big John" was able to secure from his New York connections. Lias, now not only convinced to halt Gladys' grandiose plan, but angry and heartbroken by LaRocca's revelations, had no problem throwing away what he believed to be a winning hand. However, even before the hand was dealt and just a few days following LaRocca's bombshell, Gladys was found lying on her kitchen floor with six bullet holes in her body. In FBI Report PGD 92-231, a memo to J. Edgar Hoover, a special agent transcribed testimony he took from Lias during an interview in Wheeling, wherein Lias blamed his cousin and numbers partner, Mike Russell, for Gladys' death.

Lias' claim was, in fact, the partial truth. He failed to disclose that he ordered the murder and had in fact paid Mike Russell's wife to perform the assassination. A few weeks following Gladys' demise, a formal inquest, lasting less than ten minutes, was held by the Ohio County Prosecutor, and the official cause of death was ruled a suicide. Lias is said to have complained to friends about having to needlessly pay off authorities to cover up Gladys murder: "I wasted my money. Hell, these guys couldn't find a bleeding dog in the snow."

The following article appeared in the *Wheeling Intelligencer*, illustrating a standard of the free market of crime and corruption in the friendly city:

MRS. WM. LIAS DESPONDENT OVER ILL HEALTH COMMITS SUICIDE.

Shoots Herself After Expressing Fear of Operation Ordered By Her Physician Was Visiting Relative When Act Takes Place; Prosecutor Making Sweeping Inquiry.

Mrs. Gladys Lias, wife of William "Bill" Lias, of 92 Washington Ave., Chantal Court, shot and killed herself about 11 o'clock Thursday evening. The suicide occurred at the home of Mr. and Mrs. Mike Russell, 2342 Chapline Street, relatives.

Ill health and fear of undergoing a major operation is given as the cause for the deed. Mrs. Lias had been ailing for several months and had been ordered to undergo an operation by her physician. She is said to have worried and become despondent.

Mrs. Lias went to the Russell home early Thursday to visit Mrs. Russell. Mrs. Russell had been troubled with a sinus infection and Mrs. Lias had gone to her home to comfort her. Shortly before 11 o'clock Mrs. Lias is reported to have expressed her fear of undergoing the operation. She is said to have told Mrs. Russell that she could not stand to worry and with that pulled a revolver from her pocket.

Mrs. Russell at once saw what Mrs. Lias' intentions were and jumped up. She attempted to wrest the gun from Mrs. Lias' hand, but was unable to do so. During the scuffle between Mrs. Lias and Mrs. Russell, the gun was discharged three times. One of the bullets struck Mrs. Lias in the leg, one in the shoulder and one in the chest. Mrs. Lias then pushed Mrs. Russell aside and placed the gun to her temple. The gun was automatic and several bullets crashed into her breast. One of them passed through her heart.

A call was sent for Dr. Thomas Klug, who resides a short distance away. Dr. Klug went to the home at once and upon examination found the woman dead. A call was sent for Dr. Will Cruse, Ohio County coroner. Mrs. Russell was later taken to police headquarters, where she was questioned at an early hour by Prosecutor Don McKee. Mrs. Russell, who also suffers from a heart condition was in a very weak physical condition.

A thorough investigation into the case is being made. Early this morning, George Dixon, fingerprint expert of the city police department, was called to the home and took prints on the gun and other articles about the place. Officials refused to be specific as to the purpose of taking the prints.

It has been intimated however, that there may be further developments in the case today. Fingerprints on the gun will be of little help in closing the case, in as much as the official report that the attending physician handled the gun, thereby marring prints.

The next day, the *Intelligencer* published a follow-up story headlined:

MRS. LIAS DEATH PERPLEXES CITY AND COUNTY OFFICIALS. INVESTIGATORS SAY MRS. LIAS AND MRS. RUSSELL QUARRELED OVER PHONE. FUNERAL TO BE HELD MONDAY; WM LIAS, HUSBAND, GRIEF STRICKEN BY TRAGEDY

The death of Mrs. Gladys Lias has presented many problems that have perplexed city and county officials who have been investigating the case. Prosecutor McKee has indicated that Mrs. Lias and Mrs. Russell had quarreled over the phone. However he was emphatic in stating that he was certain that Mrs. Lias shot herself and that there was no evidence that anybody else has fired any of the bullets which penetrated Mrs. Lias' body.

Prosecutor McKee said that Mrs. Russell told him that Mrs. Lias paced from room to room during her visit. He said that Mrs. Lias was seated on a bed and procured the revolver from a bedside stand and declared, "I can't stand it anymore; I am going to end it all." Mrs. Russell claims that she grabbed for the gun and pulled it down, but the other woman was too strong for her.

A post mortem operation showed that Mrs. Lias had been struck by six bullets.

Officials are also attempting to determine how Mrs. Lias sustained a broken nose and lacerations about the forehead and side of the scalp.

Bill Lias was said to have spent more time deciding what to eat than contemplating who should be killed. He first came to the attention of the FBI's Pittsburgh Field Office when the Wheeling based U.S. Attorney requested an undercover investigation into the attempted machine gun murder of a confidant of a prohibition agent assigned to the area. From newspaper accounts of the time, the intended victim of the slaying was Ray "Boots" Highland, a confidential informant for prohibition agent Roy Hundley. Sources interviewed, alleged that Anthony "six toes" Baio, an active Capone mob associate on the lam in the Elm Grove area, was contracted for the assignment. Baio was a recent Sicilian immigrant who was hiding from authorities because he was a suspect in a Canton, Ohio murder.

THIRTEEN

Soaring Twenties

In 1929, bootleg whiskey, bathtub gin, raging carnality and the stock market crash may well have served as contributing factors to the rising misery and mortality rate in the city of Wheeling. With a growing population of 56,000, the rate and cause of death for the city, among other related statistics, was published in the local newspaper. Heart disease, pneumonia and violence were the leading cause of death for inhabitants of the "Friendly" City. Cancer was the fourth leading cause, followed by syphilis, which continued to plague the nation until the discovery of penicillin fifteen years later.

Economic chaos caused fifty percent unemployment and manifested reckless, desperate behavior among those impacted by the financial crisis. This was perhaps a major factor in the uncontrollable decadence gripping the city. The benchmark for survival, or in some cases extended life, and the preservation of nobility was reserved for the advantaged. Moreover, those who were able to afford suitable and private treatment for their irrepressible passion avoided public disclosure and arrest. Those left with no choice other than treatment at a public facility for sexually transmitted disease were documented, arrested, faced fines and jail time. In 1929 records showed that one hundred and forty six were arrested and prosecuted for carrying the disease of gonorrhea or syphilis. The publication also revealed statistics from the two hospitals in the city, reporting 799 cases of current syphilis treatment, while a total of two thousand eight hundred and ninety received treatment for the disease during that year. Difficult, but worthy of note, is that reported gonorrhea victims also realized a significant rise to 752. Ironically, singer Eddy Cantor 's "Makin Whoopee" was the number two song during this time.

Pets were outliving their owners. The city of Wheeling rivaled Chicago in homicide deaths per population. Dr. Fredrick Hoffman, at the time a national leader in the study of crime in the United States, is quoted in the *Wheeling News Register* as follows: "The United States continues year after year to maintain its unenviable position as having the highest crime rate of any large country in the world." Catherine McNicol Stock, Chairman of the history department at Connecticut College wrote, "[f]aced with the worst economic downturn in history, many local politicians turned the heat up in their rhetoric. For example, the Governor of North Dakota, William Langer, a staunch opponent of farm foreclosures, told followers to 'Shoot the Banker, treat him like a chicken thief.'"

FOURTEEN

ATLANTA BARS

"Mink" Gaudio was a Steubenville, Ohio product and widely regarded as a master of Ohio Valley mob history. He boasted he could read a guy through binoculars. Mink began working in Steubenville gambling retreats before his thirteenth birthday. He recalled when Al Capone owned a Greyhound racetrack in Steubenville. Mink said that when someone had a big winner, they had to beg to get half their money. One of Mink's early duties was as a runner for the numbers king in the city; he began working for them in 1932. He said they would let him roll a special set of dice numbered zero to nine to determine the winning number. "The boss would first ask, do we have Follansbee, East Liverpool? He continued to call out every city that he covered. He made certain that all bets were in, and they held the dice, checking all of the wager slips to see what number they didn't want rolled. Following the audit, he would slap me on the back of the head and say, 'roll em' kid.' I rolled the dice until the number they wanted appeared." Mink said the boss was so cold "you could put ice in his mouth, and it wouldn't melt. His sidekick, Phil Matucci was the mastermind, and nobody messed with him. He was so short, you could eat peanuts off the top of his head, but giants opened the door for him." Phil Mattuci owned a nightclub in downtown Steubenville, and Dean Martin sang there when he was a kid starting out. Mink said that Dean sang so poorly, Phil had to pass out free drinks just to hold the crowd.

Back in the Friendly City, "Big Bill" was leaving the federal courtroom on his way to the federal penitentiary. He was convicted for violating the National Prohibition Act. This racketeer was now a twice convicted felon and faced a three year sentence in the Atlanta penitentiary. He began serving this sentence on December 17, 1931. He was shuffled around institutions and did not arrive in Atlanta until April 18, 1932, preceding the arrival of Al Capone who was escorted

DOC Photo Alphonse "Al" Capone, Atlanta Federal Penitentiary

thru the gates a month later in May of 1932 to begin serving his eleven year sentence for income tax evasion. William G. Lias wore Department of Corrections number 40752, while Alphonse Capone was assigned 40886. At the time, Capone, 5' 10 ½," weighed in at 255 lbs., out weighing "Big Bill" who at 5' 7 tipped the prison scales at 247 lbs. Lias wrote to family friends telling them that he and Capone occupied cells near one another and consorted frequently. He said, "We both enjoyed special treatment and privileges including carpeted cells, radios and special diets from the outside, delivered to our cells by prison guards." Bill also told friends that Capone had Cuban imported cigars delivered to him, but he liked the Marsh Wheeling stogies Lias shared with him. Lias spent a few months during his early criminal career working for Al Capone in Cicero, a Capone stronghold just outside of Chicago. Lias worked briefly at the "Ship" a 1920's full blown casino owned and operated by Capone. The Ship, a grand casino, offered craps, roulette, and black jack. It was a well protected enclave secured by men armed with machine guns, mounted behind shatterproof glass near the money cage.

William G.
Big Bill" Lias

"Big Bill," now fifty pounds lighter, was discharged from Atlanta in 1933 after having served just over one year of his three year sentence. Although he was a "model" inmate, his early release had nothing to do with his compliance or good time credit. The penitentiary warden and guards were annoyed by Lias early release, since they were losing the unreported income they enjoyed from Lias' benevolence during his stay. Detailed evidence from archived FBI files revealed that Lias arranged to have $500 delivered to the brother-in-law of the publisher and editor of the Atlanta Constitution for securing an early release for Lias.

"Big Bill" returned to manage his profit-soaring numbers operation, held in place by his partners George Seibert and the Russell brothers. While the majority of Americans were still waiting in soup lines, fighting over food scraps and wiping their asses with soft pages from Sears & Roebuck catalogues, Lias and his former bootlegging partner were far beyond the proletariat and bourgeois, raking in thousands a day from their multi-state "numbers" operation.

FIFTEEN

STILL NIGHTFALL IN AMERICA

It was indeed for some "the best of times and the worst of times." An example of the moral cadence of the period, a large wire-service photograph appeared on the front page, bottom fold of the *Wheeling Intelligencer* captioned, "WAY DOWN SOUTH IN THE LAND OF COTTON." The photo showed three black women dressed in protective clothing, hunched and picking cotton. It read, "Darkies are singing their old spirituals as they stoop to harvest another crop of cotton, expected to total 15,000 bales. Their burlap sacks filled, they weigh in their pickings, receiving from 50 to 75 cents per hundred pounds for their toil. The white staple is then loaded in high-sided wagons and rolled away over red clay roads to the gin. Night brings singing and dancing around the little cabins as the weary workers return from the fields. Prices this year are expected to be higher than any received for many years, so there's a good cause for singing in the South."

The newspaper headline on that same day revealed President Roosevelt's Supreme Court Nominees pledge to the KKK: "HIGH COURT JUSTICE URGED KLANSMEN TO HELP CONTROL U.S." "President Roosevelt's first court appointee made fervid pledge to hooded order after Alabama nomination to U.S. Senate." "Before the fourth annual Klorero of the realm of Alabama Invisible Empire, Knights of the Ku Klux Klan, held in the Klavern of Robert E. Lee Klan No. 1, South

Twentieth Street, Birmingham, on the afternoon of September 2, 1926, United States Senator Nominee, Hugo Black renewed his pledge of fealty to, in his own words, 'the ideals of this great fraternity to which we belong.' (Birmingham, Ala. (copyright by the North American Newspaper Alliance Inc.)) Hugo Lafayette Black went on to serve 34 years on the Supreme Court, where he distinguished himself as a defender of the first amendment, the right of defendant's to counsel and a leader in populist and liberal causes.

SIXTEEN

NUMBER'S UP

While Lias was under investigation for his numbers writing operation, a Revenue Agent issued the following report to the Federal Bureau of Investigation: "I was admitted through the electronically controlled doors that led up to the second floor. There, Lias met me at the top of the stairs. He invited me to his bar and sold me a drink of whiskey for which I paid 25 cents. The place was packed, and there were numerous card and dice games in progress. Lias told me that I could come back anytime, as long as I came alone." The first floor of the headquarters was a spacious room with custom built electronically controlled locks securing the entrance. The room was the size of a gymnasium, with a polished hardwood floor, lighted stage, a wall of safes and accommodations for hundreds of writers, vendors, and customers that gathered for the mid-day and evening draws.

Lias and his partners were forced to abandon their traditional use of stock market numbers to determine the lottery winners. They had angrily discovered that they were being duped for thousands of dollars by their New York City source who had others place bets on the winning number well in advance of it being provided to Lias. Lias unashamedly testified in court involving this matter: "We were sending $700 a week to New York to protect us from someone getting the number in advance. A guy named Joe "Whitey" Dice would come down from Pittsburgh to make the collection. At that time we got our number from the last numbers of the total shares traded for General Electric, General Motors and North American."

When the enraged Lias, discovered the identity of the local conspirator involved in the scheme to steal from his numbers operation, he allegedly accompanied the Goldberg brothers, two of his most proficient enforcers and traveled

THE OVERLORD SPEAKS

A Strong Defense Is Our William

"Overlord Speaks" cartoon was retrieved under FOIA from FBI files.

to Fairmont, West Virginia. There they found their subject, "Devil" Colantino operating a tailor shop. The victim's bullet-ridden body was discovered the following day hanging from the clothing conveyor with the last three closing numbers for General Electric, General Motors and North American etched on his forehead.

The means of selecting the winning lottery number was soon changed by the roll of dice in a special "Chuck-a-Luck" steel cage. This method not only proved to provide increased security, but raised the net profit for the operation. Lias and his partners now enjoyed the benefit of not only choosing the winning number that would yield the least payout amount, but began choosing a number that occasionally matched a ticket or tickets held by one of his crew.

The Wheeling newspaper carried headlines on January 18, 1935 with an article disclosing that the West Virginia State Police had finally succeeded in gaining forced entrance into Lias' Center Wheeling numbers operation. "They confiscated the 'Chuck-a-Luck' dice cages, poker chips, numbers slips and a record of payoffs to Ohio Valley officials that Lias identified as his 'Soup List.' The list was disclosed by prosecutors during Lias' federal tax evasion trial. E.L. Steinbecker, Ohio County Sheriff, devoured Lias' soup. Beyond his cash payments, Lias recorded a seventy dollar receipt for a suit of clothes he purchased for the Sheriff." Others among the many parasitical recipients receiving monthly bribes were the Ohio County Prosecutor Dan McKee and his assistant Tom Duval, and Wheeling Police Chief Joe Burkhart. Belmont County Prosecutor, Ohio County Sheriff Deputies and the Weirton, Benwood and McMechen Chiefs of Police also made the list. It was a Who's Who exposé of corrupt public officials. None of the bribery participants were charged or arrested, and most were reelected to office.

Hundreds of patrons and employees would arrive at the "numbers" gymnasium to await the afternoon and evening draw. Big Bill assumed his conspicuous appearance on stage near the dice machine. A former disgruntled employee explained to a *Wheeling News Register* reporter how Lias and his team would "fix" the drawing of the daily numbers: "Mr. Lias became possessed of twelve special sets of dice to be used in rolling the number. Their obvious purpose is to increase the odds in favor of the house. Before each number is rolled, every slip participating has been turned in at headquarters, and the money checked. Each pick-up man's returns are run up on adding machines, his cash compared with the record provided by his slips and the whole number verified. Before the number is rolled, it is known what numbers are 'carrying the money' hence, where the danger lies." The dice were special ordered from a firm in New York City that specialized in "loaded dice"; they were secretly weighted to avoid certain numbers. One of the State Troopers involved in the raid rolled a dice 34 times before a 2 appeared.

Lias' tri-state numbers sellers and vendors were carefully chosen. Their routes and locations included nearly every city and village within a 200 mile radius of Wheeling. Although the payoff was advertised as 600 to 1, in reality the payoff amounted to 540 to 1, with the seller and vendor sharing ten percent of the winning ticket.

Following the seizure and custody of Lias' numbers operation equipment and records, federal authorities arrested him for income tax evasion. The FBI and Internal Revenue Service based their evidence in the Lias tax evasion case on documents from his "Wheeling Book Company" for the years 1931 and 1932. The records showed Lias and his partners grossed $730,923.54 from their numbers operation for the year 1931. This, of course, was Lias' "cooked book" numbers and far from their actual profit. Nor did the estimated amount of profit include the thousands made from "fixed" draws where the ghost winner was actually a front for Lias.

Lias went on trial in federal court in Elkins, West Virginia for failure to pay $21,919 on an estimated income of $122,641.33 for the year 1931. During trial, he testified that he was imprisoned in Atlanta serving time for a liquor violation and had instructed his partner and cousin, Theodore Russell, who was secretary of the organization, to file his return.

The *Wheeling Intelligencer* published an editorial during Lias' trial expressing their outrage over Lias' admissions of bribery of public officials: "Lias testified against his partner: 'Seibert was influential politically. He used his political influence any time there was trouble. Seibert saw that we got squared off.' Thus, Bill Lias testifying at Clarksburg yesterday, explained George Seibert's connection with the numbers game. That's expressive language. It means Seibert was the fixer. The way you get 'Squared off' when running a gambling racket or operating outside the law, is to bribe public officials."

SEVENTEEN

Justice Delayed

Federal Judge William E. Baker (often referred to as the best judge money can buy), who presided at the trial, instructed the jury that if they believed Lias was incarcerated during this time and had asked his partner to file his return, he should be found not guilty. The jury bought it, and William G. "Big Bill" Lias was acquitted. During the trial, Lias retained the services of twelve attorneys (including the Judge) paying tens of thousands of dollars in recorded fees and expenses that in today's dollars would exceed a half million dollars. This, of course, was at a time when a loaf of bread cost 9 cents.

Some prominent and national attorneys made a small fortune representing Lias. However, one influential Wheeling barrister and fellow Greek-American, August Petroplus, refused Lias' repeated lucrative offers to provide legal counsel. He was among the minority of Greek-Americans who ignored Lias' wealth and influence. Friends of Gus claimed he despised Lias and his followers for their hypocrisy; "The Wheeling police would unashamedly escort Lias thru downtown Wheeling traffic. He could murder a guy on Saturday night and sit and pray in his reserved front row pew at church on Sunday morning."

During trial, prosecutors evidenced account balances for the numbers operation on deposit at the Center Wheeling Savings Bank. Lias was forced to testify and explain his enigmatic accounting system: "I put one set of books under the name of

'Joe Dayten,' that was money we took in the day. The other was 'Joe Nighten' for the night roll." He also volunteered the admission of disguising his accounts for his other activities. "'Joe Steam' was the name I used for my bookmaking money, and I kept my bootlegging money under 'Joe Barrel'."

Prosecutors revealed that the current account balance for "Joe Dayten" was $229,833, and "Joe Nighten" held $184.350. It was estimated that the Lias/Seibert numbers business grossed one million five hundred thousand dollars annually. Lias' fortune seemed infinite. (Whg. News Register)

In August of 1937, the United States government began their income tax fraud case against Bill Lias' partners in the numbers operation. His former bootlegging partner, and nexus to his social and political strength, George H. Seibert, was one who was now facing possible prison time for the same crime Lias escaped prosecution from two years earlier. The government's opening statement included, "We admit that at the trial in Elkins (Lias' 1935 income tax evasion trial), we tried to convict Bill Lias as the sole owner of the numbers business, and we believed him to be guilty, but a jury said otherwise. It was not until we heard evidence in the trial that we became aware of the partnership that began in 1930."

Seibert testified that in 1930, Lias told him that he was thinking of starting a "numbers" racket, and "he knew I had some prestige around here and good reputation, and he wanted to use me as the front man." He testified further that he allowed Lias to use his name for one-third of the profits.

The subsequent arrest of Lias' partners, George H. Seibert, Theodore and Mike Russell and accountant George W. Oldham was based upon information revealed during the earlier income tax evasion trial of Lias. Seibert, Oldham and the Russells were arrested on February 2, 1937 on similar charges of tax evasion for the year 1931. The *Wheeling Intelligencer*'s Harry G. Hoffman, covering trial, provided the following transcription: "Seibert admitted during trial that he was Lias' partner in the numbers business, but denied being involved in managing the operation. Under cross examination by U.S. Attorney Gibson,

Seibert was asked, 'What did you do with the $4,345 Soup Money?' Seibert disputed the amount and said that he only paid out, it was only about $200 a month. 'For what was it paid?' Gibson asked. Seibert hesitated. 'The man's dead,' he said. 'I didn't ask his name, I asked for what it was paid,' insisted Gibson. 'For protection.' 'Protection from the officials?' 'Yes sir.' Thus ended another attempt to learn the inside of Wheeling's numbers rackets soup list."

He continued to testify as to how and why he was asked by Lias to get in the numbers business. To the astonishment of all, Lias was subpoenaed by U.S. Attorney Howard Robinson as a witness for the government against Seibert. There was outrage among the press that Lias, "[t]he leader of the underworld was called as a prosecution witness for the government." Overlooked in their seemingly justifiable rage was the fact that the fourth estate remained unaware that Lias had corroborated with Seibert and his attorneys prior to trial. He provided assurance that his testimony would be exculpatory and favorable toward an acquittal of his life-long friend and business partner.

During Seibert's trial, Lias was informed that co-defendant Mike Russell had worked out a deal with the feds and would in return offer incriminating evidence against good friend Seibert. He became enraged and assured Seibert that the matter would be taken care of. Meanwhile, Mike's brother Theodore was being held in protective custody in fear for his life. He too was expected to incriminate Seibert in exchange for a reduced sentence. However, Theodore quickly became convinced that a plea of guilty would keep him from testifying and save his life. Thus, he acted accordingly and pled guilty before the trial began. The Russells were born in Canada under the name of Panas and adopted the name Russell when they arrived in America as alien citizens. Their mother and Bill Lias' mother were first cousins, and both Russells came to Wheeling to join "Uncle Bill" in the numbers business.

George Seibert moved closer to freedom when on August 15th, just days before he was scheduled to testify against Seibert, Mike Russell was murdered in front of his Fifteenth

Street apartment in East Wheeling. He was shot in the neck and behind the ear. Police also found four bullet holes in his hat. Sources revealed that Lias paid one of his local enforcers, Patty Bonovich, to kill Russell. Lias is said to have joked, "I could have told him to put his hat back on his head before they shot it, but after all, he was my cousin."

Less than a month later, a formal inquest was held in Ohio County Court and widow Elsa Russell, the key witness to her husband's death, asked to be excused from testifying due to sudden shock. The last person to be with the victim, Louis Goldberg, also begged to be excused because he claimed, "I have to be in Cleveland due to my health." It was reported that although a summons was issued for Goldberg, it was never served, and the prosecutor admitted that a summons had also been issued for Widow Russell, but she was later excused from appearing due to her physical condition. Lias allegedly sent word to both of them, asking for their cooperation. Bill's message was, "I hope you are feeling well enough and find the time to testify, and if you don't, I think everyone will understand and remain grateful for your loyalty."

Now the only remaining defendants in the tax evasion trial were George W. Oldham, the numbers operation accountant, and George H. Seibert. Seibert's character witnesses were sanitized Wheeling social supremacists: bankers, brokers, ministers, a postmaster, city manager and an Imperial Shrine Potentate. His legal team of Carl G. Bachman and Austin V. Wood was a powerful combination of skill and influence. Bachman was a prestigious criminal attorney, and Wood was notable and welded to the hip with the Wheeling establishment. Notwithstanding the uncertainty of the Russell brother's testimony, it was clear from the start, even to the uninitiated eye, that chances were slim for the prosecution. Under intense examination, Seibert's character witnesses remained stronger than bear's breath, defiantly defending their comrade.

On September 3, 1937 the Wheeling newspaper republished highlights from the transcript of Seibert's trial:

U.S. Attorney Gibson began questioning Seibert's first character witness, Charles Norteman.

Gibson: "Did you know that on November 15, 1919, George Seibert and other defendants pled guilty in federal court to conducting a brewery without paying government tax?"

Witness Norteman: "No recollection of that."

Gibson: "Did you take into consideration that on February 8, 1924 George H. Seibert pled guilty to conspiracy in federal court?"

Character witness, Louis F. Haller: "I took everything into consideration. I've known Mr. Seibert for fifty years, he worked for me, I trusted him and I'd do it again." Witness after witness would only attest to the good character of Mr. Seibert.

Then defense attorney Eugene Meacham called Lias, the prosecution's witness to the stand:

Meachem: "Are you still in the numbers business?"

Lias: "I don't like to admit that, I might incriminate myself and I don't lie to answer."

Meachem: "When did you first go to work after you quit school in the sixth grade?"

Lias: "Helping my people in their store. Helping in a bakery, driving a wagon. I have bootlegged all my life."

Meachem: "Where did you work besides Wheeling?"

Lias: "I've worked in Detroit, Chicago and Indiana."

Meachem: "When you came back to Wheeling did you engage in the bootlegging business?"

Lias: "I worked in my brother's store in Richland. They found two barrels of mash on the ground floor of the building where he had the store. In preference to seeing my oldest brother go to jail, I took the fall. I got six months and $1000 fine. In May 1921, I was tried for conspiracy and found not guilty."

Meachm began reading from a sheet of offenses with which Lias had been charged when the witness interrupted: "Why don't you ask me about that?"

"I don't want you to explain about it," Meachem retorted.

"You want the story of my life," said Lias. "Why don't you let me tell it? I'll tell you anything you want to know. I've got nothing to hide."

Meachem: "You've been on the witness stand a great many hours of your life haven't you?"

Lias: "This is the third time."

Meachem: "May 2, 1925, sixteen months for conspiracy, October 22, 1931, two years and ten thousand dollar fine conspiracy; October 12, 1936, income tax evasion not guilty; October 6, 1936, conspiracy, knolled." (Lias shouted yes after each charge).

Meachem: "When you went to prison, you continued to direct the numbers business didn't you?"

Lias: "Will you show me how I could direct a numbers business from a federal penitentiary? Will you show me one letter in code? Do you think they are so dumb in Atlanta that they would let you send code?" (*Wheeling Intelligencer*)

Lias endured the pounding for nearly an hour. Angry but unshaken, his intrinsic wit and street smarts took him way beyond his sixth grade of education. After two weeks of what mostly amounted to a "show trial" in front of a home town jury, a decision was reached. Records show that the jury deliberated for fifteen minutes and rendered an acquittal on charges that Seibert failed to file a partnership return and conspiracy to defraud the government. Oldham, the accountant, who sobbed during most of the trial, was described to the jury as an outstanding former member of the West Virginia House of Delegates, who was charged because he prepared the numbers return for Russell, was also found not guilty. Theodore Russell pled and was given probation.

EIGHTEEN

CAREER CHANGE

It is noted in the FBI files that, during an interview with Lias, it was clear he continued as king of the numbers racket until late in 1935, when he recognized it was time to consider abandoning his numbers operation because of increased and constant scrutiny from federal authorities and an appreciation of his narrow escape from income tax evasion charges. What further hastened his decision was news that the numbers business was made a felony by statute, imposing heavy fines and federal prison time. Choosing wisely, Lias closed the business and proceeded to harvest from his new venture.

Big Bill flexed his muscle and eventually took over nearly all of the slot and vending machine business throughout the Northern Panhandle, north into Youngstown and east to Washington County, Pennsylvania. This new venture included pinball, cigarette and candy machines, along with juke boxes. During the time of this transition, the FBI continued their surveillance, and in one interview with a former Ohio County prosecutor, the FBI agent asked his opinion of Lias' character and reputation in the community. The former Ohio County prosecutor said he knew Lias for approximately 15 years and knew him officially while he served as prosecutor. He characterized Lias as an unusual character who wielded powerful influence and accumulated substantial wealth.

Shortly after employing his new business venture, Lias worked a cloakroom strategy with his hand-picked city leaders to facilitate and protect his operation. In 1936 he temporarily succeeded in legalizing slot machines, a feat not accomplished permanently until sixty eight years later. Wheeling City Council essentially passed an ordinance that de facto legalized slots. The Council successfully defended their position, explaining it as an effort to bolster the city's revenue. A license fee of $250 a year would be charged for each machine, and for $500, an operator (like Lias) could place an unlimited number in any single establishment. Lias now owned ninety percent of the slot machines and one hundred percent of the prime locations. By assessing a stipulated and periodic "fine," the city, in effect, legalized gambling. In the first year, records showed the city derived over $119,977 in fines. Ninety-five licenses were issued in the first year, and the city realized $30,000 in new tax revenue.

After the first year, the legalization of slot machines drew profane criticism from the local press, who printed a headline calling slot machine patrons, "suckers" and illustrated the long odds of winning. They also talked about the "crooked" machines and the resulting increased crime rate in the city resulting from slot machines.

The press added fuel to their coverage by publishing an editorial claiming, "Mothers are complaining that a child, no matter what his age, is liable to play this 'one arm bandit' and as a result, many spend their money in the machines instead of buying lunch between classes. Wives claim their husbands are working and paid, but lose most of their money playing the slots before they get home." The newspaper won this round. The music from the slot reels lasted only until a federal grand jury took action, and the city adopted an ordinance declaring slots illegal. This didn't deter Lias; he simply ignored the order and continued to distribute his slot machines, while relying upon the force of bribery, circumventing laws interfering with his gambling operations.

Lias then engineered a more manageable, secret business affair to sanction slots in Wheeling. He persuaded the mayor and city manager to amend the ordinance, imposing a gambling tax on various forms of gambling in the city which would allow the city to recover lost revenue from the abolition of slot machines. The new tax revenue and resurgence of slots was accepted by opposition groups and welcomed by city leaders. Each month, the city "fined" each horse book operator $630 and imposed a fixed fine on each slot machine. In the first year of operation, the city realized in excess of one-hundred thousand dollars in new found revenue.

Lias formed Globe Amusement Company, which paid the city $184,500 in fines in its first year of operation. The federal government calculated that Lias was taking in at least $45,000 a month from his slot machine business. Louis Kartsimas, Lias' bookkeeper/race announcer at his Market Street horse book club, testified in federal court that the minimum weekly horse room payout was $20,000. Additionally, Lias was paying the city fine of $106 per month for each of his slot machines. The automatic fine assessment did, in fact, legalize gambling in the city of Wheeling.

A well respected Wheeling community leader provided the following documented testimony when asked his opinion of Big Bill: "Lias is not a gangster type, but an extremely shrewd businessman whose only interests in life are his business of gambling and his recent real estate acquisitions and his family. He has no recreations or outside activities and does not consort with hoodlums or gangsters except with his own henchman in Wheeling. Lias is considered by the city authorities as a great asset and one of its good citizens. The influence which he wields in rackets in Wheeling actually keeps gangsters and major crime racketeers out of the city of Wheeling."

NINETEEN

BETTER LATE THAN NEVER

In West Virginia, liquor was being sold exclusively in state-owned stores by the bottle and, under the law at this time, could only be consumed at home. The law stated that alcoholic beverages were not permitted to be sold to the public at any bar or public establishment. Nonetheless, Wheeling, as well as every other city in the state, was home to a glut of bars and restaurants, openly selling whiskey and beer for the past one hundred and fifty years. Wheeling was playing host to over two hundred unregulated bars and taverns; you could buy a shot of whiskey at the shoemakers. State officials recognized the public's will and were finally embarrassed by their centennial duplicity. In 1961, the West Virginia Legislature approved legislation permitting the sale and public consumption of alcohol to licensed establishments.

The FBI finally got around to conducting a formal interview with Lias. They questioned him in detail about his criminal past and enormous wealth. He candidly admitted to the agents that he made practically all of his money from gambling, illegal sale of liquor, horse booking, vending and slot machines. He proudly emphasized his new venture into commercial real estate. He further disclosed his political connections: "A former member of the West Virginia Racing Commission, whose appointment I helped secure, made me acquainted with U. S. Senator Neely who later became governor in 1940."

Lias freely admitted to the agent that he contributed heavily to Neely's gubernatorial campaign and bragged that he might have been the major contributor of all campaigns in West Virginia. Candid to a fault, he boasted further that he did not feel badly about giving police officers a little tip once in a while since, "everyone knows police make little salaries and some have lots of kids." He had made many a person by giving him opportunities to make money, and he always gave his lawyers good fees for representing him in criminal, as well as, civil matters.

FBI files quote a Wheeling public official who affirmed that "Lias is notorious, politically aligned and that when former U.S. Senator Neely, now Governor of the state of West Virginia, is banqueted in Wheeling, Bill Lias is one of the honored guests." Lias informed the agent, "I went to Charleston to meet with Governor Neely and he told me he would never make a move against me so long as the Ministerial Association, newspaper or City Officials did not object or make it too embarrassing for him." Most West Virginia politicians found it difficult to refuse Lias' philanthropy. Lias claimed one Wheeling official refused to turn down a hot stove.

TWENTY

Feed 'em and Weep

In the early 1940s, Lias decided to open an extravagant steakhouse/casino in a building he purposely chose in downtown Wheeling, not because of the location, but because of the ideal landlord. It was located just a few doors South of his Market Street horse book club. He named it Zeller's Steakhouse. An FBI memorandum to J. Edgar Hoover, dated July 22, 1947, discusses an alleged deal cut between Lias and the former publisher of the Wheeling newspaper, namely H.C. Ogden. The report reads: "According to [redacted], newspaper which formerly was headed by H.C. Ogden for years castigated Lias by editorial and news articles until Lias rented a piece of property from Ogden which he used for gambling purposes. Thereafter, Ogden became mild in his denunciation of vice and gambling in Wheeling. In fact it reached a point when Ogden at a later date, was called to testify before the Grand Jury concerning his knowledge of rackets headed by Lias, he refused to expose him." There is conflicting opinion about the owner of the building. Former Ohio county prosecutor Arch Riley claimed that former publisher Austin V. Wood was, in fact, the owner and rented it to Lias for three times the going market value."

Austin V. Wood, a curbstone moralist intoxicated with power and a dictatorial publisher of the Wheeling newspaper, enjoyed reporting opinion rather than news. Mr. Wood struggled with his relative morality, particularly when his ideology clashed with his zeal for profit. In 1952, he achieved his only election victory as a Delegate to the Republican National Convention. In one of his editorial rants he wrote: "General Eisenhower has not made his views clear upon either foreign or domestic issues. I do not believe we can afford either to choose blindly or again another candidate who will again endeavor to be all things to all people. As things stand today , however, my choice is Senator Taft, and my second choice is Douglas MacArthur." This demagoguery was heaped upon readers for years.

Within Zeller's Steakhouse, the Owl's Lounge was located on the second floor and offered customers a wall of slot machines, roulette wheels, dice, poker and blackjack tables. Dazzling cocktail waitresses flooded the area, joyfully carrying complimentary drinks to the players. Courtroom testimony disclosed that the casino needed $50,000 in petty cash for each night's operation. The lounge hosted a variety of dance routines, including exotic dancing, a musical background band and a singing emcee introducing nationally known entertainers. Zeller's drew celebrities and long-money players from Pittsburgh west to Cleveland.

The Steakhouse on the main floor hosted a spectacular restaurant with opulent décor: Irish linen covered tables, hand engraved glassware, crafted mirrored walls, leather-bound booths and table seating atop thick carpeting that accommodated exhilarated patrons. In the basement kitchen, commercial freezers held the very best imported Midwest beef and a staff of skilled butchers and cooks. Lias boasted to close associates that the steakhouse was a perfect trap for entertaining local and state politicians. It served as a landmark for conspicuous consumption. He said, "On opening night, the mayor stayed until closing. His wife stayed busy stuffing her purse with wine glasses and silverware. She ate salmon like an Alaskan bear." Lias always closed Zeller's at 3:00 a.m. sharp; that was his rule. He understood from his years on the street that nothing good happens after three in the morning. Most of the customers were by then broke, drunk or both, and nothing more than trouble. If decent stragglers were left on the first floor, he would pick up their check and tell them to take the food with them. On the second floor, it mattered not if you were up or down $50,000, it was closing time for everybody.

In an FBI interview, Zeller's was described by a Wheeling newspaper reporter as "the finest eating place, where the best people go to eat and drink. I am acquainted with Mr. Lias' gambling operation and Zeller's in addition to being an eating place, has an elaborate gambling casino on the second floor." He went on to tell the agent that he was acquainted with Lias and his family; that Lias' wife was a very fine, intelligent woman and they have two children, George and Antoinette, to whom Lias was extremely devoted. He stated that Lias was tolerated, recognized and known by the best people, despite his profession as a gambler. He said that city authorities recognized these enterprises by periodically fining him and others involved, which in effect acted as an unofficial license. He affirmed that the activities engaged in by Lias and others in Wheeling were not considered public crimes, and as for the illicit sale of whiskey, he said that Ohio County, in which Wheeling is located, has always had the reputation of being the wettest spot in West Virginia. "In the past, all attempts at curbing gambling and the illegal sale of liquor have resulted in merely driving these activities underground with no regulation or revenue for the city."

TWENTY-ONE

STRETCH RUN FOR FUN

Ohio County election records show that William G. Lias registered as a member of the Republican Party on October 7, 1944. His registration number was 38678. Bill said his choice had little to do with ideology; he well understood that corruption was non-partisan.

In December of 1945, Bill Lias acquired Wheeling Downs Racetrack at a public sale for $262,500. This was the former Fairgrounds Harness track, previously owned by the West Virginia State Fair Association. He spent millions converting this facility into one of the finest thoroughbred racetracks in the nation. Before he placed his offer at the front door of the Ohio County Courthouse, he was determined to cast the winning bid. His brother-in-law, Gregory Manos, told how the "old man" was infatuated with horses and horse racing. According to Manos, "He once told me, that every chance he got he walked to Wheeling Island to watch the races at the Fairgrounds. He was eight or nine years old when he began cleaning stalls and helped grooming horses, unaware that someday he would own the track and re-build it into one of the finest half-mile tracks in the country."

Within days, Lias recruited a construction team to begin remodeling and building major additions to the track. In less than a week following his renovation project, an injunction was filed against him in federal court in which the housing expediter charged him with using vital building materials for repairs and remodeling of Wheeling Downs, which at the time was in violation of certain Federal Housing Program regulations. Essentially, the injunction sought to legally restrict Lias from using any construction materials. Lias and his usual fleet of attorneys were successful in having the injunction hearing delayed, and Lias immediately tripled the number of employees who worked day and night and completed much of the work before the scheduled hearing. Predictably, the hearing was never held, and Lias continued work on the track for the next year.

Alice Lias hosting a lavish luncheon for Wheeling's finest, social elites at the Wheeling Downs Clubhouse

The beauty and modern features of the facility remained unmatched. Wheeling Downs had its own police force and fire department. Lias also provided skilled staff and a private ambulance service. He built exclusive water wells to serve the racetrack. This complex was essentially a city within a city. Wheeling Downs attracted leading jockeys and the finest horses in the nation. It was a beacon of tourism for the City. The track was resplendent and resembled a Hollywood setting. Lias not only excelled in the creation of classic architecture throughout the facility, but his vision and unrestrained investment provided many firsts for thoroughbred racing. It became the first track in the United States to install Tel-Autograph electric writing to the posting of prices. This feature was so successful in speeding up the process of paying off and guarding against error that it became standard equipment for most tracks in America. It was also the first track in the U.S. to compensate owners of horses so seriously injured during the course of the race that they had to be euthanized. The track was also among the first to employ two veterinarians, introduce voluntary urine tests at a time when it was not required and install a camera patrol. Lias added to the security when he employed West Virginia State Troopers to patrol the stable areas.

Lias' reputation was elevated to a new height with the purchase and successful operation of Wheeling Downs Racetrack. Alice and Bill took advantage of the luxurious clubhouse that served as an alluring venue for hosting elite patrons and celebrities. Sources attest that Big Bill had a ticket machine in his private racetrack office and "when he felt like it, he would print winning tickets after the race." He often passed out "winning" tickets after the race to visiting public officials, favorite guests, family and close friends. On early Saturday evenings, Bill and Alice, often accompanied by smartly dressed escorts, paraded through a crowd of respectfully silent onlookers as they headed for their clubhouse seats.

One example of Lias' willingness to spend whatever it took to maintain Wheeling Downs' reputation as a superior racetrack occurred during an early racing season when the track was losing precious race days due to extremely bad weather. The eroding center of the track made it nearly impossible to race and endangered the safety of the horses and jockeys. Lias rented a fleet of bulldozers, cranes and dump trucks and had crews working around the clock making repairs to avoid missing one day of racing. This effort provided only temporary relief. The track was in need of immediate resurfacing. When the 110 day meet ended, he went on the hunt for the best track soil available. Accompanied by recruited soil experts, he found his treasured soil only an hour drive from Wheeling. The problem was the owner of the property would not accept any terms other than the sale of the property, which amounted to several acres and a selling price at ten times the market value. Lias agreed and purchased the ten acres that included an Indian burial mound for $200,000. His fleet of trucks arrived carrying the golden loam soil for construction of a new racing surface. The track would be rated today as it was then; one of the best in the nation.

When Lias opened Wheeling Downs, he dried up much of the non-racing street gambling, bringing the horse players from surrounding states to the track, while boosting his off-site horse booking operation. Mink Gaudio left Steubenville and came to work at Wheeling Downs as a mutuel clerk. His appealing personality and street smarts made him a valuable commodity for the industry. He developed a solid reputation within the industry and ultimately worked tracks from New York to Florida. Mink, like so many others, held Lias in high esteem and could share hundreds of stories of Lias' moments of kindness and acts of narcissism.

One of the stories he shared was about a filly named "Annie's Dream." This horse made Lias a lot of money. She was a sprinter who loved the inside post position. He said that Lias took as much pride in being a handicapper as being a legitimate business success. He had a determined desire to have a horse he owned entered in the Kentucky Derby. It was less difficult in the 1950s to have a horse nominated or have enough cash for entry into the Derby. Big Bill did whatever it took to enter Annie's Dream in the Kentucky Derby. He confided, "I could have bought three horses in Lexington for less than it cost me to get Annie entered in the Derby."

Mink said that Annie had beaten some superior race horses, but she was strictly a sprinter and would have serious trouble going a mile. Nevertheless, Bill entered her, realizing that she had little chance against this level of competition and distance. He would be satisfied to have his name in the program. Mink said she drew an inside post position, broke near the top, but was looking at the field after the first turn.

TWENTY-TWO

IF YOU AIN'T GREEK–SLEEP IN THE STREET

Big Bill had nearly one-half of Wheeling's employable Greeks on his payroll. He remained loyal to his friends and especially reverent to those alliances with Greek heritage. His brother-in-law Greg relocated permanently from Brooklyn, New York to serve as General Manager of Wheeling Downs. Greg told a story that epitomizes Bill's reverence. Greg said that he was in Bill's office one afternoon, when the racing secretary walked in with a stranger and introduced him as George Retos, a Greek-American veterinarian, recently discharged from the U.S. Army and looking for work. Lias greeted him warmly, and Retos explained that he served as an officer during World War II and a practicing Army veterinarian. Following the war, he was assigned the task of overseeing the re-population of animals in Europe under the Marshall Plan. Impressed, Lias stood up, shook Retos' hand and proclaimed, "You've served your country, now Wheeling Downs will serve you." He hired him on the spot, paying him $200 a day, more than triple the prevailing salary for track vets.

Lias was now hoarding incalculable wealth, acquired from his unlawful temerity and near flawless ability to control exclusive gambling rights conferred upon him by a herd of pliant and corrupt public officials. Whenever a clarion call arose from the media or ministerial society to crackdown on crime in the city, law enforcement continued to selectively arrest and levy fines, to appease and temporarily silence the critics. In the year 1945, Lias, under his continued performance, paid tax on an annual income of over $600,000. In fact, Lias' earned income for 1945 was closer to one million. Friends tell me he had millions hidden in fire proof safes under the wooden staircase leading to the second floor of his 15th Street Wheeling home. He had the guy murdered who designed and built the secret hideaway. Lias bragged that he paid him before he killed him. "I hate a man who doesn't keep his word."

The following FBI report showed Lias' reported income compared to the Internal Revenue's correction of his net income for the years 1942 to 1948:

Year	Income Reported by Lias	Corrected Net Income of Lias
1942	$98,2358	$140,895
1943	$81,023	$266,635
1944	$86,109	$420,379
1945	$76,336	$662,992
1946	$135,429	$185,470
1947	$127,773	$323,985
1948	$17,928	$40,888

TWENTY-THREE

WIRED FOR CASH

Lias continued to prosper as an underworld czar and now controlled all but two horse booking establishments in the city and fifty percent of the two he didn't completely control. He also owned 1200 slot machines in Ohio County and had hundreds more spread throughout the tristate area. He operated his slot machine business under the trade name of Automatic Cigarette Company.

Lias acquired the exclusive rights to the nationwide syndicated wire service which allowed bookmakers to receive and transmit real time racing results from tracks across the country. Each bookmaker paid Lias a fee to have a ticker-tape machine installed in his place of business. The east coast syndicate was under the control of Frank Costello, Joe Adonis and Meyer Lansky. They formed the Trans-American Press Service, and with their Midwest and west coast allies, strung transmission wires on Western Union poles across the United States. Essentially, these syndicates controlled ninety percent of the horse book joints in America who subscribed to their service. The annual take from the service in 1953 was an estimated $25 million dollars.

Lias used various techniques to control the payout odds on horse racing results. There was a maximum payoff for exotic races. His goal was to minimize his risk and protect himself from "Boat Rides" (fixed races) and big bettors. Lias would have someone at the track place a big bet on certain favorite horses to lower the odds, thereby restricting exposure for big payoffs at his horse book parlors. He also fixed races to level off his liability or to take down a big win for Big Bill. Each of Lias' horse rooms cost him $636 a month, the fine assessed by the city. Of course, this amount was exclusive of the negotiated monthly cash payments to judges, prosecutors, sheriffs, police chiefs and any other formidable public figure with outstretched arms.

FBI Bureau File 92-3217 disclosed the following: "As an example of Lias' influence, in the latter part of 1946, there was a general shutdown of gambling in Wheeling on orders from the police. During this time, Lias was negotiating for wire service and was putting the pressure on all horse bookies to purchase the wire service from him, with additional fees which amounted from 25 to 50 percent interest in their horse race business." His motive was to demonstrate his power and influence to what he considered two "outlaw" bookmakers who refused to subscribe to his wire service. His wire service fee, which actually amounted to fifty percent of his subscriber's net business, was a bitter pill to swallow for most, but they feared the consequence of denial.

Lias ultimately controlled all but two horse booking establishments in the city. The two unwilling "outlaw" bookmakers were partners, Harry Clouse, a former Ohio County Sheriff, and a local restaurant owner, Harry Wiedetz. Clouse had strong political connections and a history of good working relations with Lias that went back to the bootlegging days. Clouse held office as Sheriff of Ohio County during Prohibition. Many of Lias' employees were being arrested for bootlegging, held in jail and made trustees. Clouse permitted them to take one of the department vehicles to drive out of state and pick up loads of whiskey for Lias. On one occasion, the trustees were apprehended by authorities in Pennsylvania with the car load of liquor, resulting in Clouse being indicted for malfeasance in office and sentenced to six months in jail.

Harry Weidetz owned the popular White Front restaurant at 1531 Market Street in the city. His bookmaking operation was located at the rear of his restaurant. Weidetz was a mundane, well-respected and well-mannered individual, who maintained a profitable restaurant/bar business as well as his horse book. At the end of each day, every ounce of food left in the kitchen was given away to remaining customers, strays and strangers. Clouse and Weidetz enjoyed their independence and refused to deal with Lias on whatever terms he offered. Moreover, they wanted to secure their own ticker tape machine instead of having to pay Lias rent and share one-half of their profit.

The following is a record from an FBI interview of Wiedetz and Clouse: Harry Clouse and Harry Wiedetz were separately interviewed. The former refused to state anything concerning his prior or current connections with Lias, claiming only to have worked for Lias as Manager of Zeller's Restaurant for a number of years, and that he got along very well with him. He stated that when Pearl Harbor was bombed, he entered the armed services and was discharged at the end of the war; he never had any words with Lias about going back to work for him, but decided to try business for himself; he was a partner in two horse rooms in Wheeling with Harry Wiedetz, and he was making a living in the operation. As is characteristic of persons in rackets of this type, Clouse could not be drawn into any controversial subjects in which he would appear as an informer on a fellow racketeer. He stated that he and Lias were in legitimate businesses which were "licensed" by the city of Wheeling, and so long as he was able to operate under the $636 monthly fine, he had no complaint to make.

Harry Wiedetz was less communicative than Clouse. He stated he had known Lias for 27 years and definitely indicated that he personally had no use for him. He stated he had no business with Lias and never had any business whatsoever with him. Consequently, he could say nothing about him from the standpoint of his character or reputation. Wiedetz admitted that he operated a horse book, and he had operated in this fashion for years and had made and lost several fortunes; he was not proud of his own background and could not say that anyone in this business could be regarded as a law-abiding person or one of good moral character. It was, of course, obvious from what Wiedetz left unsaid, he knew more about Lias than he was willing to say and, in the code of the underworld, would not give information against another in the same racket to constituted lawful authority.

Both seasoned veterans, they well understood the extent of Lias' wrath, but remained determined to secure the race results independently and directly from their own wire service rather than relying on Lias, who also had a reputation for transmitting delayed results and would place wagers on horses that had already won. (The term for this form of cheating in the industry is "Past Posting").

The Chief followed Lias' command and shutdown all bookmaking operations in the city including Lias', with his consent, of course. Although the effects of the closure brought Weidetz and Clouse to the bargaining table, they continued to refuse Lias' latest offer of a flat fee and the proviso that he assign a henchman to keep tabs on their operation. Consequently, without interference from the police chief, Lias re-opened his horse book stations, while Wiedetz and Clouse remained closed. When Weidetz contacted the city manager, he was told to remain closed until they reached an agreement with Lias.

Lias learned that Weidetz refused to follow the city manager's directive and had also re-opened, receiving race results relayed by telephone from an outside source located in Ohio. Worse ultimately installed his own teletype machine and secured real time results from a hijacking of the wire-service, which was accomplished by cutting into the dedicated wire-service line and recording the transmission. This gave them the time and opportunity to allow their patrons to wager prior to the recording, making the customers believe the race was being transmitted in real time. When Lias informed the east coast syndicate of the wire hijacking, they asked him to take care of the matter and expressed their gratitude and assurance to cover any costs involved. Lias is said to have engaged the services of his Cleveland connection to outsource the murder of Weidetz.

About two weeks later, Wheeling police reported that, while emerging from his car in the driveway of his home at 35 America Avenue, Harry Weidetz, age 57, was cut in half by a 12 gauge shotgun that was later discovered in a creek not far from his home. Every bookmaker in the city closed up shop for weeks following the murder of Weidetz. The closing was not ordered by police, nor did it flow from respectful mourners. The temporary closing was ordered by Lias, instructing his bookmaking clients, "Lay low until things cool down."

A Wheeling news reporter was permitted to attend a conference held by the Ohio County prosecutor seeking clues in the Weidetz killing. Lias and Clouse both agreed to attend, and a portion of the discussion was printed in the Wheeling newspaper: "One of the most startling disclosures was the operation of a short-wave set, a new racket in the Wheeling area, which it is thought might have been worked on Weidetz putting over a 'daily double' coup at odds of 200 to one. The payoff amounted to something like $25,000 or $50,000. It was brought out that Weidetz, aware of being duped, could have refused to pay off with the result being that he was murdered in retaliation." It was obvious the police were searching for a scenario that would eliminate Lias as a suspect.

The *Wheeling News Register* editorialized hope that the City of Wheeling and Ohio County would grant funding for a $5000 reward for information leading to the arrest of the Weidetz murderer. In fact, the local prosecutor contacted the governor to ask if any reward money was available from the state. No one came up with any promise of money except the guy who had Weidetz killed. Big Bill audaciously and publically proclaimed in his gruff voice, "Although me and Weidetz had fallen out as business partners, I still considered him a good man and want to see justice done. So you have my word of honor that anybody who gives the cops a lead that finds the murderer will be taken care of." It took ten minutes for an official inquest conducted by a coroner's jury to decide Weidetz died of shotgun wounds at the hands of a person or persons unknown. The murder of Weidetz, like most that preceded and followed in the Friendly City, was never solved.

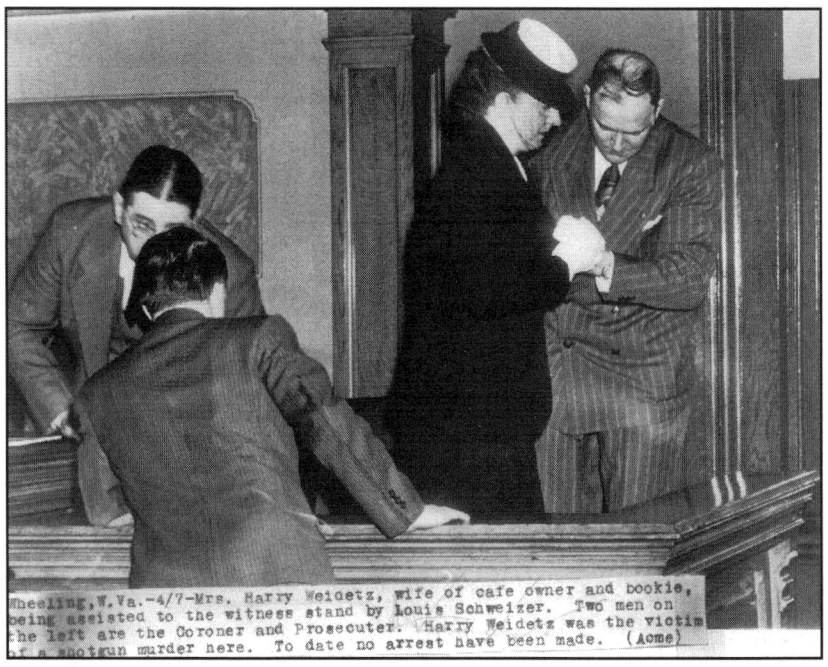

*Mrs. Harry Weidetz arriving witness stand following
coroner's inquest of her husband's murder*

TWENTY-FOUR

Spread Too Thin

Under intense pressure, the prosecuting attorney was forced to close all twenty six houses of ill-repute operating in the Center Wheeling "Red Light" district, colloquially known as "Cat House Row." All twenty six were located within a three block area of the city, which was granted a "de facto" whore house zoning variance. Twenty six madams and over one hundred "working girls" were displaced and back on their feet. Fortunately for the lonely hearted, most of the girls simply relocated to other parts of the city. It appeared, however, that the aggrieved may have been "pulled in by their catch" when the newspaper published an article describing an "upstanding, unmarried man" who was rolled for more than one hundred dollars by one of the now displaced "outlaw" whores and feared the consequences of his admission.

Chief of Police Alonzo Hixenbaugh responded to the press with the following statement: "The situation is bad, both from the standpoint of regulation of enforcement and as a public health menace." He admitted that he had many complaints, but said those making complaints did not have enough evidence for prosecution. He said the business or pick-ups on the streets, in which girls take their customers to rooming houses and cheap hotels had increased, and this was another problem difficult to overcome. He said:

"We just can't take the word of a person when he makes a complaint of this kind. The complaining person may be mistaken. We tried to keep track of the 'inmates' of the houses after they were closed, but you realize this is a big order. It's almost an impossibility. Before, we could raid an alleged house of prostitution, and we would have conclusive proof that the prostitution was practiced there. Of course a plain clothed man could be sent to the suspected houses to get evidence, but don't you think that would be asking a good bit in the line of duty?"

"Would you want it known to your wife and family that you were in houses of prostitution to get actual evidence that could be used in court? If the identity of the man gathering evidence was revealed, it would reflect on the whole police force, as far as their wives and families were concerned. When the houses were segregated in a definite area south of the creek, we had perfect control. There were no houses outside the district then. Now you can't put your finger on very many of the former inmates. Then we had perfect control and everybody obeyed or they were brought into court and punished. Then there was perfect health regulation. The girl went to the venereal disease clinic at the Ohio Valley General Hospital for examination. If they were found to have a social disease, they were taken out of the house and treated until cured. Now, there is no control from a health standpoint. The girls may all have a disease as far as we know, and this menace to the public health, in my opinion, will not diminish, it will grow. It is my understanding that when the district was a controlled and segregated area, and the girls made weekly trips to the Venereal disease clinic, they paid fees for these services which financed the clinic." [Lias actually paid for the clinic services. He had no direct interest in the whore houses but understood their value to his business].

"When a newcomer arrived in town, she was immediately escorted to the clinic and examined. If found to have a disease, she was held at the clinic for treatment. [Lias required every pimp to have his "working girls" check into the clinic the day they hit town]. I have heard that this clinic is now in jeopardy because there is a question about financing it. [Lias was giving the Chief every opportunity to get the Center Wheeling "red light" district open again, and the Chief was busy successfully silencing the cries to shut down the notorious "cat house" row]. I really believe that from an enforcement point of view and as a guarantee against the public health menace, it would be better to have the traffic segregated in a defined area, rather than have it scattered all over the city."

Lias and Hixenbaugh got their wish. Within weeks, the Center Wheeling operation reopened, and the "tenderloin" district had more red lights illuminating the alleys than Macy's at Christmas time.

Now the heat and rage were re-directed and turned up against gambling in the city. For the past five years, the city was collecting an average of $85,000 annually in periodic fines. A special grand jury was convened to investigate gambling in the city. Inexplicably, the prosecutor issued the following statement: "During the eleven years I've been in office, I have not received a single complaint regarding gambling and other vice operations in the city. I believe that the grand jury being representative of the citizens of the community, reflect the sentiment of the community. Consequently, in view of the positions taken by the grand juries, the office of Prosecuting Attorney has seldom interfered in the enforcement of law within the city limits of Wheeling." The prosecutor's admission of guilt and complicity was now on record, and he made clear his office would continue to ignore debauchery and remain sworn to complacency, injustice and ignoring public interest. Not surprisingly, the grand jury did not find any true bills of indictment that proved the commission of any crime nor impeded the continued operation of slot machines and any other form of gambling in the city.

TWENTY-FIVE

GOIN' STRAIGHT

Meanwhile, Lias' fortune-building continued to grow as he morphed into a quasi-legal entrepreneur. He began acquiring hundreds of thousands of dollars in commercial real estate holdings and expanded his gambling operations in the clubs he owned, leased or controlled. Big Bill was enjoying the good life, and adding to his pleasure was his second wife, Elmina Alice Koutroumanos, a twenty one year old beauty that the thirty-four year old Spartan married on February 24, 1935. Big Bill discovered and married his new love less than a year after the death of his "first love," Gladys, who authorities claimed committed suicide as a result of six gunshot wounds. Unlike Bill's first spouse, Elmina was not only free of self-destruction, but was a self-respecting lady with refined habits and charm.

Bill and Elmina had two children: George, born in 1936, and Antoinette, born in 1938. Both children enjoyed privileged lives; private schooling and a luxurious new home environment. Lias claimed his legal residence at 41 Fifteenth Street in Wheeling, a four story, brick fortress with a double entrance. For brief periods, he and his family, however, chose to reside at the Dodge Estate in Detroit, formerly owned by the CEO of Chrysler/Dodge. Lias recruited a dozen carpenters and craftsmen to travel from Wheeling to Detroit spending $300,000 to remodel the estate.

A letter from FBI Special Agent in Charge, E. H. Winterrowd, (File No.231) to the Director of the IRS read as follows:

Dear Sir: This will confirm information furnished to Agent of your service in Wheeling by Special Agent of this Bureau. Information has been received from a confidential source that William George Lias always carries $100,000 hidden in his automobile. The above is for your information only and is not to be disseminated outside your agency.

TWENTY-SIX

Pardon Me

Back in October of 1947, the nation was permitted to return to a voluntary food plan by the President. During World War II, in an effort to aid the war, the U.S. government urged families to reduce consumption of meat. They proclaimed "Meatless Mondays." Herbert Hoover served as head of the U.S. Food Administration. Now, President Roosevelt implemented a voluntary plan for restaurants across the nation to commit to a "Meatless Tuesday" in an effort to conserve food and feed the people of Europe. Throughout the city, "No Meat" signs adorned the windows of restaurants to comply with the President's Food Committee appeal.

In concert with the national call for sacrifice and preservation, ministers, mothers and Boy Scouts crowded the city halls of Wheeling to proclaim, "No More Corruption Day" for the city. These groups protested before the mayor and city council.

The following "Ground Hog" day, the Sheriff declared another ban on gambling, and the crackdown continued for months. City officials turned on one another, policeman accused one another of corruption, and anger and chaos prevailed. However, the local press announced then "Voice of Reason" and resolution from City Manager William Hannig, who stood before the mayor, council and groups of protestors and admonished the hypocrisy: "I want it to be on record that if we're going to enforce the law, it should not be selective. We start with the Fort Henry Club [a bastion for Wheeling's elite], the Wheeling Country Club and all fraternal organizations. Enforce the elimination of slot machines, gambling, and the sale of liquor in all of these places. I would not want to see that, and I don't believe any member council would want that." For years now, the city had been the reluctant beneficiary of hundreds of thousands of dollars in revenue from slot machines. Mr. Hannig's persuasive logic and, of course, the fear of lost revenue would soon prevail.

It wasn't long until Wheeling opened up again. Taverns and houses dispensing liquor, offering dice and poker games and the "ladies of the day and night" were also once again treated with impartiality. The law, sin and sex were separate but equal. In this year, the "Friendly City" hosted over a million tourists. The city's economy

Lias Family at their 15th Street home in Wheeling

was booming, and growth was staggering. Visitors were spending millions on hotels, restaurants and nightclubs. The racetrack and retail outlets were crowded. Worthy of note is the traffic surrounding the discreet tourist destination in Center Wheeling. Darkened alley windows displayed inviting soft red lights, and inside the "girls" were on their backs averaging ten times the weekly salary of a steelworker. Meanwhile, the local Chamber of Commerce modestly competed, exhibiting their commerce and independence with American flags and Uncle Sam pin ups in their windows, as they celebrated the announcement of the impeding Fourth of July parade.

On July 22, 1947, J. Edgar Hoover received the following memorandum from the Pittsburgh FBI Field office: "This office is currently conducting an investigation into the character and reputation of the subject, William Liakakos aka William Lias, alias William 'Big Bill' Lias, 'Big Bill,' 'Colonel Bill Lias,'

'Uncle Bill,' 'The Greek' as being of good moral character and a law abiding person in connection with his application for a pardon after completion of his sentence. As the Bureau undoubtedly knows and has been developed in the investigation thus far, Bill Lias is a notorious and an admitted gambler and operator of gambling establishments and race horse bookie for years in Wheeling and Ohio County, West Virginia." The memo omitted Lias' arrests, fines, convictions, bootlegging, numbers writing, and his alleged involvement in the attempted machine gun assassination of a federal informant, the suspected murder of his ex-wife and five other victims, and wholesale bribery of public officials. Clearly, the FBI was given room for a mild recommendation of pardon to the President. Of course, the fact that a United States senator signed off on the application could have favorably influenced their evaluation.

The adulation accompanying the pardon application was authored by reputable and prominent Wheeling figures. One affiant interviewed in connection with Lias' application for restoration of his civil rights was a journalist employed by the *Wheeling News Register*. He testified that gambling in Wheeling was somewhat officially condoned by city authorities because gambling, horse racing, as well as illegal sale of whiskey, was peculiar to this city. He went on to say that "gambling in particular is somewhat officially condoned because the city of Wheeling succeeded from a system of payoffs to a system of automatic and systematic fines which yields the city of Wheeling an approximate sum of one hundred thousand annually."

U.S. Attorney Joe F. Gibson wrote, "As Mr. Lias is paying up his old fine and is clearing up his income tax claims with the United States, I want to recommend that he be restored his civil rights. I think this is justly due to Mr. Lias or any other citizen under the circumstances."

The President of the Half Dollar Savings Bank of Wheeling wrote, "I have personally known Mr. Lias for more than fifteen years and to the best of my knowledge and belief, he has conducted himself in a moral and law abiding manner. He is a charitable man and gives baskets out to poor people around Christmas time. Lias advertises Wheeling to the world, bringing in many people from outside such as Pittsburgh, Cleveland and the surrounding area. Lias is a likeable fellow and good citizen in whom no mistake would be made if this prayer of petition would be granted." Of course what the bank chairman failed to disclose was the fact that he was also a recipient of Lias' charity. Big Bill kept deposits of hundreds of thousands of dollars in non-bearing interest accounts in his bank.

Lias lamented to the investigating agent that he realized he would be regarded as a man of bad moral character and a law-breaker in the eyes of the law outside of Wheeling, West Virginia. In Wheeling, however, activities such as he pursued were condoned, so he felt himself no worse than others of the same class who enjoyed the rights and privileges of good citizenship.

Bill Lias accompanied by his attorney (center) and brother, John Lias

Lias stated that insofar as he personally was concerned it did not matter much to him if he were not granted his civil rights. However, he was doing this only for the benefit of his two young children who were discriminated against and stigmatized by his past record. He stated that he felt that if his rights were restored to him, his children might at least be able to say that their father was pardoned by the President.

In his petition for pardon, Lias listed the following as his legitimate interests:

The Laconia building at 12th & Market Streets in Wheeling, incorporated as a real estate holding in which he owns 3900 shares; his wife Alice, 1450 shares; his son, George, 100 shares; his daughter 100 shares; his brother John, 350 shares; and his sister, Mary Pappas, 320 shares.

Property	1946 Appraised Value
Building at 1224 Chapline Street	$25,000
Klieve Apartment, 2227 Eoff Street	$30,000
Automatic Cigarette Sales, 16-16th Street	$21,000
Storeroom Building, 26-30 12th Street	$41,000
Houses, 12th and Eoff Street	$20,000
Clay Parking Lot, Eoff Street	$20,100
Southern Fire Insurance Bldg, 12-17-19 Chapline Street	$62,500
Wheeling Bank & Trust Building 1146 Market Street	$500,000
Zeller's Steakhouse, 1429 Market Street	$38,500
Community Bldg., Carmel Road & Edgington Lane	$35,000
Firestone Building, Boulevard of the Allies, Pittsburgh, Pennsylvania	$200,000
Dodge Estate, Detroit, Michigan	$64,000
Wheeling Downs, Incorporated	$262,500

The FBI report stated that the current estimated value of the aforementioned real estate, which had been enhanced and improved, had a market value of more than two million dollars. Lias' wealth was beyond measure. The average annual family income in 1946 was $3000.

TWENTY-SEVEN

Don't Fence Me In

Not only did the federal government deny Lias' petition for pardon, but within a few months of his notification of denial, he was indicted for income tax evasion by a federal grand jury. In February of 1949, William G. Lias went before a federal judge in Elkins, West Virginia to face five counts of defrauding the federal government out of millions of dollars Flanked by a battery of attorneys, he listened as the judge knolled four of the five charges against him. Federal prosecutors, well aware of Lias' resources and political influence, appeared satisfied to be holding a single count of the indictment which resulted in Lias' agreement to plead guilty to the charge. Lias was led to believe his plea would offer him a most lenient conviction of a simple fine and probation. He sat in shock and anger when the judge sentenced him to five years, once again to be served in the federal penitentiary in Atlanta. Accompanied by his $50,000 worth of attorneys, he stormed out of the courtroom and directly to his hotel room where he spent the next few hours on the phone with his congressman, the governor and a U.S. senator.

A few days later, and thousands of dollars poorer, Big Bill was back in the courtroom, standing before Judge William E. Baker, asking that his plea be withdrawn and sentence revoked. The request was predicated on Lias' attorney's contention that his client was not guilty and only pled guilty because he was led to believe that he would receive probation. Without hesitation,

Judge Baker allowed Lias' pleas of guilty to be withdrawn and summarily revoked the sentence he imposed a few days earlier. Big Bill and his entourage now marched in lock-step past the table of angry prosecutors and walked freely out of a courtroom that had only two days earlier sentenced him to five years in prison.

The news media reacted to Judge Baker's decision:

U.S. Judge William E. Baker today declared he will not be drawn into any controversies concerning William G. Lias' million dollar income tax evasion trial. From his home in Elkins, the 75 year old jurist announced he has "not a word" to say about a radio discussion of the case yesterday to Drew Pearson and will let those concerning themselves in the matter "fight it out among themselves." In his regular Sunday evening broadcast [at the time, one of the best known columnists of his day in America. He wrote syndicated newspaper columns in which he attacked notorious public persons], Pearson predicted that Baker would be replaced by another jurist when Lias goes on trial, and that his recent ruling that freed Lias from a five year sentence will be investigated by the government. (Walter Gribben Jr., News Register Staff Writer)

Following Judge Baker's decision to vacate judgment and sentence, Lias, with reckless and unmitigated candor, calmly replied to inquiring news reporters: "Judge Baker and I are close friends, and the expression of friendship made by the honorable Judge Baker convinced me that we are indeed close friends." Subsequently, the Fourth Circuit Court of Appeals accepted the prosecution's appeal of Judge Baker's decision. Nevertheless, Lias continued to enjoy his freedom and was ultimately required by the appeals court to only pay an affordable fine with no prison time.

In 1948, Wheeling was host and showpiece to the world's number one production center for the manufacturing of dental anesthetics. A subsidiary of Sterling Drug[4] transferred its entire business to Cook-Waite Laboratories in Wheeling. The

---

4   A global pharmaceutical founded in Wheeling 1901, best known for its acquisition of the American Bayer Corporation (Bayer Aspirin).

plant was located in East Wheeling and employed close to 200 workers. The *Wheeling Intelligencer* reported that in the past year, the plant had produced over 44 million cartridges of anesthetics that went all over the world and placed the name of Wheeling before 78,000 dentists in the United States.

Just to offer a further glimpse into one example of Wheeling's robust economy during this period, a federal judge ordered the liquidation of Laconia Inc., under Lias' ownership. The Laconia building is a six story commercial edifice, built in 1930 resting on the corner of 12th and Market Streets. At the time, the federal receiver valued the building at $450,000. The Laconia Building housed seventy-seven offices, Walgreen's Drug store, Western Union and the Tirre Shoe Company. Walgreen's annual lease was $18,000, and Western Union was paying Lias $5000 a year in rent. On this site in 1903 was the German Bank Building and Wheeling's Opera house. The German Bank was chartered in 1870, later merging to become the Dollar Savings Bank of Wheeling.

TWENTY-EIGHT

GROOM & SHINE

In the middle of downtown Wheeling, a burly, t-shirted black man in his mid-thirties is hunched over his shoe-shine stand, spit-shining a customer's shoes while he waits his turn in the barber's chair. "Smitty" remained oblivious to the rude remarks and cheap patronizing customers. He easily recognized the difference between insincere patronage and an honest compliment. Mr. Comas, the owner who was a Greek immigrant, operated the barber shop with his three sons. He opened the shop in 1918 at the age of sixteen. For decades, Comas Brother's was the busiest barber shop in town. Smitty shined shoes and talked sports with customers six days a week at the shop, which catered to a cross section of "Friendly City" dwellers.

Big Bill opted for private grooming. He had his hair cut at home under the vigilant eye of his bodyguard and houseboy. Chuck Comas said the bodyguard sat idly by often reading a True Detective magazine, while the attentive houseboy swept the fallen locks from the tile study. Following his first cut of Mr. Lias' hair, Chuck recalls Lias asking, "What do I owe you?" to which Chuck responded, "just give me what you think its worth." Lias barked, "I always want a price up front, and then I'll pay you what I think its worth." Chuck said Lias always paid him what he normally charged for four haircuts.

Some of those who claimed to be among "Wheeling's Finest" patronized the Comas Brother's shop. The exceptions were the few elite snobs who detested public scrutiny and the mere misery of having to consort with the general public. Among those select few, some would summon one of the Comas brothers to the enclaves of Wheeling's exclusive Fort Henry Club for an after hour grooming. Chuck said that most of them were cheap and pulled money from their pockets by the ears.

Chuck Comas later told the story of how Smitty arrived at the shop. He said Smitty had a shoe-shine stand a few blocks away from the Comas Shop at the Liberty Hat Store on 11th Street. One afternoon, Smitty approached Chuck's father and discussed the possibility of relocating to the Comas Shop. Smitty explained his dilemma to a patient Mr. Comas: "Mr. C., I can't afford to buy shoes to shine. I have to split my tips with the owner, and there's not much left for me." Chuck said his father immediately offered Smitty a job at the shop and assured him he could not only keep his tips, but retain all of his earnings. All he asked was that Smitty clean the shop after closing each day. Smitty worked at the Comas Brother's shop until his death twenty-five years later. One of the remarkable achievements of this disadvantaged, semi-literate gentleman was his acquired ability to learn to speak the Greek language. He jokingly referred to himself as the "blackest Greek" in Wheeling.

Chuck Comas often spoke about one of his more peculiar and difficult customers who was one of Lias' on-call out-of-state henchmen and reputed to be a stone cold killer, a slender, six footer with a curved nose and steely eyes. He was known among the inner circle as "Different Cities." Chuck said he reserved special time for "Different Cities," always near the end of the day. He felt it was best that few, if any, customers were present when "Different Cities" arrived, and the privacy suited them both. "He paid me extra for the special attention he wanted. I cut his hair with a tapered candle, it was called 'singeing.' I then brushed the burnt edges. He believed 'singeing' would keep oil in the hair follicles. He wore patent leather shoes with a permanent mirror like finish. Nevertheless, he always had a buck for Smitty. From the time he entered the shop until he left, he seldom spoke more than three words; he said, 'hello' and when he paid me, he said, 'okay?' Then he swaggered to the door, with his back turned, he waved and said goodbye. His bankroll, inches thick, was always tied with a rubber band. He insisted on wearing his jacket while I singed his hair. Of course, I quickly understood that he preferred to keep his gun close at all times."

Big Bill had a menacing, high-powered and skilled work force. Like any corporate executive, he knew he had to develop and manage a diverse lot of obedient and reliant staff from dishwashers to dice dealers. Lias faced a number of constant challenges in keeping things under control, but traffic to the city was not one of them.

Big Bill also provided unsolicited private security services. The thriving vice trade drew an assortment of visitors and a range of undesirables. Con-men, ex-cons, gypsies, pick-pockets, shop lifters and every form of hustler and tradesman imaginable came into the city. However, few violators returned, and fewer succeeded or escaped the wrath and punishment of the Lias organization. Bill Lias wanted everyone to know that he was the only criminal in town.

TWENTY-NINE

ONLY IN AMERICA

In March 1949, the California Commission on Organized Crime issued in their report that Frank Castiglia, aka Frank Costello, was the reputed head of the national slot machine racket which took in an estimated 2 billion dollars a year, of which 400 million was spent bribing public officials. Costello was well regarded as a political genius and referred to among his colleagues as the "Prime Minister" of the underworld. Lias, like every other slot machine operator, made regular contributions to the New York Costello family, sending payments through his Cleveland Mafia connection. Anyone who attempted to operate a hijacked or black market slot machine in Lias' territory did not become the recipients of due process--no threat, no warning, just the object and victim of his wrath. Although prone to violence, in some cases, Lias delayed its use simply because of the negative public reaction. Those who knew him warned others: "Bill will kill you for an orange." However, Lias understood the perils of violence and adopted fear as the least expensive motivator. Lias reaped tremendous benefit from the paradox he created. He controlled one of the most corrupt, but safest cities, on the East coast. You could walk safely through the dark alleys of Wheeling with your pants down.

The city virtually closed down on Sundays. Blue Laws[5] left only churches, movie theaters, Walgreens, and Islay's chipped

---

5   Sunday Blue Laws were enforced to restrict or ban some or all Sunday activities in observance of a day of worship.

ham and ice cream store open. Monday thru Saturday left "Little Chicago" wide open 24 four hours a day. On weekends there were crowds on the sidewalk through the early hours of the morning. They wandered in and out of saloons and all-night restaurants; some choosing to gamble, dine or drink before or after crowding the Center Wheeling alleys and beating the doors of the "Red Light" district.

THIRTY

SHIP THE SPARTAN

The Immigration and Naturalization Service began investigating Lias in 1932, but were unable to start proceedings against him for deportation until 1953, following passage of the McCarran-Walter Act, which forbids citizenship to an undesirable alien twice convicted for criminal offenses. In 1932, when the INS first initiated an effort to deport him, it was discovered that he could not be deported under the existing statute. Later, it appeared possible to deport him following discovery of his re-entry into the U.S. from Canada, enabling the INS to charge him with having entered the country as an alien without a passport. Authorities delayed action because of their obligation and desire to collect the prevailing tax lien against him. During the immigration proceedings, the government allowed provisions of the McCarran Act to be revoked to allow him to make trips within a twenty five mile radius of Wheeling, with the exception, of course, for him to travel to Washington, D.C. for tax hearings and to Detroit where he maintained his second home.

The McCarran Act was essentially a U.S. statute that required the registration of Communist organizations with the Attorney General. It created the Subversive Activities Control Board to investigate persons believed to be involved in "Un-American" activities. Citizens of this group could be denaturalized. This statute was meant to strengthen deportation laws and targeted what the U.S. government believed to be disloyal or subversive persons in a time of war. It was extremely controversial, and Congress overrode President Truman's veto of the bill. Truman is quoted as saying: "This bill is the greatest danger to freedom of speech, press and assembly since the Alien and Sedition Laws of 1798." Much of the law has since been repealed and ruled unconstitutional by the United States Supreme Court.

Bill and Alice Lias seated next to Gregory Manos and his bride, Elizabeth Vasilou, during their elaborate wedding reception

An exhaustive and detailed interview of Lias conducted by FBI agents regarding attempts to deport him reads in part as follows: "Lias emphasized that he has tried to extricate himself from gambling enterprises but cannot seem to get it out of his blood. He stated that he does not go on vacation or play around like gamblers in resort towns and has no recreations except making money at this type of endeavor. He stated that he has enough money and real estate to keep him and his family in the best of circumstances, and although he has tried to quit on several occasions he has been unable to do so."

From this personal interview, it was apparent that Lias was possessed with a powerful brain, was shrewd and enterprising and mad for power and wealth. He stated very bluntly that he was the cause of the city being in the black and of putting Wheeling "on the map." He stated that he had many friends in public office and in high government places and intimated that money could get him anything he set his heart on. He scoffed at honest police officers who tried to be "cops" and were satisfied with the small pittances that their jobs paid. He repeatedly stated that he was not concerned with local laws, but would never permit any infraction of federal laws. He stated that he kept scrupulous records of all his illegal businesses and paid the U.S. government every cent he owed in income taxes, and he maintained the services of a full time accountant for that purpose.

The records of the Wheeling Public School system show on one card that Lias entered Center School, Fifth Ward, on September 13, 1909. His address was given as 2208 Main Street, and his date of birth as October 16, 1898. On another card, the Wheeling Public School Enrollment Form, the date of birth for William George Lias of 2308 Main Street, Wheeling, was 1899, aged 10 years. The parent's signature given was shown as Louis Lias, brother.

During this time, Lias was tried for income tax evasion in 1936. The question of his alienage was brought to the attention of the Bureau of Immigration & Naturalization authorities, and the agency conducted an extensive investigation to establish his true birthdate and place.

During the investigation, the Bureau questioned Lias' sister, Potista, who stated that her mother told her that Bill Lias was born in Wheeling. Lias' brother John refused to be interviewed, stating that he came to the U.S. before William and did not know where he was born. Brother Louis, now deceased, gave a statement to the Bureau stating that William Lias was born in July of 1900 in Gythion, Greece, his mother wrote and told him the information, and in 1909, he sent his mother the money to come to the U.S. His mother, accompanied by his brother

William, arrived in America in 1909. Confronted with this information, Lias stated he was born in Wheeling on July 14, 1900, and his mother told him that as an infant, they returned to Greece where his father died, and his mother brought him back to the United States in 1909. He said: "There are a lot of people in Wheeling who remember when I was born, and they still talk about how big of a baby I was. I weighed almost 13 pounds when I was born. My mom told me I ate oats like a horse."

The parade of defense witnesses refuting the United States' charges against Lias ranged from childhood friends to respected physicians, public officials and prominent Wheeling businessmen. Published testimony fueled the fires of support for Lias' defense:

John Crock, a childhood friend who later became a Wheeling Steel executive, testified on behalf of Lias and recalled being with him at an early age, telling the jury that at a young age, Lias was driving a mule cart and distributing clothing and food to the needy of Center Wheeling. He further testified: "My mother and Lias' mother would go up the hill and pick dandelions together. My mother acted as a mid-wife for several Wheeling doctors, and she showed me the house where Lias was born."

The wife of former Wheeling Chief of Police Alonzo Hixenbaugh testified that they lived next door to the Lias family at 2308 Main Street and remembered his birth in Wheeling. Several Wheeling physicians followed and testified for Lias. Dr. Randolph J. Hersey told of treating Lias for burns as a young child. In all, some 26 witnesses were summoned to the stand to testify they knew Lias before 1909 when the government contended he arrived in the United States.

On September 2, 1953, deportation proceedings against Lias began in a Naturalization courtroom in Pittsburgh. However, the trial was moved to Wheeling to accommodate over one hundred defense witnesses.

By 1961, the government's deportation case against Lias had been ongoing for decades, according to an FBI memorandum dated February 7, 1961, which was initiated as a result of the increased attention toward Lias by then U.S.

Attorney General Robert F. Kennedy. The memo contained the following: "Lias, who resides in Wheeling, West Virginia, has been under investigation by the Immigration and Naturalization Service (INS) since 1932. INS was unable to initiate deportation proceedings until 1953 after the McCarran Act became effective. Although Lias claimed he was born in Wheeling on July 14, 1890, it was proven at trial that he was actually born in Greece. In July 1955, after a long trial, he was ordered deported as an illegal alien. The Immigration Board of Appeals upheld this ruling, but in 1959, District Judge C. McGarrahy granted Lias a new trial."

Following years of arrests, hearings, trial appeals and hundreds of thousands of dollars in legal fees and related costs, the news arrived: The U.S. District Court in Washington, D.C. granted William G. Lias a trial in federal district court on the basis that Lias was entitled to contest the entire deportation proceedings from the onset and have the question of his citizenship adjudicated by a District Court. Lias, unlike Frank Costello, Luciano and Marcello, remained free in the United States, enjoying uninterrupted citizenship for years while awaiting his trial in Federal District Court.

THIRTY-ONE

I LIKE IKE

The real story behind the finality of Lias' quarter century deportation battle was told to me by his good friend, Andy Zaleski. An amazingly active and well respected ninety-two year old Wheeling stockbroker welcomed me into his office for what became a lengthy and amazingly revealing interview. Mr. Zaleski shared a wealth of information from his almost fifty year personal relationship with Bill Lias. The most astonishing was the revelation involving Lias' final deportation battle. Lias has been accurately described and depicted as a gambling czar, racketeer, underworld leader and given a number of other deserving pernicious titles, but one he deserves as much as the others is that he was a fearless and laborious political genius who spent whatever he needed to do whatever he wanted.

On this fall afternoon in October 2001, I walked into Mr. Zaleski's office, introducing myself as the gentleman who had called him earlier and asking to speak with him about his old friend Bill Lias. He greeted me with reserved enthusiasm, albeit noticeably bemused by my hand-held audio recorder, which I immediately returned to my briefcase. Holding an engaging smile, he fell slowly back into his black leather cushioned chair, leaned forward and found space to rest his elbows on his cluttered desk. The wall behind him was littered with memorabilia, family photos, news articles, certificates of recognition and merit.

Mr. Zaleski told me he was thirty years old when he met Bill, and they hit it off immediately. "I owned and operated a Sinclair gas station directly across from the cathedral on Eoff Street in downtown Wheeling. I sold gas, tires and batteries to Mr. Lias for his fleet of delivery trucks. He treated me like gold. I opened my business at the height of the Great Depression, and Mr. Lias saved me. We stayed friends until he died. During World War II, he hooked me up with contacts that gave me all the gas rationing coupons I needed. I had all the gasoline, tires and battery business in Wheeling during the war. Nobody could buy gas without a coupon, and I had ninety percent of the coupons. It was like selling iced water on the dessert. I had traffic blocked trying to get into my station."

Following the declaration of war on Japan, President Roosevelt and Congress initiated the War Production Board and the Office of Price Administration. These offices were developed to control, through rationing, food and war related goods that were needed by U.S. troops. The Office of Price Administration opened nearly nine thousand control boards across America. Each county had an administrative unit (a board composed of local businessmen and politicians). It was these appointed board members in Ohio County who oversaw the rationing levels [coupon distribution] for businesses, individuals and families. The rationing went into effect in early 1942 and ended in 1946. Americans could no longer purchase the commodities of their choice. Lias used his money and influence to purchase excessive books of rationing coupons for his and his close friends' personal use.

Mr. Zaleski reminisced and told a number of remarkable stories and experiences afforded him by his close friendship with Lias. One of the two most interesting and illustrative examples of Lias' business acumen was his request of Mr. Zaleski to arrange to have T.V. celebrity Ed Sullivan accept an invitation to be Lias' guest at Wheeling Downs. Lias said he would cover his entire expenses, pay him for his time and would also name the feature race in his honor.

Sinclair Oil was the major sponsor of the Sullivan show, and Zaleski, being a Sinclair Oil franchisee, was able to make the necessary contacts and ultimately succeed in Sullivan agreeing to Lias' offer. Mr. Zaleski said he picked up Sullivan in Lias' chauffeur-driven black Cadillac at the Pittsburgh airport and brought him directly to the track where Big Bill and his entourage, including the mayor of the city, greeted them at the door. Sullivan appeared impressed with the facility and thrilled with the attention received as he stepped onto the track to be recognized by the attendees prior to the feature race. On the drive back to the airport, Sullivan commented: "I had a very enjoyable time. Mr. Lias was an exceptional host, and I must tell you that he paid me more for one day than I make in a week doing my t.v. show."

Mr. Zaleski recalled his early days at the track under Lias: "He created a job for me and paid me $50 a day to walk around. The vast majority of key track employees were of Greek descent. In fact, Zaleski said that ninety percent of the mutuel clerks spoke broken English, and preceding the first race, during the playing of the national anthem, they respectfully held their hands over their hearts and sang the anthem loudly in Greek." Zaleski said that Lias hired the "Greek School" instructor from St. John the Divine Greek Orthodox Church to teach the first generation Greek track employees how to sing the National Anthem in Greek.

Andy Zaleski then told me the story that distinguished Lias from all crime bosses that ever were or ever will be. One early Sunday evening, he was invited to Lias' home on Fifteenth Street and sat in the company of Big Bill and his nationally renowned deportation attorney, Charles Wasserman. They remained seated at the dining room table following a dinner of Greek salad, baked lamb, grape leaves and rice prepared by Alice Lias. They munched on homemade baklava while Bill opened a bottle of imported ouzo, announcing, "Let's get down to business." Lias was haunted by the U.S. Immigration Service for twenty years

Lias told his attorney: "Charles, this deportation thing is getting on my nerves, have you heard from Justice?" Wasserman, shamefaced, apologetically responded that he had not. Whereupon, Zaleski said that Lias removed the unlit cigar from his mouth, struggled as he stood to pull his wallet from his hip pocket and stated: "Let me find my note. I've got Eisenhower 's number. He plays poker on Sunday nights and told me this is his private number to call to reach him." Zaleski said he unfolded the note, handed it to his unnerved attorney and told Wasserman to call and tell the President to make a call. Wasserman examined the note, picked up the phone and repeated the number to the operator. In less than a minute, composed but excited, Wasserman opened the conversation: "Hello, Mr. President, I am calling on behalf of Mr. Bill Lias. My name is Charles Wasserman, and I represent him in the deportation matter. He's here with me and asked that I call you to express his concern that he is patiently awaiting word from District Court on final disposition of his case." Wasserman grinned as he listened to the President's brief response and said, "Thank you Mr. President." When he hung up the telephone, Zaleski said Wasserman turned to Bill and said, "I've been practicing law for thirty years and represented some of the major corporate giants across America and on the other side of the coin, powers like Luciano, Costello and Joe Adonis, but none of them had the private phone number of the President." Lias, biting down hard on his cigar, was unimpressed by his attorney's revelation and barked, "What did he say?" Wasserman replied: "He said to tell you that it's in the works and not to worry because the Judge that will make the decision will be there long after he leaves office." Bill stood up and stuck out his hand. "I'm going to bed, you guys stay as long as you want."

Zaleski recalled an unusual tirade from Lias during the end of their evening conversation with Wasserman. He qualified the bitter exchange, attributing it to the late hour and the empty bottle of ouzo. Zaleski said, "My best recollection of Bill's rage was against the establishment; he railed uncontrollably, 'I'm no angel. I break the law, but I'm no phony either. These

"Mayflower" people with long money and power, they'll step on your face and blame you for screwin' up their shoe shine. They'll keep food off your table and buy their wife a coat she don't need. A poor guy gets a dose of the clap, and they print his name in the paper and throw em' in jail. When they can't piss, they wait until dark and go to the hospital in an ambulance and are treated like they have the flu. They wanna' drink bootleg whiskey until they can't stand up, crawl to the whorehouse and the next day they're preachin' against vice and prostitution. The poor people send their kids to schools where the janitors smarter than the teacher. Yeah, the weak will inherit the earth alright; six feet of it. Someday they'll legalize it all: craps, bookmakin', booze and whores. Then they'll run it all and still be carryin' their bibles and holdin' their noses up in the air. Don't get me wrong, it's still a great country, and I'll fight for it and always love it. I just don't want these phonies knockin' me for sellin' what their buyin'."

During the meridian of Lias' "interests," he was represented by a host of prominent Wheeling attorneys and his career barrister who extended his criminal career, Charles J. Margiotti, a nationally famed Pennsylvania attorney. Margiotti served two terms as State Attorney General and served Lias up until his death in 1956. Lias then retained the renowned Charles Wasserman to represent him in his Deportation trials. Near this transition of legal counsel, the *Wheeling News Register* wrote of his former attorneys descending upon the U.S. District Court with an array of petitions requesting court approval for bills for fees and expenses owed them by Lias. "At least three attorneys representing Lias' interests indicated they were withdrawing from pending cases growing out of government income tax claims against Lias and his companies in the amount of more than $2 million. Withdrawing were Attorney Carl Bachman and Attorney Charles Ihlenfeld of Wheeling and also Thurman Hill of Washington D.C."

The end finally came in 1961. The United States District Court in Washington, D.C. ruled in Lias' favor. The case was dismissed on June 30, 1961 by U.S. District Court Judge

Alexander Holtzoff, who confirmed that the United States had failed to establish that Lias was not a citizen of United States and thereby declared him to be a United States citizen.

On September 22, 1961, the following memo was sent to FBI Director Hoover by Special Agent Joseph H. Hannon: "Judge Alexander Holtzoff, U.S. District Court, Washington, D.C. has dismissed this case (deportation) on 6/30/61 indicating that the U.S. has not established a preponderance of evidence that subject was not a citizen of the U.S., and he has submitted a recommendation to the U.S. Department of Justice that this case not be appealed."

The Judge further declared: "Matters relating to his deportation and ownership of money on deposit in Canadian banks in the names of members of his family and an associate have been resolved. In view of the aforementioned, no further investigation will be conducted in this matter by the Pittsburgh office of the Federal Bureau of Investigation." (FBI file PG 92-231).

Lias allegedly contributed heavily to John F. Kennedy's presidential campaign, but more to Eisenhower's presidency than Henry Robinson Luce, owner of *Time magazine*. Lias' brother-in-law Greg recalls that he once accompanied a Lias devotee and Baltimore native, Tommy "The Gat" Stassinopolous, who delivered a suitcase of cash to a contact stationed at 408 Charles Street in Baltimore. The contact was believed to be an associate of the Battaglia/Trotta family who arranged to have the cash delivered directly to the White House.

THIRTY-TWO

GO ON RED

Back on Market Street, there was a new game in town. The *Wheeling News Register* caught a Wheeling city councilman trying to defend himself from his reported presence at the YALE restaurant during a police raid of an illegal dice game. The headline story read: "The News Register learned in an authoritative way that a policeman testified he had declined to make a gambling raid because a member of council was allegedly present in a restaurant while a so called '26' dice game was in progress." One of the policeman assigned to the raid told the reporter that he was instructed to "back off" when they arrived and found the councilman. The 26 game was illegal and unlike other licensed devices, e.g., tip boards, pinball and slot machines, the 26 game was prohibited. This was another of Lias' inventive traps. He allowed several Wheeling outlets to operate the game in which he collected 25% of the profit for rental and protection. The 26 game was brutal. It offered a player to roll ten dice and choose one or more numbers from his roll. In order to win, he would have to roll the number or numbers he chose 26 times in 13 rolls of the dice. The odds heavily favored the house who covered all bets. When one owner asked Lias about the player's chances of winning in the "26" game he laughed, "They'll get fatter eatin' apples."

Technology brought some relief, but also increased operating costs at the brothels. Before the advent of Listerine and paper towels, the "working girls" practiced oral and basic hygiene needs by gargling and rinsing with cheap whiskey. They also spent hours between work details, scrubbing tattered and recycled cloth bath towels. Nevertheless, the big picture never changed. In the fall of 1953, W.H. "Cliff" McWilliams, one of the more prolific journalists for the Wheeling newspaper, wrote the following, headlined: RED LIGHT DISTRICT REOPENS IN WHEELING:

The rag weeds are trampled on the railroad tracks. Men of three states are on the move. Painted beauties of yesteryear smile and nod through the little peepholes of the doors as the sultry July breezes whip around them. In other words, 23rd and Water Street looks like a cross between the days of Nero Claudius Caesar and visitation nights at the bowery. Cabs shuttle between the districts and downtown Wheeling bringing visitors and customers back. Crowds of gawking males mosey along the dusty sidewalks peering into first one window and then another. They sit on the railroad tracks and laugh, and mill men or miners, many in work clothes and unwashed, some are servicemen in immaculate uniforms, some are blushing boys out on their first unfortunate adventure.

Cliff McWilliams was a capable journalist, but he probably should have, on at least one occasion, left his pencil and camera in the car and experienced firsthand, the "unfortunate" adventure he pejoratively described as being thrust upon the "blushing boys." His painted beauties description of the "working girls" was disingenuous. They were closer to tomorrow than "yesteryear." Many, in fact, were young natural beauties. The "peering thru the windows" description Cliff offered was at best imaginative, since the girls were hidden, the rooms were darkened, and the windows draped. The Wheeling "Cat House" owners had a product to sell, and they discreetly advertised with red lights and green painted doors. They didn't recruit grandmas.

Wheeling city officials were without shame in their spurious claims of sincerely attempting to eliminate prostitution. They conducted coordinated periodic raids, arresting a few of the prostitutes only to allow them to return to their beds the following day. The calculated raids served to help silence the critics while reinforcing the belief that law enforcement was committed to cracking down on prostitution. More importantly to law enforcement, it also reminded pimps, madams and owners of the imperative to continue their protection payoffs. At times, law enforcement exercised even more, less disruptive procedures. Once during the raid of only four of the twenty-six active whore houses, only eleven women were arrested and taken into custody. They were photographed, fingerprinted, paid a fine and immediately released.

In the 1950s the Wheeling police chief presented the results of a survey conducted by the American Social Hygiene Association, giving Wheeling a top rating for its efforts to curb prostitution. In this release, the Chief admitted that several of the houses of ill repute were currently opened afternoons and evenings. He went on to say the brothels were open seven days a week and reported doing a turn-away business on weekends. He continued: "A girl at one of the houses said they had been open for the past four years, missing only a day or two." The survey revealed that the girls ranged in age from 20 to 40, and their prices were as high as $50 on weekends.

In a *Wheeling Intelligencer* article, Dick Bowden quoted the Wheeling police chief as follows: "A few traces of prostitution are still evident in Wheeling and the only possible way to clear it out is through constant vigilance on the part of police. Wheeling is fast approaching the irreducible minimum which exists in all cities in America." In 1953 television arrived in Wheeling. Cliff failed to mention that prostitutes outnumbered the TV sets in the homes of "Friendly City" residents. "I Love Lucy" took a back seat to "Round the World" with Raven. Wheeling, at this time, had the highest percentage of whore houses per capita than any city in America. Former Wheeling Chief of Police Ed Weith estimated that at one time the city of Wheeling harbored as many as forty houses of prostitution. Among those forty were two occupied by black prostitutes who, like their white counterparts, prohibited black male customers. This whore house policy remained immune from forthcoming civil rights legislation.

THIRTY-THREE

BYE, BYE AMERICAN PIE

In 1948, Lias was indicted for criminal tax fraud on charges of income tax evasion for the years 1942 through 1948 totaling $2,012.00 (equal to about $24 million today) plus penalties. He was acquitted of the criminal tax fraud on July 2, 1949; however, the civil tax liability remained. Lias argued his tax case before the Fourth Circuit United States Court of Appeals, covering the individual

"Big Bill" Lias reading over the IRS Income Tax Indictment

tax cases for the years 1942 to 1948 inclusive. William G. Lias' federal tax trial rivaled the "Andrew Mellon"[6] tax case. Records showed that Lias' tax case exceeded the magnitude of any in the history of the United States. The taxing authorities in the Lias case called the matter "startling."

Records from the Commissioner of Internal Revenue Respondent reveal that for the year 1945, the year of the maximum tax deficiency, the total net income reported by the "Lias Family

---

6   A federal tax suit against James Couzens, a Republican Senator from Michigan who was reportedly the wealthiest member of Congress at the time. The suit evolved from an ongoing dispute between Couzens and Andrew Mellon, Secretary of the Treasury. The amount of tax involved was 10 million dollars.

Group," as adjusted by the revenue agents, was $121,977.54, and the net income reported by Lias was $76,336.18, or a total of $198,313.72. The net assets of the Group increased by $540,575.21 during that year, and total expenditures of $245,456.03 were made, indicating a consolidated net income of some $780,000. The Respondent found the amounts of net income found by the tax court were omitted from Lias' tax returns, and the circumstances under which the omissions were shown to have occurred were amply sufficient to support the fraud penalties. Since fraud had been established, the statute of limitations did not apply. The Internal Revenue Service, under the Net Worth Expenditures Method for the entire Lias family group, together with additional interest and penalties, found this deficiency would amount to an estimated three million dollars.

Lias told the U.S. Tax Court that he kept $219,000 in his sister's private safe and other thousands in bank accounts listed under fictitious names. The fifty seven year old gambler said his gambling associates used these funds when he was serving a term in the penitentiary. During Lias' Hearing before the IRS Commission, he refused to furnish the agents with a net worth statement. During their quest to determine his net worth, agents discovered that mutilated currency in the amount of $124,000 was delivered by an employee of the Racing Association to the Wheeling Half Dollar Bank for deposit or exchange. In the following month, an additional $15,000 in mutilated money was turned over to the petitioner (Lias) by an employee of his Market Street Club. The money was allegedly hidden in a file cabinet in Zeller's Steakhouse. This amount was sent to the United States Treasury for redemption and was allowed to be credited to his tax liability. Lias inexplicably and fearless of self-incrimination further testified that in 1926 he had $229,000 in concealed currency and by June 1936 it had grown to $620,000. "The petitioner was on the stand for several days, affording the Court an opportunity to observe his demeanor as a witness. He was evasive, contradictory and unresponsive. As a result of his many litigations arising from his disregard of law, petitioner had evidently acquired a technique of evasiveness and confusion that made him a very difficult witness.[7]

Ultimately the decision of the Tax Court was upheld by the Fourth District Court of Appeals, and the United States Supreme Court refused Lias' request to review the case. Lias offered the government $1.6 million to settle the claim, but the government rejected his offer. Beginning in 1951, the IRS assessed Lias' debt at six percent on a final tax claim of $3,009,728.84, which amounted to $180,000 a year. In the complaint, the bulk of his assessment came from the IRS estimate that Lias was averaging $45,000 a month income from his slot machine operations. Meanwhile, they seized all of his real estate, business operations and whatever cash they could find.

On December 2, 1951, to prevent what the IRS feared as possible dissipation of Lias' property, including Wheeling Downs racetrack, pending determination of his civil tax liability, the IRS brought proceedings in District Court to appoint receivers for the property. To the shock and anger of many, the receiver (his old friend Judge Watkins) subsequently determined that it would be in the best interest of the receivership to operate the racetrack at a summer meet in 1952 and to hire Lias as General Manager since he was well qualified to run the track.

Judge Watkins, who was appointed to the federal bench by Lias' dear friend, Senator Mathew Neely, approved the hiring of Lias as General Manager at a salary of $35,000. Two "unbiased" experts were hired by the court to appraise the value at private sale of Wheeling Downs racetrack. It was noted in the appraisal that a new owner who did not have the expertise of Lias would render the enterprise a going value of $3,100,000, but with the elimination of Lias, the going value at private sale would be reduced to $2,125,000. These experts contended that it had been worth nearly one million dollars to retain Lias. An FBI Memorandum to Director J. Edgar Hoover read: "Lias is still the owner of Wheeling Downs racetrack and operates it as General Manager under federal receivership. Judge Clarence P.

---

7   William Lias, Petitioner v. Commissioner of Internal Revenue. United States Tax Court, Docket Nos. 27264.27762

Lemire of U.S. Tax Court handed down a decision after hearing lengthy testimony that Lias was liable for back income tax and penalties amounting to $2,012,000. The decision stipulated that Lias and the Internal Revenue Service must determine how much interest is owed to the government."

Among the outraged was famed radio columnist Drew Pearson. He lamented not only Lias' success in becoming General Manager of Wheeling Downs, but was furious about Lias' involvement in the recent Presidential Primary campaign in Ohio. He stated: "William G. Lias, Wheeling Downs racetrack owner, phoned Democrat leaders in Ohio to thwart the presidential ambitions of Senator Estes Kefauver." Pearson was only half right. Lias may have phoned Ohio Democrat leaders to oppose Kefauver, but in addition, made arrangements to deliver the bags of cash he would provide them.

On the floor of the Senate, U.S. Senator John J. Williams of Delaware warned: "William G. Lias is one of the nation's most prominent racketeers." *Time Magazine* produced an article titled, "THE UNCIVIL SERVANT." It read in part:

"Delaware's watchdog, Senator John J. Williams, had a shocker for his colleagues: Were they aware that the United States Government is operating a racetrack and has employed a nationally known racketeer? Were they aware that the government is paying a former racketeer an annual salary of $35,000, placing him below only the President ($100,000) and the Chief Justice ($35,000) on the U.S. payroll? Republican Williams' target is a pudgy bulls-eye he has blasted before, one time bootlegger and numbers king, William G. "Big Bill" Lias whose badly distributed 360 lbs., cause him to resemble the false-bottom gasoline truck he devised in the 20s to haul West Virginia moonshine. Forsaking crasser operations, Lias in 1945 bought Wheeling Downs, a half-mile track on an island in the Ohio River at Wheeling. To protect the tax claim, the government put Lias into receivership in 1952, then decided Big Bill probably could run the federalized track more efficiently than anyone else. Lias, who paid himself $65,000 a year as General Manager, asked a modest $55,000 to do the job for Uncle Sam. Federal Judge Harry Watkins, supervising the receivership, scaled the request to $35,000. The Internal Revenue Service makes no apology for allowing Wheeling Downs to operate with Big Bill at its helm: "We're a collection agency," said an IRS man. "If he's got the connections and know-how to make it pay, well..."

In response to the criticism, Charles K. Rice, Assistant Attorney General for the United States Tax Division, included the following in a memo to FBI Director Hoover, responding directly to a complaint issued by Congressman Dante B. Fascell of Florida:

"Lias has served as General Manager of the race track since July 18, 1952. Two race meets were thereafter held in 1952, one in the summer and another in the fall. A total of $16,930.72 was handled during those meets. The races were attended by 288,567 persons and the state of West Virginia received $700,000 from the two meets. Over $500,000 was realized in profits to the receivership. It should be noted that the operation of the track has preserved the assets subject to the lien of the United States against Lias back taxes and also benefitted the Federal Government, the State of West Virginia and the City of Wheeling through collection of taxes on profits earned during the receivership. The receiver has reported that for the period of February 24, 1952 to April 30, 1956 the receivers of the two corporations have paid a total of $4,121,257.21 to these taxing authorities."

Although critics could not deny Lias' success as appointed manager of Wheeling Downs, the outcry continued. Another article appearing in the *Coronet Magazine* by Deane and David Heller in April 1958, titled "How the Senator Made the Racketeer Pay," read:

This year approximately $46,610,239 in federal income tax will pour into the treasury. The money will come from 60,186,000 taxpayers. Some will pay with a sense of resignation; others with a feeling of patriotism, and a few under protest. Nevertheless, they will pay. For as citizens they think they should. Contrast this then, with the attitude of triple chinned, 360 pound Bill Lias of Wheeling, West Virginia.

Described by the FBI as a racket czar of West Virginia and Southern Ohio, bootlegger, slot machine mogul, numbers operator and gambler, he has amassed millions. But for years he cynically scorned even to file an income tax return, and thereafter, although he went through the motions of filing, he resorted to every gimmick, dodge and loophole that a racketeer with political connections can use to thwart our tax laws, according to United States Senator John Williams of Delaware.

Some of the assertions made by Senator Williams were that Lias bragged about bringing prominent Congressmen into the office of the Internal Revenue Commissioner to plea for assistance. It was in fact that Lias was permitted to settle one of his federal income tax claims for about ten cents on the dollar, which outraged Senator Williams who branded Lias as the 'Worst Example' of tax enforcement against the nation's big-shot racketeer.

Alice Lias and her children, Antoinette and George, waiting outside D.C. Courthouse during "Big Bill's" Tax Hearing

Senator Williams confronted Lias during an undisclosed conference in D.C., admonishing him for his failure to pay or file any tax return. The fearless and contemptuous Lias cupped his hand to his mouth and responded in a half-mocking, indignant retort: "I thought taxes were only for 'law-abiding' citizens."end of quote

On July 5, 1957, Wheeling Downs racetrack was sold at public auction for $1,780,000. The proceeds from the sale went towards the 3.8 million dollar tax claim now pending against Lias. There was little doubt that Lias had more than enough cash to pay the $3.8million lien against him, but the catch 22 of having to justify his available cash would have simply exacerbated his problems. Lias grieved the loss of his hallmark of success. The government netted nearly one million dollars from the sale with the remainder granted to Mrs. Lias and her two children.

THIRTY-FOUR

MOTOR TO THE FRIENDLY CITY

Just two weeks before his death, I ran into Big Bill's nephew, George Caravasious. Mr. Caravasious practiced law in Wheeling for nearly fifty years. He was a 1945 graduate of Linsly Military Academy in Wheeling and within seven years, received his undergraduate and law degree from Harvard University. He was a Korean war veteran and a member of the Harvard, Yale & Princeton Club of Pittsburgh. His mother, Katherine Lias Caravasious was a silent partner with Bill and George Seibert in the numbers business. Uncle Bill spent time and money grooming George for a political future that did not come to fruition. George was bashful, introverted and enjoyed debating the works of ancient Greek philosophers, but found it difficult ordering from a menu.

George and I had a lengthy and candid conversation about Uncle Bill. He was eager to boast that his uncle had accomplished what no other vice-lord was able to do. "He won two federal income tax criminal trials and one deportation trial. Most federal tax trials were settled for ten cents on the dollar, but when Uncle Bill offered to settle his last case, the IRS would no longer accept settlements of that magnitude. This policy followed the discovery of a federal judge on the take in St. Louis that brought national attention and embarrassment. Uncle Bill took the 'rubber band' off when it came to hiring the best attorneys in the nation. Charles Wasserman was the best deportation attorney in the country. He represented Lucky Luciano and Carlos Marcello in government deportation efforts. I stayed close to Uncle Bill. I attended every day of every one of his trials. He was in this country for almost seventy years and still spoke broken English." Before he departed, he smiled and remarked, "And by the way, Uncle Bill was born in Greece."

Immediately following the sale of the track, the FBI became extremely suspicious of the process and ultimate award. A special agent from the Pittsburgh office informed Director Hoover that U.S. District Court Judge Harry E. Watkins confirmed the sale of the track to Hazel Park Racing Association Inc. out of Detroit, Michigan, asserting they were the highest, most qualified bidder, when in fact, Yonkers Raceway, Yonkers, New York, had bid $1,830,000, an offer of $50,000 more than Hazel Park. However, Judge Watkins refused to accept their bid claiming Yonkers did not show "good cause" as to why the bid was not entered at a previous court hearing. In confirming the sale to Lias' choice, Hazel Park, Watkins said the award to the Detroit faction was, "in the best interest of all concerned." The August 9, 1957 FBI Memo disclosed "[a]ccording to newspaper accounts in Wheeling since the date of the award, there has been an indication that the Yonkers Raceway, Inc., which actually offered a bid of $50,000 above the bid made by Hazel Park, but which was not accepted by the court, would appeal the ruling."

The Yonkers group did not appeal the Judge's decision. The same agent sent a follow-up memo to the Director on August 9, 1957 indicating that Hazel Park owners were connected with the former "Purple Gang" from Detroit, and those current owners were members of the Mafia. The remaining bidders, including Jack Kelly, father of famed actress Grace Kelly, was represented by a young and aspiring fellow Irishman, Wheeling attorney Jeremy McCamic. A later memo to Hoover, sent August 14, 1957, indicated that Yonkers Raceway was informed, "[m] any of the officials and stockholders of the Hazel Park Racing Association were connected with the Detroit Mafia and that they are fearful of what will happen to anyone who opposes this group." Serving in the U.S. Senate at this time was Lias' friend, Mathew M. Neely, who appointed Judge Watkins to the federal post to the Third Federal District. When Watkins arrived and took his seat behind the bench, it was "shoot till you win" for Lias. The evening before the bid, Lias allegedly arranged a private meeting with Judge Watkins and the Hazel Park group at the home of a Wheeling businessman, where they reviewed the bids, rehearsed the bidding process and completed the sale.

Tocca and his crew retained my friend Mink Gaudio, who would ultimately become President of the track union. The Building Service Employees Union sought to organize Wheeling Down employees immediately following the sale to Hazel Park. The International seized upon what they believed was an opportunity to increase wages and benefits for the pari-mutuel clerks and other employees, a demand they would not dare make under Lias' rule. Obviously, they were unaware that the new owners made Lias look like Pee Wee Herman.

Ninety percent of the 145 employees signed membership cards. Tocca became outraged when learning of the threat from the employees. He called in a hit ordering the murder of the president of the union. Mike Gallo, one of Tocca's top enforcers, always traveled with him. Counsel for Hazel Park, James V. Bellanca, interceded, convincing Tocca of a better plan. Bellanca began his move, recruiting locals from the Teamsters Union to move in and organize the parking lot service, while Teamster representatives from Pennsylvania were simultaneously organizing waiters and waitresses at the tracks restaurants. Sheer numbers and power allowed Bellanca to discreetly put the Teamsters in control of the Union membership and elect Mink Gaudio, president of the local union.

Cheating is endemic to the casino gambling industry and millions are spent trying to protect owners and patrons. Horse and dog racetracks have also served as proving grounds for con-men, pickpockets, counterfeiters and every conceivable opportunity for cheating the system and the vulnerable public. Jockeys are often suspects involving fixed horse races that result in a prohibitive favorite losing or a long-shot winning a race. In contrast, competitive racing without a jockey results in equivalent public reservation. A greyhound racing trainer was once asked what he could do to make his dog win a race, he replied, "I can't do anything to make sure he wins, but if I want, I can make him lose." Some examples and forms of cheating that occurred at Wheeling Downs during this period, besides the schemes devised by colonies of jockeys, trainers, scale clerks and judges, included the daily double which was a low hanging fruit. This scam included the clerk at the ten dollar window who was in on the play. The cheater would purchase a ten dollar win ticket and go to a nearby trailer where he had access to stolen ticket paper and a printer. All that was needed was the race code printed on the original ticket. He then printed a number of tickets with every combination for the daily double (winning horses for the first and second race) in time to redeem them at the finish of the second race, thereby cashing in on the daily double.

Mink, in discussing corruption and thievery in and around racetracks, highlighted the Ciero brothers of Wheeling as the best con artists he ever saw, including those he met at Aqueduct, Hot Springs and Cleveland. When first meeting them, they shared one of their basic practices with me: "Always keep a buck in your hand whether or not you're behind the window. When a customer drops cash on the floor, you can pick it up, palm his drop, and if it's a $5, $10 or $20 give him the dollar." The brothers then instructed Mink on how to count win money for a customer: "Always count it slow and give them the lowest denomination first. Customers are intimidated and always in a hurry and many can't count or simply multiply. For example, if a guy has sixteen dollars and change coming to him, go slow-- bring the one dollar first and watch his reaction, if he's holding, bring the five and then stop, often he will run away from the window and you made him for the ten."

Mink said that "New York" guys worked at Aqueduct, then went South in the winter to New Orleans to fill out the year. "I enjoyed working with them. They were all connected and wired men. Some were made guys and picked the top jobs. They were all arrogant and brutal. I saw one guy slap a customer and they threw the customer off the track. I worked the $10 window at Aqueduct and would tout customers. Nearly every race I would make an interested customer give me $10 to buy a ticket (which I pocketed) in exchange for my 'hot tip.' If there were 10 horses in the race, I made sure I touted a different horse for each customer hoping one was a winner. Often I would end up with $40 or $50 and that was big, big money back then."

Hazel Park eventually put the track up for sale, primarily because they were unable to compete with the politically entrenched owner of their competitor, Waterford Park Thoroughbred Racetrack, located about 30 miles to their north in Chester, West Virginia. Jim Edwards, the owner, had powerful connections with legislative leaders and the current governor. Moreover, he was a Huntington, West Virginia native and enjoyed the benefit of the Hazel Park organization as being looked upon not only as outsiders, but gangsters. The WV Racing Commission controlled the allowable race days and post times for each race day. The Legislature refused to approve year round racing for any track. Subsequently, the three track owners in the state tried to squeeze as many racing days as possible for season meets. Edwards enjoyed a constant advantage in this regard, which adversely affected Wheeling Downs, its employees and vendors. Moreover, Edwards made it difficult for Tocca and his crew to employ and maintain reliable and skilled personnel. He persuaded the Racing Commission to allow him to start his races at a later time each day, which prevented his employees from working week-ends and evenings at Wheeling Downs.

Wheeling Downs employees delighted in the treatment they received under the Tocca ownership. Tommy Mathews, who retired from racing from his position as mutuels manager at Wheeling Downs in 2004, began his uninterrupted career in 1956 under Lias. He held great respect for Lias and even a greater respect for Tocca, who raised his salary from $15.00 a day to $35.00 and relocated him to supervise the count room.

Prior to the sale, Bellanca assured Mink and others locals who had demonstrated their loyalty to Hazel Park that the track would not be sold to Jim Edwards, and they were negotiating with a Bostonian sportsman named Jay Mathews, who assured them he was representing the willing new owner Tom Maren out of New England. However, it was discovered following the sale to Maren that both individuals were fronting for Jim Edwards who became the owner of record of Wheeling Downs.

A Department of Justice Report disclosed the following: "On July 30, 1962, a source advised that it is being freely discussed all over the Wheeling area that William G. Lias has re-purchased Wheeling Downs race track. Although the reports which were made public that it was sold to Thomas Maren, a Boston, Mass., Sportsman, who actually bought it as a favor to Jim Edwards, the current owner of Waterford Park race track, because Hazel Park would not sell it to Mr. Edwards." Further investigation failed to substantiate the rumor that Lias was the new owner. Mink vividly recalled soon after discovering that Maren had fronted the sale for Edwards, he received a phone call from Bellanca who said: "Mink, don't talk too much. I just want you to know that we have confirmed the double-cross pulled on us by these 'cake eaters,' and I'm making this call to assure you that we never go back on our word. Please tell our friends that I will always respect their loyalty and apologize for being fooled." Within months, Mink got word that Jay Mathews and his wife were found murdered; his son, who was living in Germany, and his daughter, who resided in Venezuela, were also murdered.

Mink said the only thing that saved Jim Edwards was Bill Lias' intervention. Lias, to some degree, convinced Edwards that he had persuaded Tocca to back off. Nevertheless, Edwards immediately hired bodyguards and had trouble sleeping for the rest of his life. Edwards purchased a failing Wheeling Downs in 1956. A few years later, after unsuccessfully operating the track, he was allegedly responsible for the fire that destroyed the clubhouse, adjoining buildings and closed the track until 1969. In 1969, he sold the track to Ogden Corporation, who in 1976 introduced Greyhound racing, which continues today. Literally and figuratively, Wheeling Downs went to the dogs.

To most, it looked like the end for Lias. The government had him on the ropes, stripped him of his real estate holdings, and brought a 3.8 million dollar tax lien against him, accumulating at six percent interest. They took possession of his race track and whatever cash he was unable to hide. But, Big Bill had a hole card. It wasn't a gold mine, but he turned it into one. He had retained an undisclosed and hidden interest in a restaurant/bar at 23rd and Main Street in Center Wheeling, sharing one-half interest with a hardened ex-con named Nick Miller. The Pirate Café was a small scale, but highly profitable business, located in the center of the "Red Light" district where they drew business from locals and week-end warriors. Nick Vosvick Miller managed the gambling end of the business, which included slot machines, poker and a black jack table.

THIRTY-FIVE

Mutiny in the County

Undaunted and left with little choice, Lias decided to approach Miller with an offer to take controlling interest in the Pirate Café. Brother-in-law Manos said that Miller reacted with fierce contempt asking Lias, "How in the hell can you do this to me? We've been partners since day one, and I've never given you a bad count. This is all I've got and now you're throwing me out in the street?" Bill impassively explained, "I'm gonna give you more than it's worth and you'll have your money in a few days." He gently returned his unlit "Bogarted" cigar back to his mouth and swaggered out the door barking, "When you get your money, I want this place cleaned out. Don't even leave the toilet paper." That same day, Lias filled a bank bag with cash and had it delivered to Miller. Within the hour, the courier returned to Lias' home with the bag full of money and disturbing news. "Boss, he said he didn't want a dime, and he's keeping the joint and don't care what happens."

On August 22, 1957, a week following Nick Miller's repudiation, his body was found stuffed in the trunk of his abandoned Lincoln on a quiet street in Wilkinsburg, Pennsylvania. Authorities claimed it was impossible to determine the cause of his death. Miller had been arrested 37 times and suffered 32 convictions. He served two terms in Ohio penitentiaries. News accounts described Miller as being "[c]lad in shorts and his body surrounded by three baseball gloves, a softball and a monogrammed sport coat." Detectives were told that a five carat diamond ring, a diamond studded wristwatch and thousands of dollars were missing. Police and press reports also revealed that inside the Lincoln was a brown felt hat bearing the label; "Louis Hat Shop, Cadillac Square, Michigan" (FBI files & *Whg. News Register*). The detectives testified that it was unlikely that the killer would leave his hat in the car. Of course, who other than Big Bill Lias, who seemingly enjoyed signing off on his accomplishments, would exhibit such audacity? By all accounts, Lias demanded that his hat be returned and explained to authorities that he borrowed Miller's car and must have forgotten to take his hat. Lias was seen wearing his hat at Miller's graveside services.

Paul Nathaniel Hankish and a notorious Pittsburgh contract killer, Al Ross Zied, were alleged to have accompanied Miller on the day of his murder, on what was supposed to be a gambling trip to Pittsburgh. There was more speculation than outrage in the community, and authorities did not aggressively pursue the investigation into Miller's death. It was, however, reported that authorities interviewed Lias for three hours, and his best public denial was, "Miller was a friend of mine, but I have not had any business with him since I sold the Pirate to him 12 years ago." Within a month following Miller's funeral, Lias, who owned the building, secured licensing, and the Pirate Café became "Billy's."

The year is 1957. Big Bill's emotional wounds were slowly healing with the comfort of the growing success of his family. His son George was attending his first year of law school at Ohio State University and recently wed. His daughter Antoinette was residing at home with her parents and attending Mt. DeChantal Visitation Academy, a prestigious private school in Wheeling. Worth mentioning, is that in 1957, America had launched a lunar exploration mission in an attempt to circle the moon, while women were catapulted into fair treatment in the "Friendly City." It was announced in that year that women became eligible to serve on juries in Ohio County.

THIRTY-SIX

GREEK TOWN

Wheeling's vice op-
erations remained free and
continued to expand. Nearly
$40,000 was spent by busi-
nesses in the city purchasing
federal gambling stamps issued by the Internal Rev-
enue Service. These "tax
stamps" allowed the owners
to participate in gambling,
including but not limited to

*Bill, Alice and special guests at
their wedding anniversary*

slot and pinball machines, numbers writing and bookmaking,
without fear of reprisal. It was Dodge City in suits and skirts.
The IRS unashamedly explained that the stamps were not a license to gamble, but only a tax.

Throughout the city of Wheeling, there were well over two
hundred licensed gambling and liquor stamps issued. Illustrative
of the neon illuminated icons serving food, fun and/or liquor to
Wheeling residents and visitors were the Bartender's Lounge,
Duck Inn, Sailor Joe's, Colonel's Sausage, Spaghetti Village
and the Dinner Bell. Spread among the eateries, taverns and
"knockout joints" were Greek coffee houses. These were ethnic
sanctuaries where many first generation Greek-Americans
consorted daily, often returning for the evening hours.

The bare wooden tables in the coffee houses were cluttered with Greek newspapers, stained coffee cups and decks of pinochle cards. Rabekah Karelis, a Wheeling native, writes in "*Greektown*" on the shores of the Ohio, "Greek immigrants settled in Centre Wheeling, earning its name '*Greektown*' by some locals. They were traditional coffee houses and Greek men were often found sitting on the sidewalks talking and playing cards. It was supposedly like walking in downtown Athens for these short blocks"

Some of the Greek-American patrons who were also owners dominating the licensed eateries in the city; Pandelos, Pappas, Demas, Dormas, Mamakos, Sklouvanakis and Vasilou. To their credit, none of the foregoing was listed among the routinely published and cited by the health department for a high bacteria count. The Wheeling news article revealed four of the twenty-six restaurants in the city checked for bacteria count by the city health department during the recent monthly inspection, showed excessive bacteria counts on glasses, knives and forks. There were likely more bacteria in the Wheeling eateries than stored in the Center for Disease Control.

THIRTY-SEVEN

Paradise Found

Big Bill had finally completed remodeling of his last gambling garrison, Billy's. A news reporter was first to describe the new facility:

"The doors that guard the back room at Billy's open only to those people who are acceptable. In a hallway leading from the restaurant proper to the kitchen is a metal door into which is set a one-way mirror. Carefully hung, the door's ease of operation masks its massiveness as it swings open into a hallway some thirty feet long and eight feet wide. At the far end is a familiar door fitted with a mirror that becomes a window when looked thru from the inside. An elaborate system of locks and lights guard against any unauthorized opening of either door. A sign on the wall informs patrons that only one door can be opened at a time; that when a light is burning above one door, it will not open. Consequently, patrons having gone through the first door, must wait in the hallway and be inspected from the back room until the locks have slid home." (FBI files & *Whg. News Register*)

The back room was a paradise for high rollers. Slot machines, poker and blackjack tables were always full, but the Barbuit table was the elephant in the room. Barbuit is a Greek dice game that was the life blood of the enormous profit from

Billy's. The game is played with two dice and originated in the Middle East. The dice were passed around the table, giving each player his chance to roll. The player to the right of the shooter is designated the Fader. He has first option of placing the amount of the wager. The shooter then has the option of covering part or all of the bet, and players make side bets with one another. In the event a player's wager was not covered, Lias or one of his subordinates was always present to fade (cover) the wager. Lose rolls were 1-1, 2-2, 4-4 or 1-2. A player's win bet was 3-3, 5-5, 5-6, or 6-6. No win and no lose rolls gave the players a chance to increase their wagers. The house raked in 2 ½ percent which amounted to thousands of dollars. The dealers -- Tommy "Tomo" Tsoras and "Tut" Beatrice -- possessed skills beyond the dreams and expectations of modern day casino owners. There was no overhead surveillance, no box men, stickman or pit boss; just one dealer, keeping track of as many as a dozen players making compounded wagers, paying winners, collecting from losers and computing payoffs following every throw of the dice, while calculating the 2 ½ percent rake.

Among the long-money gamblers on hand one evening was Johnny Joseph, a man who epitomized the purest form of addiction to gambling. Johnny was a gruesomely handsome, zoot suiter and former heavyweight professional boxer, whose numerous concussions and resulting fixations may have caused his obsessive traits. Among his obsessions was insisting his wife iron his socks and underwear. He was respected, but known to those in the loop as a guy who gambled to lose.

John woke each day thinking about his first bet. He shared a fitting, albeit grim, illustration of his gambling addiction. He related the following: "I was playing one night and was up about four thousand. It was getting close to midnight; I was tired and way ahead. I decided to quit, drove straight home and went to bed. I put the four grand and my watch on the night stand. I couldn't sleep, kept thinking about the game. I rolled over and took my watch from the night stand. It was 12:30 a.m. I got up, dressed and went back down to the game. Within an hour I blew it all, the entire four grand. I drove home with change in my pocket, went to bed and slept like a baby."

The following incident is indicative of the power and respect that Lias commanded as an underworld enforcer. On a Saturday morning at about 2:00 a.m., the Barbuit table was surrounded, crowded shoulder to shoulder with long-money weekend players; some holding their money fist tight, others in paper bags resting on the rail. These morning players were wagering as high as one thousand dollars on the first win or lose roll. Big Bill had assumed his usual position at table end where he was provided with a stool and ample space on each side of his 350 pound frame. At the opposite end of the table, stood "Coast to Coast," another less severe, degenerate gambler. His final roll would bring his total winnings for the night to just over ten thousand dollars.

Al Diekman, Mutual Manager of Wheeling Downs; Bill Lias; Thomas Flynn, Manger Wheeling Downs; Greg Manos, Lias' brother-in-law; Jack Dempsey, Heavyweight Boxing Champ receiving a charitable contribution; Wilson Seibert, Son of George Seibert; Austin Wood, manager of the local newspaper.

I had a fourteen block newspaper route that covered nearly one half the city of Benwood. I negotiated four separate drop offs with the news truck driver to lighten the unbearable weight of the Sunday paper. The canvass shoulder strap from my paper bag wore my skin to the bone. On Sunday mornings after finishing my deliveries, I was welcome to stop at the Flamingo Grill to get my usual bottle of coke and a nickel's worth of pistachios from the peanut machine. The owner, Antonio "Undo" Sparachane, was empathetic and permitted me to patronize the bar during Sunday morning clean-up. I had finished my coke and was rubbing and licking the red pistachio shell stains from my fingers when "Coast to Coast" walked through the door. I recognized him immediately. He was one of my more generous paper customers, so I hung around expecting him to buy me another coke.

He asked Undo if he could "slip" him a shot and a beer. Puzzled, Undo asked, "Man, what in the hell brings you out this early?" Coast told him that he couldn't sleep, "You aren't gonna believe what happened to me last night. I won ten thousand playin' Barbuit at Billy's. I'm still shaken' and can't sleep. I left Billy's about two thirty this morning. I was up big money, and I walked over to Lias and told him I was going to leave, but my car was parked about two blocks away in front of Alma's Red Barn. I told him I was afraid someone would rob me. He asked, 'Where do you live?' I told him Benwood and then he asked how much cash I was carrying. I told him about ten thousand. He grunted, 'Go get your car and drive home to Benwood and when you get there, call me. If you don't have ten grand, you come in tomorrow, and I'll give you twenty.' When I got home I called and thanked him. Now I ain't scared of being robbed, I'm nervous about havin' so much cash." He downed his shot and bottle of beer, pushed a ten dollar bill at Undo and told him, "Keep the change." Undo thanked him, then pointed over toward me and said, "Don't forget the paper boy." Coast to Coast walked over and handed me a five. That was the equivalent of two weeks pay for me.

THIRTY-EIGHT

Beat 'em Till They Weep

Up until the mid- 1950s Wheeling remained virtually lawless. Nobody played games with the cops or the underworld, and neither played fair. The following article appeared in the *Wheeling News Register* on March 4, 1953: "THIRD DEGREE NO LONGER USED IN WHEELING TO OBTAIN CONFESSION

The writer confessed:

"I can recall years ago when the howls of pain, cursing and the noise of battle issued from the city jail conference room in the basement under police headquarters. But the beaten prisoners were never seen since they were confined in a cell adjoining the questioning room out of sight of others than the detectives. Some policeman used to brag of their accomplishments. "He talked when we got thru with him" one would say to another in headquarters. The old third degree composed of lashing a prisoner with the buckle of a belt or a rubber hose. Often police would stand at the four opposite walls of the questioning room. One would punch the prisoner and when the blow knocked him to the opposite side, he received another blow. This practice has disappeared. The current Chief of Police has served for 25 years, and he cannot remember when a subject was given the third degree while questioned for a crime."

The truth was, not only was beating suspects or apprehended violators commonplace among the police force during this time, but many lawbreakers, pimps, cheating gamblers, thieves and disruptive drunks were left to Lias' crew of enforcers to dispense justice. Sources named Center Wheeling inhabitants Charlie Kupchak, Shorty Fragale and the Ringer Brothers as Lias enforcers. For more serious work, Lias retained the services of the Goldberg brothers, David and Hymie. Those close to Lias claimed the Goldbergs were mean and unmerciful, both former star Wheeling high school athletes. Lias claimed Hymie could tear a man's arm off like it was a chicken wing. Lias was directly responsible for numerous contract killings, among which were his horse book competitor, Harry Weidetz; former numbers partner, Mike Russell; Gus Petrakis; Nick Frank; Whitey Dice; Nick Miller; "Buckeye" Joe Papine; "Iggy" Sebulsky and his first wife, Gladys Bradley.

THIRTY-NINE

MOREY COMES TO WHEELING

Among the city's notable characters was a flamboyant, brimmed hat New Yorker who arrived in the city during the Great Depression. He wasn't looking for sex or a dice game, he was sent to buy out destitute clothiers for as close as he could get to ten cents on the dollar. What Morey Rivlin soon discovered was that even ten cents on the dollar was becoming a bad investment. His coke bottle glasses often fell near the tip of his cigar. Seldom attired without one of his favorite Hart, Schaffner and Marx suits, his flash and out of town swagger was a giveaway. Morey quickly fell in love with the city and offered the following self-characterization, "I was confident that a young, enterprising New Yorker could double down on these hillbillies before they knew what hit em." Morey envisioned a city with a lot of "low hanging fruit" ready to be picked. "I never saw anything like it. I've traveled the whole east coast, but these people were different. Most were out of work, scratchin' their ass with their elbow, some without heat and electricity and lined up for flour and sugar commodities. But the poor bastards stayed tough and proud. They just kept their heads down, kept quiet and did what they had to do to try and beat the odds. On the other side of the tracks, there were plenty of 'white shirts' carrying around pockets full of face cards (Ten & Twenty dollar bills), lookin' for action and that's what caught my interest."

Morey, however, saw the lawless opportunity in this wide-open city, but knew he had to exercise caution and patience before making a move. He said, "While I was sittin' tight before making my move, I started looking around the city for a nice Jewish girl." His first trip to the synagogue offered him an introduction to his future wife, Lilian Levin. Morey tells the story that his infatuation for Lilian grew following his discovery of her dad's Dun & Bradstreet credit rating.

Morey leased a building downtown and opened a horse book on 14th Street. "I had a pretty strong bankroll and a new wife with more cash than I could dream of. This joint was a 'hole in the wall,' I had a coke and peanut machine out front and eight chairs, a couple of tables and a chalkboard in the back room where I booked cinch bets. I was opened for about a week, when the Greek introduced himself. Two apes came thru the door and told me Mr. Lias asked them to tell me I must have forgot to get his permission to open a horse book. They said, 'Mr. Lias knows you're new in town and wants to let you know that you'll start paying him $250 a month for wire service and 30 points on your net.' I told them that kind of chop will break me. They just walked away, and one of them stopped, turned and told me, 'If you can't afford it, you shouldn't be in business.' I put a lock on the door the following week."

In the mid-1960s, Morey opened the Executive Traveler's Club. It became one of the most popular night clubs in the city, known for fine steaks, shrimp and chopped chicken liver appetizers and imported strippers. Eventually he added a black jack table and a high stakes poker game. It was "shoot till you win" for Morey. 'Big Bill' was now preoccupied and happy, busy going straight with his race track and paid little attention to independent nightclub or gambling operations in the city. Morey, his young mistress Jan and wife Lilian opened and closed the ETC.

One of my favorite Morey Rivlin stories revealed his powerful wit and sense of humor. He once complained, "You know kid, people are always asking me, 'Morey, how's business?' I tell 'em, they come to town with a twenty dollar bill and the Ten Commandments and the bastards don't break either of them."

FORTY

Don't Ask I'll Tell

U.S. Attorney General Robert F. Kennedy sent a representative from Washington, D.C., along with an unnamed Wheeling attorney and U.S. District Attorney Robert E. Maxwell, to interview Lias concerning the Teamsters' Union and its association with the Mafia. Lias had a reputation for only telling on himself. He told these individuals that he was not acquainted with the activities of the Italians; that he did not like them; that he had very little to do with them. He indicated that he might be in a position to furnish information of possible value, but feared reprisal against him or his family. (FBI Report 92-3217, 11/24/61) The FBI then sent an informant to Lias in an attempt to determine whether he was telling all he knew about the Mafia and the Teamsters. The informant reported the following to the FBI: "(Lias) told me that a representative of the United States Attorney General and the U.S. Attorney for the Northern District recently interviewed him concerning the Teamsters Union and the Mafia, but he could not furnish information that Jo Jo Pecora is a front man for Gabriel Kelly Mannerino, from New Kensington, Pennsylvania and is operating gambling establishments in West Virginia and that the West Virginia Governor is permitting gambling operations in the state; and that the city and county officials in Wheeling are either corrupt or inefficient."

The informant advised that the foregoing statements were taken on October12, 1961. The report then went on to describe details and names of active criminal events:

"JoJo Pecora, Pittsburgh, Pa., is a front man for the notorious Mannerino Family from New Kensington, PA., in the Club 30 in Chester, West Virginia. A new club on route 30 in Chester known as the "Red Dog" built ostensibly as a gambling casino in Chester has opened. The Governor is permitting a gambling casino in Morgan's Halfway house located on U.S. 40 near the West Virginia-Pennsylvania state line at Valley Grove, W.Va. He married well, taking the daughter of "Big John" Larocca as his bride. For years the rackets in the northern panhandle of West Virginia were locally operated. Lias is somewhat concerned with the infiltration of out of state racketeers into the area. During the past year or so, while Lias was busy preparing his trial in Washington D.C., certain individuals figured he was "on the boat" and were taking measures to take over. Jo Jo Pecora was listed by the Pennsylvania Crime Commission as the "underboss" to Michael Genovese of the Pennsylvania Mafia. He controlled gambling for the mob in the upper Northern Panhandle of West Virginia. He ultimately became underboss of the Pittsburgh family of the Cosa Nostra."

Over the years, the Pennsylvania Crime Commission has listed Pecora's underworld business involvements. It says Pecora was involved in a West Virginia vending business, that he was a partner of Anthony A. "Wango" Capizzi of the North Hills in Pittsburgh in a mob-run Las Vegas gambling junket business and that he ran several illegal gambling clubs along a five mile strip of Route 30 in West Virginia between the Pennsylvania and Ohio borders.

The following is taken from FOIA, FBI Memorandum dated September 22, 1961:

For years the rackets in the northern panhandle of West Virginia were locally operated. Lias is somewhat concerned Lias' close friends deserted him, and have begun to associate with Paul Hankish. There was one report that Hankish and some of his friends were planning to rob his restaurant which resulted in Lias telling Hankish and other to keep away from the restaurant (Billy's). Efforts were being made to syndicate the rackets in Wheeling. A madam of a local house of prostitution was told that she would have to pay the syndicate in order to keep operating. Lias and Hankish were now locked in a battle of criminal wills."

Al Ross, aka Abe Zied, Pittsburgh, Pennsylvania, who is frequently seen with the new crowd, is strictly an executioner. Among close associates of Paul Hankish are Johnny and Jimmy Mathews, local slot machine repairmen and thieves, who act as finger men for jobs pulled by Hankish or his associates. Lias told the FBI agents that the owner of Wheeling newspapers is in favor of an open town. The only crusader against vice conditions on the newspaper is the Editor, Harry Hamm.

Western Pennsylvania Mob Boss Jo Jo Pecora was soft spoken and easily ingratiated himself to those deserving of his friendship. However, he carried out his underworld obligations without reservation. Jo Jo was skilled at controlling his emotions, leaving few to suspect his dark side. Those close to him would tell you that a drop of his blood would kill a rattlesnake. Jo Jo and his wife lived quietly in a modest home near the base of his operation in Hancock county. Just across the Ohio River was the veritable well of organized gambling: Steubenville, Ohio, a city that significantly contributed to the Americanization of the casino industry and the forerunner of Las Vegas. From that city came the recruitment of one who became the envy and treasure of that enterprise; Pete "Kang" Griffo. Kang began his career dealing dice at the Baron Café located in the heart of downtown Steubenville. Shortly thereafter, Kang elevated his career and went to work for Pecora, first at the Club 30 in Chester, West Virginia and then to the Red Dog, a newly constructed casino only a short distance away. Kang stayed at the Red Dog working for Pecora until it was shut down following an FBI raid. He then found himself in Havana Cuba working the crap tables as a Pit Boss for Myer Lansky and Sam Giancano at their recently constructed Havana casino. Griffo and hundreds of American casino operatives fled Cuba upon Fidel Castro's takeover in February 1959. Back in the United States, Griffo was sought out by Frank Sinatra and Skinny DAmato to manage the gaming at the Cal Neva resort in Lake Tahoe. Once there, he sent for his teen-aged brother-in-law, Dewey "D.J." Guida to join him and work as a parking valet at the casino. D.J. recalled this youthful experience, "I was treated like gold. I routinely picked up the McGuire Sisters (Christine, Dorothy and Phyllis, a singing trio that earned six gold records between 1952-68) for Mr. Giancana. I made a fortune parking cars for Sinatra, Dean Martin, Peter Lawford and a ton of Hollywood celebrities." In 1963, the Nevada Gaming Commission revoked the casino license for the Cal Neva because of their finding of Giancana's affiliation. Griffo ended his career as General Manager of the North Shore Club in Tahoe.

FORTY-ONE

FAIR TRADE

One evening I was having dinner with friends at the Union Grill in Washington, Pennsylvania. Our host was Bernard Folio, a wealthy Clarksburg, West Virginia businessman. Besides beer and wine distributorships, Bernie owned a dynamite manufacturing plant. Bernie's enterprises demanded intense political involvement, as he relied heavily upon state contracts and franchises for his wine and beer distribution. He shared the following story:

"In 1978, former Governor Arch A. Moore decided to oppose incumbent U.S. Senator Jennings Randolph. Robert E. Maxwell was a Lyndon Johnson Judicial appointee to the United States District Court for North Central West Virginia. He approached me for my financial aid and family support for Jennings Randolph. We cut a deal, I went for Randolph against Moore in exchange for federal parole for Jo Jo Pecora. Moore was defeated and Pecora was paroled. It was then, and remained for decades; "Wild and Wonderful West Virginia."

The mafia's influence and control spread throughout the state. My good friend J.J., a respected Hancock County businessman, offered me precious stories of mob control and its characters. J.J. related the first FBI raid of the notorious Club 30 in Chester:

Undercover agents had been in the club for weeks prior to the raid. They drank, gambled and knew all of the dealers and most of the customers. One Saturday night, an army of agents and cops arrived. They beat the door down with a sledge hammer and came in with a doctor, two nurses and a movie camera. All the guys were hiding their guns in women's purses. They took cash, tables and dice, and the newspaper declared gambling dead in the County. The Club was back open in three weeks.

He said that Benny Phillips, a "Machine" operator (juke boxes, cigarettes, pinballs and slots), had his slot machines in the Club 30. He was so strong politically that the Mafia had to give him part ownership and one-half interest in the slot operation, because they needed his influence with the current West Virginia Governor Wally Barron.

William Wallace Barron served as Governor from 1961 until 1965. He and several others in his administration were charged with bribery and conspiracy under the federal anti-racketeering law. All were convicted of the charges except Barron. The governor was later convicted for jury tampering and sentenced to five years in the federal penitentiary. Prominent among the string of powerful defense attorneys participating was the nationally respected Edward Bennett Williams and a member of his firm, Peter Taft, grandson of President William Howard Taft.

Steubenville, Ohio was without question the original proving grounds for high stakes and professional gambling. When Bugsy Siegel opened the Flamingo in Vegas, a majority of the dealers he recruited were the best of the best dice and card mechanics from Steubenville. As Vegas and Havana Casinos began to flourish, Steubenville products were heavily recruited for management and table operations. Consequently, in the early fifties, Wheeling began outdistancing their competitor as a gambling and vice mecca. Meanwhile, Wheeling and Steubenville competed peacefully in their gambling and vice. Although both were considered tough mob controlled cities, Steubenville was controlled on-site by an assigned La Cosa Nostra Capo. Jimmy Tripodi maintained the title and control of eastern Ohio for fifty years. Those who knew him addressed him politely as "Boss," while privately, but respectfully, referring to him as "Lupo" (the Wolf).

FBI sources speculated that up until the 1960s, any mafia contract killing in the Ohio Valley had to receive prior approval from Tripodi. Immune, of course, was "Big Bill," who received direct orders from Cleveland. Tripodi was endowed with that responsibility and authority from the New York families. Some claim his territory stretched from Youngstown to Western Pennsylvania. Jimmy Tripodi was devout, very private and, despite his discreet but exceptional underworld attachment, a respected figure throughout his community. He was reserved and deferential, and it was said that he never missed offering his Sacrament of Penance and taking Holy Communion at Sunday Mass. His close friends admitted that the Priest waived Tripodi's obligation for cleansing of his sins through confession before receiving the Eucharist.

He was an "old school Mafioso, a true "Moustache Pete." His name may have appeared in the news twice during his reign and that would include the announcement of his death. I once had dinner with Jimmy and friends at his preferred and only public hangout, the Venetian Restaurant in Steubenville. I recall that during the entire dinner, he spoke only four words in English. He politely informed the waiter, "We need more bread."

FORTY-TWO

POLITICS AS UNUSUAL

The Mafia had Hancock County locked up in the 1960s. The mob owned the Sheriff, Dick Wright, who was the designated "bag" man for the Kennedy's. The mob built a motel across from the Club 30 and gave it to Dick Wright. A former Weirton bank owner was among the donors and complained, "I had to come up with a thousand cash, and they refused a check. I asked Wright, will you take anything besides cash? He said yep, gold!" A Kennedy appointee and former JFK political coordinator for the northern panhandle of West Virginia who served a decade as a state senator and was appointed United States marshall by President Kennedy talked about Kennedy's father flying into Pittsburgh airport and driving to Weirton where he and a guy named McDonough gave the Sheriff (Dick Wright) $50,000 to cover the Northern Panhandle. McDonough, who was head of the West Virginia "Irish Mafia" for JFK's primary election, is said to have passed hundreds of thousands of dollars around the state prior to the 1960 Kennedy-Humphrey primary election.

Federal authorities believed the mafia cash contribution orders came from the Pennsylvania mob boss, John Larocca, under instructions from the New York families. The Kennedy forces had no difficulty in convincing all eastern Ohio, western Pennsylvania and northern West Virginia mob interests to contribute to Kennedy's campaign.

162

The Kennedy faction not only collected well, but paid well. I recall discussing the 1960 West Virginia Kennedy-Humphrey primary with a former Wyoming County, West Virginia state senator. He told me the following story: "Dad was sheriff during the 1960 primary, and the Kennedy guy came down to see him, asked him what it would cost to win the county. Dad told him he could 'lock it up' for five thousand. The guy came back a week later with the five, and a few days before the primary he returned and asked dad how it looked. Dad showed him the results."

The FBI continued their interest in Lias, who was now resigned to operating Billy's. FBI Report File No. 166-2 revealed that informants disclosed that Lias frequented Billy's Restaurant & Bar during the late evening hours and usually remained there until 7:00 or 8:00 a.m., after which he went home to sleep. They advised that he dressed in a suit, sport shirt, hat and chewed expensive cigars. They said he continued to speak with a heavy Greek accent, was extremely overweight and was reported to have some form of diabetes. The informant made mention of the fact that he was an extremely religious man and contributed heavily to the Greek Orthodox Church in which his wife was an active member. These informants disclosed that Lias did not carry any weapons, and although he usually traveled with an associate, he was not known to use a personal bodyguard.

FORTY-THREE

Hakeem's Near Death Experience

On January 17, 1964, an automobile briefly occupied by Paul Nathaniel Hankish violently exploded in front of his residence in Warwood, West Virginia. Terrified neighbors quickly emerged from their homes to view the scene. Shrill sounds of sirens preceded the arrival of police, firemen and other medical personnel. As the smoke cleared, small scattered flames burned atop

Hakeem's Near Death Experience. Photo belongs to the Wheeling News Register

fragments of a smoldering, decimated automobile with nothing remaining above the arched steering wheel. Paul Hankish was helplessly ensnared and dying in this tomb of steel and rubble. It took nearly an hour to free him from the wreckage. Hankish entered his 1963 Oldsmobile, and when he turned the key, the charge of what was later determined to be several sticks of dynamite exploded. The attempted assassination resulted in Hankish's legs being amputated above the knees, his left ear drum being ruptured, both hands shattered requiring plastic surgery, his thighs torn to the buttocks, both eyes lacerated and full body injuries from flying metal. Upon arriving at the local hospital, witnesses said he remained periodically lucid and was first attended by Dr.'s George Kellas and Angelo Daniels. Hankish is said to have screamed, "Get these fuckin' Greeks away from me." Fortunately for him, the Greek skilled surgeons remained on duty and helped save his life.

When local FBI agents arrived at the hospital and began questioning Wheeling police officers, they affirmed that Hankish was a well-known gambler and racketeer and alluded to the feud between Hankish and Lias. They detailed the most recent confrontation between the two resulting from Hankish opening a Barbuit game in direct competition with Lias. When I asked Lias' brother-in-law Gregory Manos what made Bill finally go after Hankish, he elevated his tempered Brooklyn accent and said "Uncle Bill" had no choice.

When Senator Neely died, he lost his power connection with the "squares." He was in big tax trouble; his health was failing, and the FBI stayed on his ass. All the old man had left was the Barbuit game at Billy's. Then Hankish went on a suicide mission. He opened a Barbuit game trying to compete with us. He had a blown-up picture of Bill hung on the wall in his joint with the word's, "My mother always told me never trust a man whose ass is wider than his shoulders." Bill knew the end was near, but he thought he could put it on auto-pilot, and he wanted his successor to be anybody but Hankish. But that "Camel Driver" wouldn't quit and the final blow came when the old man got word that Hankish went to Jersey to connect up with a guy they called "Demus" who had juice with the New York outfits. It was over. Bill got the okay from his Cleveland people to take him out. How Hankish survived that explosion was more than a miracle. There was enough dynamite under that car to kill six people.

FORTY-FOUR

Symphonic Criminal

Paul Hankish was raised in abject poverty. He began attending parochial grade school in Wheeling at the age of six, and during this time, his parents were separated. His mother moved to Detroit, and Paul went with her attending Campo Grade School in Hamtrack, Michigan. He later returned to Wheeling to live with his dying father. While back at Central School, he suffered unbearable humiliation when a Brother at the school stood him before his class and criticized him for wearing the same dirty shirt for three consecutive days. He left school after completing part of the ninth grade. At the age of fifteen, Paul caught a bus for Texas. He got employment at a Schoonerville restaurant in Austin, Texas where he worked for nearly two years as a dishwasher and stock boy. He was earning $30 a week and his meals. At the age of seventeen, he returned to Wheeling and worked at "Nick the Greek" Stefano's Bivouac Club as a bartender earning $25 a week. From that time on, he secured various jobs, including at Buelah Park Racetrack in Columbus, Ascot Park in Akron and finally Wheeling Downs Racetrack as a money runner and ticket seller. He complained that the owner, Bill Lias, treated everybody like slaves, except the Greeks.

Although Hankish miraculously survived the attempted assassination, there remained little doubt that Lias, notwithstanding his diminishing power and poor health, was and would remain in control. Less than a month following the Hankish car bombing, the February 6, 1964 edition of the *Wheeling News Register* carried a front page story in which Dr. Forrest Kirkpatrick, a high ranking official of Wheeling Steel Corporation, addressed a civic meeting and mentioned Lias while discussing the economic problems of the community. He indicated sarcastically that Bill Lias was more widely known as part of the Wheeling image than the Wheeling Symphony Orchestra.

The FBI commented on this article and Lias' response (PG 92-231): "The February 16, 1964 issue of the *Wheeling News Register*, in the column devoted to letters to the editor, contained a reply from subject in which he took exception to these remarks and referred to himself as a life-long resident of Wheeling and a family man and stated that he was proud to say that there were many people in all walks of life who knew him and considered him an honorable man, regardless of what they had read about him in various publications, whose profits were based upon readers interest. He went on to state that it is true that there is some lawlessness in Wheeling, as everywhere, and no one should be heard to speak in favor of it, that certain law may be unnecessarily restrictive and should be changed through the democratic process, but existing laws should not be violated. He went on to analyze, what in his opinion were the reasons for the economic ills of the community and criticized the Wheeling Steel Corporation as well as other civic and business leaders in this connection."

Nevertheless, Bill began to concede his powerful image and popularity. He became victim to his age, fatigue and failing health. On April 20, 1964 he entered the Ohio Valley General Hospital for treatment, and his condition continued to decline, but his popularity in the community remained equal to the Wheeling Symphony whose acclaim remained dormant. The following month, his daughter Antoinette was married to Pete Parous, an unemployed Pittsburgh resident, who charmed Bill's daughter and was granted consent by Big Bill only because of his Greek heritage. Bill took the rubber band off and provided them an extravagant wedding reception, followed by a honeymoon trip to Greece, Italy, France and Switzerland. When they returned, Lias put his son-in-law in charge of Billy's. The operation languished under Parous' management. Bill was resting in his Florida condo when he got word that Billy's was forced to close on December 28, 1964.

There was credible doubt about the reopening of Billy's, because of pressure exerted by the newly elected Ohio County Prosecutor Arch Riley. When sworn into office, Riley declared the prohibition of large scale gambling in Wheeling. However, in spite of these threats, Billy's was able to reopen in March 3, 1965. Prosecutor Riley advised the FBI that he intended to pursue the necessary steps to have his office take further action. On March 22, 1965 an early morning raid of Billy's was conducted jointly by the Wheeling Police Department and the West Virginia State Police under the direction of the Prosecutor's office. A state police officer from the Clarksburg detachment (Joe Trupo), working undercover, had earlier gained entrance to the back room, and at the time of the raid, he was able to prevent anyone from destroying incriminating evidence. Then, on June 2, 1965 the beer license of Billy's Bar & Restaurant was revoked, and Billy's closed forever on June 24 1965.

Big Bill and his wife Alice remained in their condominium on Collins Avenue in Miami Beach. FBI agents interviewed Bill in Florida, and he indicated that his plans on returning to Wheeling were indefinite. He said he had a good doctor in Miami, and he was of the opinion that the climate in Miami was more agreeable to his condition. He claimed that he was doing nothing illegal at the present time and intended to do the same in the future. There is no record of Lias being interviewed by local, state or federal authorities regarding the attempted assassination of Paul Hankish.

Gregory Manos related many experiences about his years working for his brother-in-law, who he referred to as "Uncle Bill." He maintained that Bill seldom expressed feelings other than anger.

He showed great affection for his family and treated me like gold. He seldom spoke about his childhood, expressions of self-pity and despised weakness. He was now a beaten man; he had health problems and tax problems and had lost many of his close friends. Worse, he was losing the thing he coveted more than cash, he was losing respect. Let me tell you something people don't know about the old man's heart. We were sitting in Billy's late one evening. A young man was mopping the floor and cleaning tables. The kid was overweight, dressed like a bum, working his ass off. Bill pulled his cigar from his mouth and said, "Greg, see that kid, don't underestimate him. I started when I was 12 years old, fat, ugly and spoke poor English. I started out at the bottom rung of every ladder. All those Wheeling German kids made fun of me, and I had to take it. I let kids make fun of me because I thought they would like me better. When I got the hammer and took the city, everybody had to act like they liked me. Now, I feel like I'm going back to where I started. I feel like that poor little fat kid again. Greg, you know this is a tough business. You gotta be on your feet every day and be ready to do what you have to do to hold your power. You know the Italians are runnin' it all. They're hungrier, tough, and they got good leaders. You know the "Rock" (John LaRocca), he told me before you can become a member of their outfit, you have to kill someone with your bare hands. He said that when he was asked to do it, he wasn't sure if he could. You know, choke a guy, an old friend or some stranger, maybe somebody you're not even mad at. You know what he did? He lived on a farm, so one day he said he went out and choked a Billy goat for practice. He said it was a lot easier after that. He says now, every time he sees a goat, he wants to choke it. Now I feel that same way about some people. But I'm a tired old man.

FORTY-FIVE

Mafia Takeover

Ferdinand Lunderg, in his book The Rich & The Super Rich, quotes U.S. Senator Estes Kefauver, who in 1950 headed the Special Senate Committee to Investigate Crime, "Underworld characters with political protection are acquiring legally established businesses as 'fronts'. Such characters, it is held, have made a bundle in the underworld through gambling operations, houses of prostitution, bootlegging, assassination, smuggling, the narcotics trafficking and they are now pyramiding their illicit gains in the labyrinth in the corporate world."

An elevated era of organized crime, associated with leading Mafia figures from New York to Florida was about to be introduced to the city of Wheeling. The editor of the *Wheeling News Register* feared the consequences of a Hankish takeover and voiced his concern in a detailed letter to the newly elected West Virginia governor. Harry Hamm, a highly respected journalist, wrote the following on November 6, 1964:

Dear Governor Baron: Enclosed you will find material just as we received in the mail today. I thought it best that you handle this information in connection with the investigation of the parole system. We shall not pursue this until we hear from you. Meanwhile, congratulations on the great Democratic victory in West Virginia. I am most pleased with the outcome in the state and particularly the fine showing made by Ohio County in the recent election. Yours truly, Harry Hamm, Editor, *The Wheeling News Register.*

The following Confidential Information was included in Hamm's letter:

PAUL HANKISH first came to public attention in the mid '50s when he was connected with a place known as "Scoreboard Billiards," a known gambling establishment in downtown Wheeling. The U.S. Senate Crime Investigation Committee headed by Senator Estes Kefauver in 1956 reported Wheeling was linked with big-time gambling syndicates over the country. Senator Kefauver named one of the places in Wheeling as the "Scoreboard Billiards." Hankish was listed at that time as the bartender for the establishment. Bets could be made on any sporting event at this place.

By 1959 Hankish appeared to have moved up in the racket circles. His headquarters became the AMVETS Post at 14th Street, Wheeling, second floor—once the notorious Pony Club—a gambling and bookie parlor. Another favorite hangout was the Saddle Oyster Bar at 16th Street, operated by Howard Allen, a known bookie. It was in 1959 that the News Register exposed the operations of the AMVETS Post as a front for big-time gambling. The National AMVETS conducted an investigation and immediately suspended the Post charter. A copy of the letter from national headquarters stating the results of the investigation should be on file with that organization in Washington. The letter is dated August 17, 1959. Associated with Hankish in the AMVETS Post operation were other racket characters including Bobby Watkins, Louis George, "Catfish" Joseph and Abraham Zeid, alias Albert Zeid, alias Al Ross of New Kensington, Pennsylvania. With the closing of the AMVETS establishment, Hankish seemed to set up headquarters at the Saddle Oyster Bar with his close friend Howard Allen. This place became the headquarters for known racket figures from the tri-state district; high stakes crap and barbuit games on weekends drew hoodlums from all over.

Meanwhile, reports circulated that Hankish was involved in horse booking, the numbers racket and a syndicate dealing with betting on various sporting events. Confidential investigations by the Ohio County Sheriff's office, then under Sheriff Warren Pugh, disclosed that Hankish ran up sizeable telephone toll calls to such points as Detroit, Cleveland, New Kensington, Steubenville, New Jersey, Pittsburgh, Nevada and New Orleans. Other associates of Hankish in 1959, included Carl Yaquinta, long connected with horse booking in Wheeling. Yaquinta was subsequently arrested in nation-wide raids by Internal Revenue Agents on gambling establishments. He was seized at Baton Rouge, LA. Also associated with Hankish was Anthony "Tony" Zambito of Wheeling. Zambito operated the Jolly Bar and Convertible Club, upstairs at a downtown location.

An FBI confidential informant stated that Hankish muscled John Snyder of Martins Ferry, Ohio, out of the numbers business. A man identified as Bill George aided in this move and brought in an unidentified muscle man from New Jersey to pull it off. While the Jolly Bar operated, visitors were seen gathering there from such places as Michigan, Alabama, Youngstown, Pittsburgh, etc., according to a check of cars. In 1959 a raid by the local police on the Convertible Club brought the arrest of Zambito and Eckard Brown of Benwood. Brown was charged with operating a chuck-a-luck gambling table. He had been seen frequently in the company of Hankish and was caught several years earlier with gang counterfeiting race track tickets at Wheeling Downs. It was said that Brown was a runner for Hankish in the numbers business. Reports all indicated Brown was part of a gang robbing slot machines in the area. In the late summer and early fall of 1959, it was reported that a man identified as Norman Farber (may be an alias) arrived in Wheeling and became a constant companion of Hankish. Farber reportedly is a well-known, heavy gambler from Baton Rouge, New Orleans, Pittsburgh, etc., said to have wide connections with criminals throughout the country and handled fencing of stolen merchandise including jewelry, clothing, etc. Farber had three rooms on the fifth floor of the Windsor Hotel in Wheeling. Some gambling operations were said to have been directed from the hotel as well as other criminal activities. Authorities had Farber under surveillance at the time, but he suddenly moved out and left Wheeling on the Sunday morning Hankish was arrested at Fairmont, West Virginia while robbing a supermarket safe.

On August 24, 1959, the Wheeling Country Club's safe was cracked, and $3,000 was stolen. The night watchman, Russell Morman, a Negro, complained that he was assaulted with a revolver by one of the thieves. Morman identified Hankish as one of the four men who handcuffed him to a radiator while robbing the Club's safe. Following Hankish's indictment for the robbery, and in a surprise move, defense counsel filed an affidavit on which Morman said he was mistaken in the identification of Hankish. Defense counsel then indicated it has a mystery witness who would testify that Morman made the identification to cover his own "illegal" activities at the club, but that testimony by this witness might result in self-incrimination. Immunity from prosecution was requested for this witness, who had not yet been identified (and never was).

*News Item: 1-8-60 POLICE FIND MORMAN ---RELUCTANT WITNESS ARRESTED. CHANGED STORY THAT HANKISH ROBBED CLUB. Russell Morman, sought on charges of false swearing and perjury after the Paul Hankish case collapsed in Ohio County Intermediate Court last month, today was arrested in a Wheeling Rooming house. It was the testimony of Morman which resulted in a directed verdict of acquittal for Hankish, tried for a $3000 armed robbery of the Wheeling Country Club. Morman subsequently pled guilty to willfully, falsely, corruptly and feloniously testifying before a grand jury. Money and fear of reprisal for honest testimony exceeded Morman's concern for prison time.

On September 4, 1959, a News Register reporter, checking on conditions, reported that two out-of-town light colored Cadillacs were spotted on Market Street. A man referred to as "Pat" or "slope belly" was driving one accompanied by a blonde female companion. Al Ross or Al Zeid was reported the owner of the other Cadillac. The word around town was that these persons were part of a safecracking gang. It was on September 6, 1959, that Hankish was caught by police at Fairmont and charged with armed robbery in connection with safecracking of a supermarket. The charge was later reduced to breaking and entering. In his company were known hoodlums with long arrest records including George Floria of Detroit, Joseph Arrington of Cleveland and Vincent Innocenzia also of Cleveland. Safecracking tools were found with these men.

Hankish was driving a 1957 Oldsmobile at the time he was arrested. It was owned by Louis George of Wheeling, a known police character arrested on numerous occasions for horse booking. Inside the car were bags of numbers slips. It took a jury of seven men and five women 20 minutes to convict Hankish of the charge of breaking and entering. The judge sentenced his two co-defendants to sentences of 1 to 15 years, and Hankish received a sentence of 1 to 10 years since he did not have a previous record. Following their convictions, all three were released under bond of $15,000 for appeals. All of the sentences were intermediate sentences, which meant they could be paroled after serving one year. Vincent Innocenzia's decomposed body was found shortly following his sentencing. He, like Hankish and Florea, was out on bond pending their appeal. He had been shot three times in the back of the head. A resident of Parma, Ohio, a Cleveland suburb, Innocenzia had been arrested for 18 felonies during his criminal career. When his body was discovered, there was $100 in his pocket. He was fully clothed, and his hands were in his pockets. Summit County authorities questioned Hankish, who later told a News Register reporter, "I don't know anything about it. You know more about it than I do. All I know is that he was a nice boy."

*State of West Virginia Report on Parolee, James C. Frame's Investigation, March 31, 1963

"A couple of weeks ago, just prior to the Paul Hankish bombing, Jim Scott, ex-convict and pal of Paul Hankish, checked in at a rooming house in Huntington. He rented the room on the word of Emil George who vouched for him. It was reported that while Scott was in Huntington, a wealthy uncle of Emil George, who resides in that city, was robbed of a large sum of money when his safe was blown. After Scott departed the rooming house, police checked his room and found a large supply of burglary tools there. Also it was reported that prior to the Hankish bombing, a man identified as Mr. Hitt from Fairmont was robbed of $118,000. Informant says police traced numerous calls from Hankish to certain parties in Fairmont prior to the robbery."

The *Wheeling News Register* and editor Hamm were outraged when Hankish was granted parole for the breaking and entering conviction. Hamm publically called for Governor Baron to intercede and investigate what he strongly believed to be wrongdoing and chicanery. The West Virginia State Police, upon the direction of the governor, conducted an investigation of the West Virginia Board of Probation and Parole and Paul Nathaniel Hankish. On December 29, 1964, Sergeant K.J. Neely provided the following report to Governor Baron:

Pursuant to your instructions, the undersigned has conducted a confidential investigation concerning certain activities of the State Board of Probation and Parole. In his original instructions, the undersigned was directed to inquire particularly into the case history of Paul Hankish. Mr. Hankish was sentenced to the Penitentiary on July 9, 1962 on the conviction of Breaking & Entering for a period of 1 to 10 years.

Mr. Hankish was further sentenced by the Federal Court in Wheeling for a one year conviction on Gambling to run concurrent with his State sentence. In June of 1963, Mr. Hankish was granted a parole and released on said parole on September 4, 1963.

Immediately upon his release, Mr. Hankish was employed by the Auto Ranch, Incorporated, located at North River Road, Wheeling. The Auto Ranch Incorporated is operated by Mr. Ed Tolbert. Chief of Police Louis M. Kulpa, Lieutenant William J. Thomas and Detective Noll of the Wheeling Police Department advised the undersigned that Mr. Tolbert is connected with the rackets in Wheeling. The Police Department has on occasion turned up stolen property on his premises and they have information that Mr. Tolbert is financed by some of the slot machine operators in the Wheeling area. It might be further noted that when Mr. Hankish went to work for Mr. Tolbert, he had in his employ at the time, one James Scott who was on parole from the state penitentiary and is currently wanted as a parole violator. Soon after Mr. Hankish's release on parole, he was observed by the three previously named Wheeling Police officers in the company of "Big Red" Richardson who is a known gambler and operator of houses of prostitution. Richardson was recently convicted by the Federal Court in Wheeling for federal income tax evasion and is currently confined to a federal penitentiary.

In December, 1963, Mr. Hankish got permission from the parole board to visit Joseph Covello in Bellville, New Jersey. (NOTE: Joseph Covello has a criminal record dating back to 1937 for gambling, book making and assault.) This was verified by transcript which is currently in the possession of the Wheeling Police Department, furnished by the city of Bellville, New Jersey. In April of 1964, Mr. Covello was arrested by the Federal Bureau of Investigation on a charge of telephoning interstate for bets and wagers. In August of 1964, he was arrested by the Newark, New Jersey Police Department for the New York Police Department for assault on a policeman. This record has been verified with the FBI by the undersigned officer.

On January 17, 1964, Hankish got in his automobile, which was parked in front of his home, and when he turned on the ignition and attempted to start the car, an explosive charge was detonated. As a result of his injuries, he was confined in the North Wheeling Hospital until May of 1964. Since his release from the hospital, Hankish has been accompanied by James E. Mathews almost constantly. Mathews was convicted of Breaking & Entering in Ohio County during 1938 and was placed on five years of probation. Mathews is in constant association with the underworld element in the Wheeling area. Chief Kulpa of Wheeling stated that he had recently learned that Hankish was operating a poker game in the city and he sent two officers to stop the game. Chief Kulpa further stated that he was contacted by Tom Padden, Sheriff of Ohio County, and Sheriff Padden attempted to intercede for Hankish and asked that Hankish be permitted to continue operation of the game. Chief Kulpa further related that he had Hankish's home under surveillance and a number of automobiles registered in the names of people with criminal records and disreputable characters had been seen parked at or near his residence and the occupants of these automobiles have been seen entering his home.

A few examples of this activity are as follows:

A vehicle belonging to John F. Allen, 1896 Ridgefield Road, Cleveland, Ohio who is an ex-convict visited Hankish's residence on August 11, 12, and 13, 1964.

A vehicle owned by Ronald J. Bries, 168 29th Street, Wheeling, who is known to the Wheeling Police Department and has been suspected of handling stolen property visited the Hankish residence on August 9, 12, 18, and 29 and September 2, 1964.

A vehicle registered to Roger Cocco, Bellview, Kentucky, who is a known underworld character and has a criminal record dating back to 1936 visited the Hankish home on September 16 and 26, October 12, 18, and November 7 and 8, 1964.

A vehicle registered to Mike Z. Kotellos, Martins Ferry, Ohio, who has been convicted of operating a Keno Board and for operating gambling devices, visited Hankish's home on September 6, 1964.

The report being circulated in the Wheeling area that Hankish had rented a box at Forbes Field in Pittsburgh was checked by Trooper S.S. Satterfield and found to be untrue. During this investigation, the Wheeling Police officers previously mentioned indicated that there was a rumor circulated among the criminal element that Hankish was offering a reward for information revealing the name of the person or persons who had informed the Weirton Chief of Police, Edward Frankovich that Hankish was to be in the Weirton area on the night of November 23, 1964. The investigating officer contacted Chief Frankovich in Weirton and Frankovich stated that he had gotten his information from a confidential informant that Hankish was to visit the Sports Lounge on the night of November 23, 1964. Frankovich related that he staked out the Sports Lounge on that night about 10:30 p.m., Hankish arrived in a green Chrysler Imperial, bearing license U897B, which was registered to Mike Moses. (NOTE: Mike Moses is a known gambler and a procurer for houses of prostitution. This information was provided by Chief Kulpa). The woman accompanying Hankish at this time is believed to have given a fictitious name she was not known to the Weirton officers, but from her description, Chief Kulpa identified her as Patricia Worsham of Elm Grove, who is Hankish's girlfriend. She is a former employee of the Planning Division of the City of Wheeling.

Frankovich, accompanied by Lieutenant Fred Risovich, entered the back room of the Sports Lounge immediately after Hankish and his two companions entered the premises and found Hankish at a table with Emilo Julian and Al Magrini. On the table was a bottle of whiskey and a towel covering something which Frankovich later learned was jewelry. Chief Frankovich advised that the Sports Lounge is involved in book making and is operated by Al "Mags" Magrini. Mr. Magrini has a criminal record with the Weirton police department. On October 5, 1963 he was charged with Permitting the operation of a Lottery; on July 23, 1964, Gambling; and on December 2, 1964, operating a Lottery. Emilio Julian, who was also present when Chief Frankovich entered the premises, has been arrested by the Weirton police department on two separate occasions for operating a Lottery. Hankish gave his reason for being in Weirton was to contact Mr. Magrini and Julian in an effort to borrow money from them. Upon closer questioning by Frankovich, Hankish admitted that this was not the real purpose of his visit. Frankovich advised Hankish that he was not welcome in Weirton and for him to leave town immediately and not to return.

On December 18, 1964, First Sergeant, R.L. Bonar and the undersigned contacted Mr. Harry Hamm, Editor of the *Wheeling News Register*. (NOTE: Mr. Hamm has, from time to time of the original announcement of the parole of Mr. Hankish in June 1963, been editorializing on this action of the parole board. Copies of these editorials are attached to this report. Also attached is a confidential narrative from Mr. Hamm concerning the activities of Hankish and other underworld characters in and around Wheeling) Mr. Hamm further related that when he received information concerning Hankish being in Weirton, he directed his City Editor Al Molnar to contact Norman MacEwan, who is the Parole Officer charged with supervising Hankish, and learn from Mr. MacEwan if Hankish had violated his parole by leaving Ohio County. MacEwan advised Mr. Molnar that Hankish was not in violation. (NOTE: Parole regulations require the parolee to have written permission from the Parole Board before he can leave the county in which he has been paroled. It was further developed during this investigation that the Parole Board, upon the recommendation of Mr. MacEwan, had issued continuous travel permits to Hankish, permitting him to travel in the State of Ohio and in a radius of 35 miles from Wheeling. These permits started immediately after Hankish was paroled and were continued up until the time he was injured in the bombing of his automobile).

In summarizing the activities and circumstances concerning Paul Hankish, it is well established that Mr. Hankish is currently associated with underworld characters, which is a violation of the rules and regulations promulgated by the Board of Probation and Parole, and it is quite clear that he is being poorly supervised by his Parole Officer. Certain allegations were made that Mr. Creasy and other members of the Parole Board were receiving monies for granting paroles.

This information had circulated by rumor through both the State Maximum Security Penitentiary in Moundsville and Medium Security prisons. Receipts and other documents were supposedly available to the investigating officer to verify these rumors. A letter purported to have been signed by Mr. Creasy as Chairman of the Board to Walter W. Dillon, offering a parole to George F. Mellott, WVP-44336, if Mr. Dillon would pay $15,000 in cash to Mr. Creasy has been examined by Lieutenant C. G. West and pronounced a forgery. The receipts mentioned earlier were found to be non-existent with the exception of one in the amount of $30 purported to have been signed by Robert Dean,

Parole Officer for Raleigh County. This receipt was also examined and pronounced a forgery.

The undersigned talked to several inmates at both the Maximum and Medium state penitentiaries and was unable to find any evidence which would substantiate rumors of monies being collected by Mr. Creasy or any member of the Parole Board.

FORTY-SIX

Beating City Hall

The Wheeling news-paper was unmerciful in their opposition to Hankish's parole. Day after day, headlines demanded scrutiny: IS HANKISH READY FOR PAROLE! SHOCKING! NEED FOR PROBE! HANKISH RELEASE SURPRISES

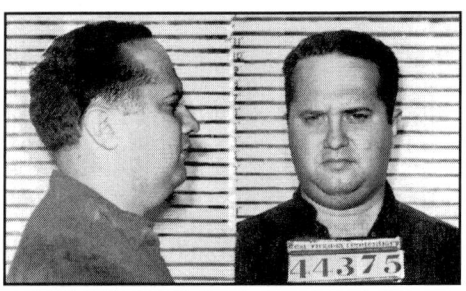

DOC photo, Paul Nathaniel Hankish

OFFICER! Despite this crusade, respected community leaders, elected officials and law enforcement personnel defiantly supported Hankish's parole. The following is a short-list of the many that encouraged parole for Paul Hankish and provided their sentiment to the parole board:

James Byrum, established Wheeling barrister and prosecuting attorney, wrote "I have known Paul for the past four years and have known his wife considerably longer and they are fine people. I have always liked him and he is very devoted to his family and I consider Paul and his wife good friends of mine. I represented him in his federal case and the local draft board told me his score was the highest ever turned in."

Thomas Saad, Assistant Prosecuting Attorney, Wheeling (Ohio County): "I have known Paul for twenty years, we were both raised in Center Wheeling. I always got along with him and he was good to his father. He has a wonderful wife. He is good to his family. He is a person who does not lie. He drank moderately and I have never known him to be intoxicated. He has always been a good hearted person and he got in with the wrong outfit. He was never in trouble in this country and I would recommend him to be paroled when he has served his minimum time."

Tom Nagem, 9 Vermont Street, Wheeling, W.Va. Tel Cedar 3-0277 (Bartender, Ft. Henry Billiards): "I have known Paul since he was a baby. I lived in the same neighborhood with his parents. His parents did not get along well and his mother left and Paul was pretty much on his own when he was small. I always considered him to be honest as when he was a kid and hungry, I would give him a buck and he would always pay it back. He has always been loved and respected by everyone and he has a very pleasing personality and has been that way since he was a kid."

Tom O'Brien, Ohio County Prosecuting Attorney: "He was not convicted in Ohio County. He will tell you the truth. Good to his family."

Tom Padden, Sheriff, Ohio County: "I have known Paul for years and I have always liked him. He is a good family man, operated several book shops and race track establishments. He is not a bad fellow at all. I would recommend that he be paroled after serving his minimum time."

Joe Colangelo, Deputy Sheriff: "I have known Paul Hankish for over 20 years. He is all right as far as I know he has never been in any trouble in Wheeling. He has worked operating book making. This does not make him an undesirable citizen."

Unrelenting pressure from the media and Wheeling police officials continued their cry for revocation of Hankish's parole. At Hankish's request, a parole conference was held on July 8, 1964 in Charleston before members of the West Virginia Parole Board. The Chairman opened the conference to explain his purpose for accepting Hankish's request for the conference.

Mr. Creasey: Paul, you had written permission from Parole Officer MacEwan to come to Charleston for the purpose of this conference.

Hankish seized the opportunity to defend himself and vilify his adversaries.

Hankish: He, Mr. MacEwan came to my home July 2nd or 3rd well, on or about that time, I'm not really accurate of the time and he went over the rules. "Two of the rules were not to patronize a place selling alcoholic beverages and not to go into gambling establishments. As far as violating my parole for this, I have probably been on parole for ten months and I have probably violated my parole every day for five months of that time as I have taken my family out to eat in restaurants and every one of them sells beer at all times and possibly whiskey too.

When I go to Allen's Coffee Shop, 1500 Market Street, Howard Allen owns this place and the Academy Billiards and they do sell beer. Before I went to the hospital, I have gotten in the habit of going downtown and going into the Sportsman's Bar. Prior to being on parole, all my life, I have spent in and around gambling. These places have "Baseball Tickers" and they bring in results. I have sat there at nights until 10:30 or 11:00 just watching, and then I'd go home. I know for a fact they have taken my picture coming out of these places, but I didn't do anything wrong as far as I could see. As far as drinking, I have never taken a drink in public. As far as gambling I have played Bridge in my own house for small stakes. In Wheeling there is a man named Cliff McWilliams, possibly he is editor for the evening Wheeling newspaper, I think the News Register. When I was in the hospital, and I want you to know I'm not referring to this for sympathy, he was walking down the alley to the News Register and there was an open manhole with some lumber over it and he fell through it and was held there by some lumber. Now if I had my limbs, I would have gladly stood on the lumber and held him there. What actually happened was, he was dead drunk. Well this guy McWilliams, has been very antagonistic to me. While I was in the hospital for the first three weeks, I was unconscious, the newspaper quoted me every day after the second day I was there.

They even printed that my arm had been removed. There was no truth to what he put in the paper. If I said anything it was in my sleep or while I was under heavy sedation. They put quotes in there saying that I had identified this fellow or that. I have never said anything. I was out about two months and had a permit to go into Belmont County, Ohio. A cousin of mine owns a bar over there. Cliff used to go to his bar. One night he was drinking-my cousin is the same one who owns the Charter House and he happens to be in there and when Cliff gets half-high, he tells Pee Wee George, "we are keeping a dossier on him and before it is over, we will have him back in the penitentiary-we will have the parole board fired and the parole officer fired or the action of the board changed. After this happened, I have been a little bit of a hot head all my life and this got to me and I called Ogden Wood and asked him if I could come down there and he told me what he thought of me and I told him what I thought about him. I told him about Mr. McWilliams going into his place, bar and drinking and getting half high and he said he wasn't responsible for him. He said, "As far as your parole, I think a favor was granted." I said, "I broke into a supermarket and I have never gotten into trouble before. With all the bad publicity you gave me, I almost did not make parole. He, Austin Wood, said that when someone is coming up for parole, they should put it in the paper. I said, when I got my parole you said there wasn't even an investigation made and this is not true. There were many letters written on my behalf. Bob Riley, one of my attorneys ran into Austin about two weeks before I was getting out and said to him, 'Why don't you quit picking on that boy. The only reason you are picking on him is because a certain man named Lias is telling you to.' Well they both got mad. Austin said, 'Well it won't make any difference if he gets out, he will be dead in a few weeks anyway.' I just hope someone doesn't push me as I am very ill-tempered and it might sound silly to you, but this I can't change. That's the way I am and that's it. I am full of hate, eaten up with it.

The Chief of Police in Wheeling (Kulpa) was made by the newspaper. He is extremely friendly with Austin Wood and the newspaper. Prior to becoming Chief of Police, he would take money from a blind beggar. When he got to be Chief of Police, I know of one particular arrangement when he was receiving money from someone and after about six months he got scared and cut that out. All the time he was on the Police force his closest friend was Johnny Lee. Lee runs a house of prostitution on 23rd and Main, the address would be 2318 Main, but it is torn down now. Now Lee is running this other house of prostitution and he gets arrested and placed on probation for one year.

The Chief of Police was in Dallas, Texas to some kind of convention; when he found out that Lee was arrested, he came back immediately and made some arrangements not to harass certain places if they gave Lee probation, which was done. Since that time Lee was arrested again for running another house. Nothing was done about it. This is common knowledge to everybody in Wheeling. I have abused him in gambling and would do it again if I had the chance. This should be investigated. How come the newspaper makes no issue of that-because to do this would hurt Kulpa – Chief of Police, and they know Lee would talk and if he went to the penitentiary he'd take Kulpa with him. Now, if I'd get caught speeding, I'd make the headlines.

Creasey: Paul, I think we should make it clear that we want you to stay out of these places for the remaining period you are on parole.

Hankish: I will do that.

Creasey: This will be not only in your best interests but it will keep your friends out of a bad light.

Hankish: I will do that.

Creasey: This is not only for you, but for all parolees in Ohio County and for that matter, in the whole State of West Virginia.

Hankish: I can do it. If you told me I had to stand on my head for eight months, I could do it. Austin Wood told me this is directly against me and partially against the parole board. He said the parole board laws should be changed.

Creasey: Paul, it is clear what you have to do regarding these rules MacEwan cautioned and warned you about. Do you understand this, and what could happen to your parole if you don't abide by the rules?

Hankish: I understand. I understand my obligation to these parole rules.

Hankish: Mr. Creasey, you told me you were going to answer the newspaper. I will not repeat this to anyone. I will say I hate to see you do this. You will be the loser.

Board Member: Paul, you realize that before we can answer the newspaper, we must be sure and certain that we have all the correct answers, we must be right.

Hankish: You can't win. I may have deserved this but I'll tell you, I have seen them take innocent people, nice people and cause them to commit suicide. There was a man who worked at Wheeling Steel. This man married a woman who was the widow of a deceased bookmaker, and because of this they harassed him and he finally committed suicide. They said he drank himself to death, but he didn't. A very good friend of mine, Harry Richardson, his wife runs a house of prostitution. I associate with him quite frequently. He and Lias were friendly and Lias called Richardson and cursed him out because of me. Lias does these things. He puts the finger on everybody and they keep putting this in the paper what others are doing and never anything he does. When they took me to the hospital, I was conscious, I didn't even go into shock. I don't want any sympathy. You see, there were all these doctors there at my side and I looked up and said, "I don't want any damned Greek touching me." Two doctors turned around and left. I later apologized and they came back. I was half out of my mind.

Creasey: Paul, we want you to hang on. We want you to complete your parole period successfully. These rules are a matter of the Board's policy. We may not get involved with the controversy with the paper until you are off parole. Paul, we hope this meeting has been of some benefit to you in helping you know and understand better the rules of parole which you must abide by. Do your best to live by these rules. They are for all parolees.

Hankish: Yes, I know. I understand them but I can't see why these things can be done in Ohio and not in West Virginia. Can I go across the river?

Creasey: You talk to Mr. MacEwan about this Paul. Good luck to you and we want you to know that the Board is wishing for you only the best of everything.

On January 4, 1965, Curtis Trent, an executive assistant to West Virginia Governor Barron, called Parole Board Chairman Alexander J Creasey to his office and informed him that the Governor wanted Hankish's parole revoked, and his parole officer fired. In their zeal to have Hankish's parole revoked, the media influenced the Governor to require the West Virginia Board of Probation & Parole to convene a Special Board Inquiry challenging the opinion and conduct of Hankish's parole officer, Norman MacEwan. Mr. MacEwan was the first African American and to date, the last to serve as a parole officer in the state of West Virginia.

The hearing was convened on January 5, 1965. The following are selected excerpts from that hearing:

Board Member: Mr. MacEwan, we called you down here because of the receipt of certain investigating reports relative to the activities of Paul Hankish. We shall ask you some questions on this matter as it is serious and we hope you will give us a fair answer. We believe when Hankish was released on parole he went to work for the Auto Ranch, operated by Mr. Ed Tolbert. Chief Kulpa advised us that Mr. Tolbert is connected with the rackets in Wheeling. Do you have any information relative to this?

MacEwan: None whatsoever. I have known Mr. Tolbert for years as a reputable car dealer in Wheeling and I have no knowledge of him having any prior criminal record or connection with the rackets in Wheeling. It is my opinion that if he did, he would have been prosecuted long before now.

Board Member: Do you know a person up there referred to as "Big Red" Richardson and if you do, give us some information about him.

MacEwan: I have met Mr. Richardson on three occasions and at the time of this meeting he had no criminal record. Later he was charged with income tax evasion and sentenced to eighteen months in the federal penitentiary. To my knowledge, "Red" Richardson has no record of felony convictions, but I have not looked up his record on operating a house of Prostitution.

Board Member: The investigation report indicates that Hankish has been operating a poker game in the city of Wheeling. The report also indicates that Police Chief Kulpa dispatched two officers to stop the operation of such game or games. Do you have any knowledge as to whether Paul has been operating a poker game or games in the city of Wheeling)?

MacEwan: To my knowledge no. If Paul Hankish would have been operating any form of gambling in Wheeling, Chief Kulpa would have had him arrested immediately. Chief Kulpa dislikes Hankish very much and would do anything to have him arrested or put in jail for anything at all. Paul is registered with the Bureau of Police in Wheeling and is known to every policeman in Wheeling. As to consulting with Chief Kulpa, I had on one occasion to present a ticket for overtime parking to be okay'd by an officer. I was in the City County building conducting my work in connection with the Police department. I handed the ticket to Mr. Kulpa and he said, "Why should I do anything about your ticket after what Creasey did to me?"

I replied, "What was that?"

He said, "He made a fool out of me. He then turned and walked away.

Board Member: I am interested in knowing what information you can give us as to why the extreme interest in the parole board is being shown by the Wheeling Newspapers?

MacEwan: I think the papers in Wheeling are the most ruthless papers in the world. I don't know if they are out to hang

Paul Hankish, me or the Parole Board, but it is inconceivable that anyone would go to the extremes that they are going.

A subsequent parole hearing was held for Hankish to determine if he had in fact violated conditions of his parole, and Hankish was found not to have caused any violations. Mr. MacEwan was also exonerated from any charges. Much to their chagrin, the Chief of Police and Wheeling newspapers failed in their effort to have Hankish's parole revoked, and his parole officer fired. Hankish continued parole for the next eight months and successfully discharged his sentence.

FORTY-SEVEN

THE BIGGER THE BETTER

Paul's father, Peter Killi Hankish, was born in Beirut, Lebanon and naturalized a U.S. citizen in his early teens. He was a retired steelworker and suffered from pancreatic cancer, which took his life at age sixty five. Paul Hankish was born on July 18, 1931 in Wheeling, West Virginia and was one of three children. He married Patricia Jean Rose on July 2, 1956, following a five year courtship. The ceremony was performed by Reverend Charles Aurand at 35 16th Street in Wheeling. Patricia Rose Hankish was born May 6, 1930 in Wheeling and completed her senior year of high school in Oakland, Maryland. Mrs. Hankish worked as a cashier at Kroger supermarket, Leatherwood Lane in Wheeling from 1955 to 1956, at Figaretti's restaurant in Elm Grove from 1952 to 1955, the Far East restaurant from 1951 to 1952, and her first employer was the Rose Bowl Café on 16th Street in Wheeling from 1949 to 1951. In 1959, Paul and Patty moved to Wheeling Island, residing at 326 North Huron Street, a first floor brick apartment, paying $82.50 a month rent. At the time, Mrs. Hankish was receiving $50 a week from Echard "Whitey" Brown, owner of the Sunset Club in Ohio. Paul was a silent partner in the club. Paul always affectionately referred to her as Patty 1.

Two children were born to this relationship: Rosemarie, an accomplished graphic artist, born on November 29, 1958 and Christopher Paul, born June 19, 1962. A congenial, lasting relationship existed between Hankish and his first wife, Patricia Rose, through their divorce and up until the time of his death. Paul's youngest son Peter, from his second marriage, was the godson of Youngstown Mafia Godfather, Joey Naples. Peter was a graduate of the prestigious private Linsly Military Academy, where he excelled academically and was an outstanding athlete. He went on to acquire a Bachelor of Science degree from Villanova University. Naples was said to have been connected with the Pittsburgh Genovese family and ran gambling operations from Pittsburgh to Youngstown. He and his two younger brothers were victims of shotgun and car bombing murders. Naples allegedly was murdered on the orders of Pittsburgh mafia chieftain, Lenny Strollo, who believed that Naples had turned informant and was meeting regularly in Bridgeport, Ohio with a Wheeling based FBI Agent.

Federal Authorities have confirmed the long standing suspicion concerning the assassination of Youngstown Mafia leader Joey Naples and the motivation behind his murder. In the investigation following Naples' killing, it was learned that he had become an informant and was meeting regularly with an unnamed, hard-charging, Wheeling based FBI agent. The two were said to have met secretly in parked cars in a parking lot beneath the Route 7 overpass in Bridgeport, Ohio. According to Justice Department sources, Naples provided valuable and incriminating information about activities of the Western Pennsylvania Mafia. Sources indicate that Naples' decision to turn informant, his motive and quid pro quo for the information exchange resulted in extensive investigation by the Department of Justice. Following Naples' death, Pittsburgh Mob boss, Lenny Strollo immediately seized command over the Youngstown Mafia. He also subsequently turned informant following his federal arrest and conviction.

Rosemarie Hankish's godfather was Joseph "Demus" Covello, a powerful Capo in the New Jersey DeCavalcante family. An article published in the *Miami Herald* in 1984 discloses the arrest of Covello, who they described as a "reputed member of the New York, Gambino Family." They claimed that his bookmaking operation handled between $100,000 and $200,000 a day during football season, and he also covered bets for baseball games and horse racing. Christopher Hankish was endowed as the godson of Gabriel "Kelly" Mannerino, who at the time, was partners with Tampa, Florida boss Santo Traficante in the Sans Souci Hotel and Casino located a few miles outside of Havana, Cuba.

This was one of only two casinos operating in Cuba at this time. The Cuban Information Archives, written by Lefty Clark described the Sans Souci Hotel/Casino as the most elaborate, accommodating 3000 guests, most of them who came from the United States. "Elegant gaming facilities and lavish show rooms. Once inside the opulent entrance, the Sans Souci had showgirls recruited from all over the world, performing constant productions. There was 'Wild Ballet' based on American show dance styles and dance troupe that specialized in wild uninhibited dances on native themes."

"Kelly" Mannerino, operating out of New Kensington, Pennsylvania, held enormous power. He was acclaimed among the New York Families. He and Trafficante alone, convinced the boss of bosses, Vito Genovese, to sanction the assassination of Albert Anastasia, boss of the Gambino Family and founder of "Murder Inc." Mannerino was among those who escaped while attending the infamous New York "Applachin" Summit of the American Mafia in 1957. It was during this meeting that the decision was made to kill Albert Anastasia for territorial interference. He took the Fifth Amendment when he appeared before the United States McClellan Hearings in 1958. This was the U.S. Select Committee on Improper Activities in Labor and Management. Robert F. Kennedy was counsel for, and Mannerino was one of 343 who invoked the Fifth Amendment. Kennedy was focused on the Teamsters Union.

Mannerino was a frequent and welcomed guest at Joe Sonken's Gold Coast Restaurant & Lounge on Ocean Drive in Miami. An article written by Deborah Ramirez for the Sun Sentenial describes the aura and reputation of what she called the Legendary Restaurant: "If the walls could talk at Joe

Sonken's they might whisper Cosa Nostra. Gold Coast has been in business since 1948 keeping police and FBI agents busy with surveillance activities and investigations of mob activities. Some of the restaurant's patrons read like a Who's Who in the underworld." Hankish was a frequent patron of the Gold Coast.

FORTY-EIGHT

THE REAL DEAL

Mannerino relished his many visits to Sonken's and, on one occasion, shared private stories and memories with a dear friend of mine who resided in Miami. One special story he shared with me is particularly revealing. He told me that when the subject of Jimmy Hoffa came up, Mannerino always expressed sorrow and disappointment:

Fitzimmons was like having your grandfather in charge. He stayed right and never made us punt. Jimmy made us millions and had *Palle de ferro* (iron balls), but when the Kennedy's went after him, he was history. Of course he didn't do anything to help himself or anyone else. He jumps in front of a TV camera and knocks the Attorney General of the United States. Now he gets hot because he had to wait an hour for Kennedy to show for an appointment and brags about threatenin' to work him over. We used up big favors to spring him early from the joint and he gets out and thinks he can put a Santa Claus suit on and climb back in the ring. We called in black markers for this guy. We had a real good relationship with a guy named Chuck Colson [Special Assistant to President Nixon]. This guy was close with the President. We worked a deal with him for the President to pardon Jimmy. Now they tell me that Jimmy signed the pardon, and they had language in there that kept him from ever goin' back to the Teamster's Presidency. When he found out, he went nuts, got hotter than fried grease. He started makin' threats, I'm gonna' do this, I'm gonna' do that. Well, all he did was quit breathin'. Now they're lookin' for him. Don't get me wrong, I don't know what they did with him, but you can bet, they'll get fatter eatin' apples if they think they can find one of his shoes.

There was a Greek coffee house near Mannerino's, Catoris Candy Store in New Kensington. He often spent time in the coffee house, chatting with friends or meeting out of town visitors and associates who treated him with ceremonial courtesy. On this day, he was lamenting and reflecting upon his rise to power and the obligations of a "made" man. A visitor from Youngstown came to the table asking him for a favor. Following a cryptic, whispered exchange, the visitor departed groveling and expressing his gratitude, walking backwards on his way to the door. Then Kelly said: See that guy, he's loyal and stand-up and we've done business for years. Now there are a lot of guys like him. They go out of town, make big scores, fifty or sixty grand. You think they would stop by and drop something off, buy a damn box of candy from me. No, the only time they come by is when they're in a jam and they want me to use favors I bought to get them out. But I can't complain, this is the life I chose and it's been good to me. Tough, but good. I remember the night they called me. I was twenty five. I knew I had to go. I looked around the house, my wife, kids, and I knew I had to do what they asked. Back then, it was not anything like it is today. Now, when you get the call it might be for some Mexican who doesn't even have a birth certificate. Back then, if you had to cut a guy, it might be your uncle.

Mannerino was implicated but never indicted in a 12 million dollar heist of Canadian government bonds stolen to help finance Castro's revolution in 1958. The mob had to play both sides in an attempt to save their interests in the Cuban casinos. Castro promised, then betrayed them. Mannerino and Trafficante were promised exclusive rights to operate slots in Havana once Battista was overthrown. They hated Castro for his betrayal much more than they despised President Kennedy. Gabriel Kelly Mannerino ruled western Pennsylvania for nearly thirty years and had a thirty five year arrest record, but never served a day in prison.

Harry Hamm, for the duration of his career as Editor of the *Wheeling News Register*, persisted in attempting to expose the scope and level of Hankish's national role in organized crime. Nevertheless, for the following twenty years, Hankish ruled with near impunity from the back room of his Market Street "Regal Coffee Shop," just two blocks away from the federal building.

Back on February 28, 1965, Hankish began relying upon receiving a check for $254.00 from the Social Security Administration for permanent disability. His monthly benefit would be $254 -- $113 for himself, $47 for his wife and $94 for his son and daughter. Hankish, while receiving these disability entitlements, made a connection with Irving Slobtkin, owner of a wholesale jewelry company at 111 South 8th Street in Philadelphia, Pennsylvania, where he purchased jewelry for resale and continued this trade until he chose to devote all his time to his criminal career.

One of the most impressive among his choice of Wheeling attorneys was James Byum, a respected and successful criminal attorney and Wheeling native. His judgment and friendship was sacred. Once during lunch, Jim began discussing Paul's problems and mentioned his remarkable ascendance to power and the respect held for him by major, national crime figures. He said, "Paul is brilliant, I only wish he would have devoted his time and talent to a legal profession. I was told he has an estimated I.Q. of 130. There is no doubt in my mind that had he not suffered the injuries that now plague him resulting from the bombing, he would be among the top crime leaders in the nation. Of course he still ranks up there with the best, but he is severely restrained by his poor health and disability."

The FBI identified and targeted Hankish early as a close associate of the New Jersey Cosa Nostra family. An FBI Special Agent Memo sent to Hoover in the early sixties noted, "Hankish is a long-time Wheeling, West Virginia hoodlum and is in contact with LCN members in various areas of the country. For years, the FBI maintained constant surveillance, but were able only to secure a beer hijacking conviction that was handed to them by an informant. The conviction was overturned on appeal following Hankish's incarceration."

FORTY-NINE

EYES ON THE PRIZE

On July 14, 1967, agents of the Internal Revenue Service raided Hankish's operation base, the Academy Billiards at 1502 Market Street. They also raided his residence at 343 Hazlett Avenue. They seized bookmaking records and wagering paraphernalia. On October 10, 1967, Hankish was indicted by a federal grand jury on seven counts of failure to pay excise tax on wagering. The IRS placed an assessment against him for $115,254. Most of the assessment was ultimately dismissed. From that day forward, the FBI conducted extensive surveillance of Hankish, the transcripts of which revealed embarrassing performance and pathetic narrations, laced with ethnic slurs. I have herein produced a brief portion of a one day, transcribed surveillance illustrating the inefficiency and misplaced mentality of the day.

The following activity was recorded by a Special Agent hidden atop the Half Dollar Bank, located directly across the street from the Academy Billiards.

(March 25, 1970) At 10:30 A.M., the Negro who chauffeured Paul Hankish around on the previous day and who now has been identified as Jesse Anderson, was seen entering the Academy with another male, 5'8" tall, 35 to 40 years of age, heavy build, dark hair, appeared to be of Lebanese or Syrian extraction. At 12:30 P.M., two men who had previously entered and left the Academy on approximately five different occasions during the past 15 minutes, left the Academy and entered a 1964 or 1965 Plymouth, white over turquoise in color. This car left being driven North on Market Street. The driver is described as a white male 5'8" tall, wearing glasses, a hat and had a fat face medium dark complexion and Jewish features. At 1:15 P.M., Jesse Anderson helped the aforementioned "Jewish looking" man load some of the packages into the Plymouth. A man described as a white male, about 5'11" tall, 30-35 years of age, dark hair, neatly cut and wearing a bluish grey suit, either Syrian or Italian extraction, emerged and entered the Plymouth.

At 3:41 P.M., the individual who has the physical appearance of a "gorilla" leaves the Academy and walks across Market Street. (April 8, 1970) Surveillance began at 8:35 AM. Jesse Anderson, the Syrian and the "Hawkish" looking man enter the Academy. 1:00 PM, view of Academy is obstructed by Budweiser truck. 2:07 PM, Syrian or Italian extraction individual mentioned earlier, observed carrying 25 to 30 women's dresses with tags still hanging into the Academy."

This segmented FBI surveillance continued daily, often from 8:00 AM until midnight for the following six months.

FIFTY
_____

DEATH AND TAXES

William G. Lias died from congestive heart failure at Ohio Valley General Hospital on June 1, 1970. Charles Callaway, *News Register* staff writer, noted in his obituary that on file in the Ohio County Clerk's office was a lien for $2,442,944.61, which was put on record in 1967. The original tax lien was filed by the federal government for 3 million dollars in 1951. At one time, the interest on the balance was running at $300 a day. When I asked Gregory Manos if Bill died broke, he shook his head and chuckled, "If Alice started burning hundred dollar bills every minute of the day, for the next ten years, she'd run out of matches before hundreds." Prior to his death and for probably thirty consecutive years, William G. "Big Bill" Lias was the wealthiest individual in the state of West Virginia.

Hankish, Lias' adversary, continued to suffer daily from the wounds and memory of Lias' seven year old unsuccessful, assassination attempt. What made it worse, Paul was told by Pennsylvania Mafia Capo, Gabriel "Kelly" Mannerino that word was received from Cleveland that no act of retribution in any form was to be taken against Lias or any member of his family. The closest Hankish came to violating his oath was when he had one of his henchman attend Lias' wake and steal the visitor's registry from the funeral home. Hankish wanted to witness those who paid their respects to his enemy. Jesse Anderson told me that initially, "Paul wanted me to break into the funeral home and lift Lias' body from the coffin and dump it on the floor."

In this year, Bill and Alice Lias suffered the devastating loss of their daughter Antoinette, who died from natural causes, and their young son, George, perished a few years later from a heart attack. Alice remained respected within the community. This charming lady continued her active Matriarch role in the Greek Church and civic involvement while devoting her life to raising her deceased daughter's son.

FIFTY-ONE

UNLIMITED CORRUPTION

During the 1970s, Hankish tightened his influence and control within and outside his Mafia connections. In Ohio County, it was almost common knowledge that he literally owned the current irrational Prosecuting Attorney, a handful of cops and one or two Magistrates.

The Prosecutor was said to have suffered from an extreme alcohol addiction, which only contributed to his depravity and vulnerability. Hankish referred to him as "The Nut." During Dennis Naum's term in office, Hankish once complained to his attorney, "'The Nut' just witnessed a murder in the 'My Club.'" The My Club was a bottom rung, Center Wheeling illegally operated strip club. The owner of the club "Corky" Corchran often forced his "Dancers" to have sex with special customers. In this instance, Corchran was accused of savagely assaulting and murdering one of his "Dancers," Anita Kay McLaughlin on the night in question. The following is taken from a West Virginia Supreme Court Citation: Naum V Halbitter, 309 S.E. 2d 109 (W.Va 1983).

On 24 May 1982, petitioner Dennis Naum, Prosecuting Attorney of Ohio County, was called to testify before a grand jury. Mr. Naum testified that his only knowledge of Anita Kay McLaughlin was that she was a waitress at a bar he occasionally visited. On 6 April, 1983, the petitioner (Dennis Naum) was indicted for False Swearing. McLaughlin is now dead, an apparent victim of homicide. In rebutting petitioner's claim that he had only passing knowledge of Ms. McLaughlin, the special prosecutor relied upon statements allegedly made by Ms. McLaughlin to friends and family. The prosecutor claimed those statements indicated that the petitioner (Dennis Naum) had intimate relations with a deceased prostitute, on at least one and perhaps more than one occasion. Mr. Corchran ultimately pled to the crime and served time in prison. The indictment of Prosecutor Naum was terminated.

Hankish purportedly supplied cocaine to a Coroner, who in one display of his compromising will, was said to have covered up the intentional poisoning of a house of prostitution owner in conflict with Hankish. He was also alleged to have the eyes and ears of a bribery addicted sheriff along with various other local officials. Hankish developed his personal brigade of criminal talent which ranged from shoplifters to contract killers. Many of his soldiers possessed diverse talents that contributed to the racketeering trade which strengthened his empire. Jesse Anderson served multiple roles for Hankish, among them an enforcer and bag man. Paul called him Mandingo. Hankish loaned him out to bankers, lawyers, hospital administrators and anyone else deserving of Hankish's assistance. Anderson's services were diverse and expensive and ranged from collecting an overdue debt to threatening the lover of a cheating wife. Understanding that information was power, he put in place an efficient intelligence system. His data base held the identity and details of cheating spouses and closet gays to a collection of secretly filmed whore house episodes of prominent Wheeling officials. He was also the master of the "dry snitch."

Jesse Anderson boasted that he routinely collected from slot machine and whore house operators from the tip of the Northern Panhandle to the middle of the state. Thereafter, he continued south as instructed and took the cash directly to the kitchen door of the Governor's Mansion where he was greeted by a member of Governor Moore's executive security staff who presumably took the bag of cash directly to the awaiting Governor. He said, "Paul would count the cash before I delivered it and always took a piece of the action." If someone failed to pay, Hankish would instruct Jesse to convince them, and in some cases, he chose to punish them by reporting the default to contacts he had with city police, county sheriffs or state police, who would retaliate. Jesse said, "The 'Monster' always found a way to verify the amount I dropped off. Sometimes I would steal a $20 just to jerk him off."

FIFTY-TWO

ALMOST HEAVEN

Prior to the takeover of the Gaston Caperton administration in 1989, the state of West Virginia was on the verge of bankruptcy. The gas meter at the Governor's Mansion was "red tagged" for non payment and empty handed legislators were resigned to accepting salami sandwiches from lobbyists. Worse, the state lagged behind the rest of the nation in everything but corruption. Beginning in 1989 and within a year thereafter, two State Senate Presidents and the Governor were convicted of criminal misconduct and sent to federal prisons. They were convicted for a multitude of crimes ranging from tax fraud to extortion. Two of the three were residents of the Wheeling area: Governor Arch A. Moore's home was in Glen Dale and Dan Tonkovich was a High Street, Benwood boy.

Years prior to the legalization of Video Lottery and Casino gambling in West Virginia, a former prominent Las Vegas casino manager arrived in Wheeling to seek interested and influential parties to assist in legalizing casino gambling in the mountain state. Anthony Tony Torcasio, a charismatic bon vivant, converged upon the 1986 session of the West Virginia legislature (accompanied by potential investors from the Northern Panhandle to Newark, New Jersey) to attempt to secure passage of legalized gambling. Blinded with optimism, Torcasio first discovered a hotel for sale in Weirton, West Virginia. He convinced his investors to buy the hotel, named it the Grande and appointed himself manager with promise and plans to convert it into a casino.

It wasn't long before his grand plan met defeat and disaster. Torcasio was indicted for paying $17,000 to the Senate President for the purpose of attempting to influence the passage of a statute that would legalize casino gambling. Following his four day trial, he was convicted of perjury and aiding and abetting Dan Tonkovich, the Senate President, who had earlier pled guilty to committing extortion under the Hobbs Act.[8]

Prior to the legislative session in November 1985, State Senate President met with the investors to decide the economic benefits of legalized gambling.[9] Then in December 1985, Tonkovich and Torcasio met for the first time. Fred Perrone, one of the investors inquired whether Tonkovich, who owned a small public relations firm, would be interested in mounting a public relations campaign directed to increase the public interest in legalized gambling. Tonkovich at first, rejected their offer, but then agreed on a $15,000 contract which he suggested be put in the name of his administrative assistant, Robert Cain. Tonkovich also testified during trial that Torcasio gave him $1000 cash for his newborn son and later $1000 cash as a Mother's Day gift for his wife.

Dan Tonkovich was at one time, every parent's dream. A respectful and scholarly young man who excelled as an athlete and distinguished himself with a Masters degree from Syracuse University. He served gallantly as a Viet Nam Infantryman, returning home to be elected the youngest President of the State Senate in state's history. His once boundless future ended in theatrical tragedy. Tonkovich served his final term as President of his Democrat controlled Senate under the leadership of Republican Governor Arch A. Moore.

Pam Belluck, Inquirer Staff Writer, describes Torcasio during an interview days before his commitment to Allentown

8   The Hobbs Act, codified at 18 U.S.C. 1951 states in part: Whoever in any way or degree obstructs, delays or affects commerce or the movement of any article or commodity in commerce by robbery or extortion shall be fined not more than $10,000 or imprisoned not more than twenty years.

9   Court of Appeals for the Fourth Circuit, Case No. 91-5316

federal penitentiary, "I used to run the Tropicana in Vegas." said Torcasio, his burly face turning red with excitement. "I brought in Joe DiMaggio (DiMaggio testified on his behalf during his Charleston, West Virginia trial. He might have had more success had he chosen Willie Nelson) Joe Namath and Jerry Vale worked for expenses because he owed me a favor."

The best memory Torcasio said, is the day he convinced Dean Martin to present a baton twirling award to his daughter, Becky on a Las Vegas stage, after which Martin warbled, "Everybody Loves Somebody Sometime." Belluck goes on, "Tony was a kid in a time and place when backroom casino gambling was getting its start in the 1930's in Steubenville, Ohio, the hometown of Jimmy "The Greek" Snyder and Dean Martin." "I was born and raised with Dino" he said, taking out a copy of the recent Dean Martin bibliography, Dino. "My name is in there about ten times"

Somewhere in all this, Torcasio skirted the edge of the ABSCAM scandal of 1979. (An FBI sting operation stemming from an investigation of valuable stolen paintings and bribery of public officials from Pennsylvania to New Jersey) Torcasio was sent by Penthouse publisher Robert Guccione to Florida where he had a meeting with a man who was supposed to provide money for the planned Penthouse Casino in New Jersey. The man turned out to be Melvin Weinberg (Christian Bale in American Hustle) the con man who turned key FBI informant in the ABSCAM investigation. Torcasio however, was never charged. A 1983 U.S. Senate Committee review said that Weinberg was trying to bribe New Jersey officials for money for the Penthouse casino.

Torcasio's extortion and perjury charges were upheld by Federal Appeals Court and the United States Supreme Court refused to hear the case.

In 1990, facing 36 years in federal prison, former governor Arch A. Moore pled guilty to five felony counts and was sentenced to five years and 10 months in prison. Amazingly however, for the base of his supporters, it remained difficult for them and many others to dislike Arch. He was a WWII wounded purple heart, decorated veteran and a charismatic master politician, quite capable of governing. In 1967, during his term as Congressman, I visited his office and caught up with him in the Capitol Judiciary Room where he served on the Judiciary Committee with Chairman, Emanuel Celler and Peter Rodino. They were conducting an Impeachment Hearing for Congressman Adam Clayton Powell.[10]

I sat patiently and conspicuously in a near empty Judiciary room. Following a break in the hearing, Arch sent a page, informing me to meet him back at his office. I was his luncheon guest at the Rayburn Cafeteria where he disclosed his plans to run for Governor. He said, "George, I know you're a democrat and I don't want to put you in a box, but I'm going to clean our state up and put us on top where we belong. If you can find it in your heart to help me, I'd like to bring you to Charleston."

I chose to remain loyal to my party and supported Jim Sprouse, his opponent who lost to Arch by 12,000 votes. Thirty years later a second Republican, Cecil Underwood was elected Governor of West Virginia. He was first elected Governor in 1957 at the age of 35, the youngest governor ever elected, and forty years later in 1997 became the oldest Governor to serve the mountaineers. Underwood served his two terms without scandal. Nevertheless he never allowed justice to interfere with politics. While serving on the Parole Board under his administration, I witnessed and participated in a classic example of outrageous preferential treatment in our justice system. In November 1997, Underwood's Chief of Staff received a call from a high ranking State Senator asking the governor to intercede In the Parole Board's decision regarding an inmate from his district who was serving time for involuntary manslaughter. The Chairman advised the board that the subject was a major contributor to both the Senator's and Governor's election. The subject was originally indicted for first degree murder in the shooting death of his wife. She was killed during breakfast as she sat across

10   Adam Clayton was the first black person elected to Congress. Following his exclusion in 1967 on allegations of corruption. He was however, reelected losing his seat to Charlie Rangel.

the table from him. He claimed he was cleaning his rifle when it accidentally discharged. He was found guilty by a jury of second degree murder and sentenced to 5 to 18 years in prison. He appealed this conviction and was granted a new trial and change of venue. Appearing before an "understanding" Judge, he was granted the right to take an Alford Plea to Voluntary Manslaughter and his sentence reduced to 1 to 5 years.[11] Thus, this chain store owner and once convicted murderer, who was able to retain famed pathologist Cyril Wecht, to testify on his behalf, spent one year "incarcerated" in the local county jail. Throughout those twelve months, he was permitted to leave daily to manage his business and return at night to sleep in his bunk. In his first appearance before the Board, he was granted Parole.

---

11   Alford Plea allows the criminal not to admit to the crime, but admit that the prosecution could likely prove his guilt. Essentially, it allows the defendant to plead guilty even though he is unwilling to admit guilt.

FIFTY-THREE

You Are Who You Eat With

The very best of local and out of state attorneys were retained by Hankish. He understood the importance of keeping the very best closest to him. His premiere bookmaking/wagering counsel included a mathematical whiz, who commanded national respect as a near genius sports handicapper. Hankish retained stone cold killers, drug smugglers, an arsonist and a maniacal, but creative and efficient, cross-country shoplifter. Hankish's team benefitted from his working relationships with members of the Gambino, Luchese, Bruno and Decavalcante families. Naturally, his most powerful mentor was Gabriel "Kelly" Mannerino, who by his national reputation conferred widespread and lasting power upon Hankish, which enabled him to operate with near exclusion and impunity in many parts of the country. Hankish developed his close relationship with the Gambino family during his imprisonment at Lewisburg Penitentiary Camp, where he spent his days and nights with the likes of Tony "Pro" Provenzano, exchanging smuggled kibbe and stuffed grape leaves for lasagna and salami.

Hankish drew enormous interest and respect for providing remarkably accurate sports betting lines to select East Coast mafia leaders residing with him in Lewisburg penitentiary. They utilized and shared his betting lines for their wagering activities inside and outside the prison. Upon his release, his personal odds maker and bookmaking associate had amassed thousands of dollars for Hankish and built up a trade that subsequently enabled Hankish to expand their operation. Hankish was booking and wagering hundreds of thousands a week on college and professional sports. Among his largest sports betting customers were Wheeling physicians and attorneys. One exception was Hankish's friend, Wheeling businessman George Boury, who is alleged to have wagered as much as five to ten thousand a game on weekend professional football games with a Kentucky bookmaker, who was an ally to Hankish. At one time, Boury was unmatched in his success as a ruthless Wheeling businessman. Mr. Boury was the son of Lebanese immigrant parents who struggled as early Wheeling merchants. Among his family interests, he owned a string of Elby's Big Boy restaurants in multiple states. During Hankish's trial, George Boury's secretary, Dorothy Simon, offered damaging testimony against Hankish. Prior to Hankish's trial, Youngstown Mafia boss, Joey Naples offered to have a member of the Youngstown De Bartolo family "walk into George Boury's office and tell George, 'I hope the rumor I'm hearing about your secretary testifying against Paul is just bullshit.'"

College basketball games, as well as professional football, became as crooked as horse and dog racing. Professional odds makers admitted they were routinely fixed. Shaved points and thrown games; players, coaches and referees were at times in on the play. In college basketball, I was told that often times there were as many as ten fixed games a week. In professional football, a Hankish cocaine distributor alleged that one or two professional football teams played around with the point spread and the over and under. Hankish and San Francisco Forty Niner's owner, Edward J. DeBartolo Sr., were said to have been associates, but no proof or allegations ever surfaced about football improprieties. A former college basketball official told me that in the fifties and early sixties, "We fixed more basketball games in West Virginia than elections."

FIFTY-FOUR

LOOK AT MR. Z.

One of Hankish's early associates was Tony Zambito, an "old school," major league gambler and night club operator. Tony later shed his underworld ties and became a well-respected Wheeling businessman. Tony was a successful nightclub operator and owned the popular Jolly Bar located in downtown Wheeling on the north plaza. He was a WWII veteran, an absolutely devoted parent and a delightful gentleman. Tony had operated nightclubs in Wheeling since the early 1940's. The Wheeling newspaper published a raving review of Tony Z's formal opening of the Jai Lai Night Club in the early 1950's: "The largest and one of the most fashionable night clubs ever created for Wheeling will have its formal opening tonight. The new club is located on the second floor at 1407 Market Street. The club has a 200 seat dining room. The club is arranged to meet all entertainment demands. A specially built check room is located immediately inside the club's entrance. The stage is effectively across the end of the room to provide a complete view from every table. As a special introduction a movie starlet will be the opening attraction. Barbara O'Brien, most recently seen with Laurel & Hardy but who began her film career at Echo of Our Gang comedies will be the star of the opening show. Miss O'Brien is an excellent vocalist. She recently has been singing in New York and Canada and comes here for a special engagement."

Tony Z developed solid connections with outfit members during his military service. In the late 1950s, Tony opened the Jolly Bar. It opened its doors at 11:00 p.m. and closed at his will. The room was always packed at midnight. A green tongued Sammy Bettini was at the piano, complying with his physician's order that he imbibe only from the bottle of Crème De Menthe at his side, which would do his vital organs less harm than his ordinary preference; a bottle of Canadian Club whiskey each day. All seats were full at the blackjack table with a flashy blonde female in the dealer's seat. On this day, a crowd of onlookers hovered behind the players, not entirely interested in the game, but excited to watch one of the players. Seated to the dealer's right (third base) was the immortal Bobby Lane, quarterback for the Pittsburgh Steelers. In the early 1960s, the Steelers used the football facilities at West Liberty State College for their training camp. This facility was only a brief drive to downtown Wheeling. They partied almost nightly throughout the city, with the exception of teammate, "Big Daddy" Lipscomb. Because the city, for the most part remained "de facto" segregated, "Big Daddy" spent his night life in Steubenville, Ohio. There were only six black players on the Steeler team that year. They finished 9 and 5 and second in the Eastern Conference, qualifying them for the playoff bowl. It was Art Rooney's first ever post season game.

FIFTY-FIVE

PAY OR PRAY

Dynamite bombs were exploding all over Wheeling and parts of Eastern Ohio. The newspapers were guessing at the cause calling the "blitzkrieg" a "Pinball War." In fact, it was the Cleveland mob shaking down operators and owners of pinball machines and juke boxes throughout the Ohio Valley. They expected pay for the mandatory protection they created for any electronic gambling or vending machine. They dispatched someone monthly to collect from the owners. One of the reluctant, targeted vendors refusing to pay was Charlie Zambito, Tony Z's brother and owner of the Bella Via restaurant, which harbored a mini casino on the second floor. His son, Charlie Jr., who helped manage the business, approached his Dad one Saturday afternoon and expressed concern to his father, "Dad, I just got word that we're on the target list for a bombing tonight. It's our Saturday night, and we'll be packed. Should we close to protect our customers?" His dad calmly responded, "Just stay open and keep away from the windows."

FIFTY-SIX

Rockin' Round the Clock

During Wheeling's faltering post-"Victorian Era," much of the downtown and "below the bridge" area resembled the French Quarter of New Orleans. In fact, it was in many ways superior; it was less expensive and safer. Of course, there were no marching bands with brass and military horns, but the sights and sounds of jubilation were music to the ears of festive crowds crowding the streets and sidewalks, all eager to cabaret and starved for action. The recidivist locals were joined by hundreds of tourists excited to share the variety and vice of "Little Chicago." The success of those in the food and beverage business could be measured by the enormity of trash and garbage obstructing their contiguous alleyways.

On Monday mornings, you would find pyramids of empty whiskey and beer bottles, the vestiges wrapped in newspaper, flanked by overflowing Wheeling Steel garbage cans. The garbage collectors used industrial brooms and feed shovels to collect the rubbish. Often, stray animals competed with rodents for edible scraps. Weekdays were reserved for locals. Soon after 5:00 p.m., the sidewalks were lined with departing shoppers and employees. Only a few hours later, many would return to the darkening city for "after hour" action. A short walk up Market Street offered adjoining rows of unmatched opportunity for dining, drinking and entertainment, ranging from "bust out" joints to a few fashionable restaurants and taverns. Downtown

Wheeling hosted eight movie theaters within a six block area; however, their marquees were dwarfed in comparison to the alluring neon displays of BARB'S BONGO, DUCK INN, GYPSY'S, NOSEY'S, WEST VIRGINIA SNAKE'S CLUB, PINK ELEPHANT and the CAROUSEL.

"Below the bridge" was a euphemism for the whore house district. The city of Wheeling once held the distinction of being the "Whore House Capitol of the United States." The latest count had the number at twenty six in a two block area that was patrolled by Wheeling policemen who only said no to prostitution when you asked them if they had enough. The following is a list of some notorious and recorded houses of ill repute, described either by their location and/or trade name: The Loop, Green Lantern, Aggie's on South Penn, Stone House, The Menu, Big Red & Janet's, Vicky's Green Door, Alma's Red Barn, Floss Hotel, The Torch, Roy & Nellie Garrison's, Looch & Helen's Cedar Bar, Raven's Roundhouse, Forty Winks and the King of the Road.

These seductive landmarks drew patrons arriving in every form of transportation attainable. They took trains, buses and taxi cabs, while some walked and others ran. The traffic flowed every day of the week from noon until the early morning hours. "Big Red" Richardson and his wife Janet owned and operated the crème de' la' crème of the Wheeling cathouses. It was located directly behind Billy's Bar at 23rd and Main Streets. On a typical evening, you would find Janet, the Madam, seated at a chrome legged table. While waiting for the doorbell to ring or to escort an attended customer to the door, vigilant Janet would remain at her seat, committed to her black coffee and playing head to head Hollywood gin with one of the "Sponge Boys." Beyond her diverse obligations, including collecting the cash, timekeeper and security, she emceed the lineup call to the anxious customers seated in the crowded waiting room, about to make their choice from several scantily dressed, available parading prostitutes. Once chosen and behind closed doors, the "working girl" escorted her customer and drew him close to her bedside lamp, removing the shade whereupon she conducted a cursory examination of her client. Forsaking her best interest and absent the presence of some startling empirical discovery, she would proceed to solicit their commercial interest: "Honey, a straight lay is ten dollars, half and half is fifteen, straight 'French' is twenty and 'around the world is fifty' what's your pleasure?"

These young women were indentured servants, subjected to inhumane control by pimps who took half of their earnings and served as their masters. The pimps supposedly offered them protection and security, when in fact they did no more than mistreat and exploit them. Most, if not all, of the prostitutes became addicted to amphetamines, which their pimps graciously supplied. These lonely, misguided young women become vulnerable and ideal Stockholm syndrome candidates for their procurers. During this period, there were very few prostitutes working without pimps. Those independent few were referred to in the trade as "Outlaws" and scorned by their peers.

All the Madams enjoyed the security of on-site "hired muscle." Unruly or menacing customers were often, literally, thrown out the door, and those too slow or reluctant to quickly depart the brick alley upon which they landed were often arrested for disorderly conduct by cooperating police who diligently paroled the area. One Wheeling policeman recalls a disgruntled arrestee complaining, "Hey man, whatta arresting me for, they're sellin' pussy in there," to which the officer replied, "Can't do anything about that unless you got a receipt."

Janet's diligence would send her to the foot of the stairs where she would emit the euphemistic call, "Your time is up, honey you okay?" When the response was an affirmative "Comin' down," Janet waited to escort the "John" to the door. One of Janet's bodyguards was Fritz Falcone. Fritz, when not on duty at Janet's, worked the door for various night clubs in the city. He was a rugged, dedicated family man who held a full-time day shift at Bloch Brothers tobacco as a machinist. He shared the following story: Big Red and Janet reserved Saturday mornings for "special" patrons, those who expected privacy such as Wheeling's elite businessmen, ministers, public officials and many others who were openly diametrically opposed to prostitution. Fritz said he often worked the Saturday morning detail and to his surprise, an unannounced police raid occurred during which time the Wheeling city manager was occupying one of the bordello bedrooms. The cops were hammering at the door, shouting, "Open up Janet or you'll be buying a new door!" Janet ordered Fritz to rush upstairs and "get that crazy ass City Manager out of here."

The "City Emperor" now clothed, rushed down the stairs only to be confronted by a contingent of uniformed officers. True to his profession and moral turpitude, he marched directly toward them, pointing his finger and shouted, "Where in the hell have you guys been? I've been waiting here for an hour." His theater and untied shoe laces proved less than convincing, but a call to the Chief hindered his arrest. More appetizing was the police chief's desire to capitalize on his catch and the opportunity of holding a black marker over his boss. The manager departed unrestrained in the company of the police officers, six prostitutes, the madam and two mortified patrons: a handcuffed druggist and a retired school teacher. The city manager remained in his post at Wheeling a short while before deciding to relocate to the state capitol in Charleston, West Virginia, where you might find prostitutes serving with diplomatic immunity. Following a few years of failure as a practicing attorney, he was duly elected Circuit Judge for Kanawha County. His stay on the bench was as brief and ill-timed as his visit to the Wheeling bordello. He was, before completing his first term, impeached and removed from office on ethics violations, sexual harassment and appearing on the bench in a toxic state. For the judge, it was Almost Heaven, West Virginia.

A mastermind pimp and otherwise successful Wheeling businessman, "Big Ray" Thalman shared his entrepreneurs skills, leasing his young girlfriend to houses of prostitution. Big Ray revealed the enormous wealth he acquired from his "turned out" beauty. He owned one of the most popular and attractive prostitutes ever to inhabit a Wheeling brothel. This stunning red-headed beauty, a recent local high school graduate, soon adopted the trade name "Pepsi." When asked how she chose the title, Big Ray explained, "She originally worked under the name "Rusty." While working at the 'King of the Road' truck stop whorehouse just off I-70, the Madam owned a dog named Rusty, an Irish Setter she kept in the brothel. The Madam approached Ms. Rusty and told her she would have to change her name to avoid the confusion and disruption. She went on to explain that when she summoned Ms. Rusty the dog would react, often dashing about anxiously awaiting patrons. Ms. Rusty quickly agreed with the Madam's request, and as she pondered her trade name change, looking across the room and recognizing the Pepsi Cola vending machine, she raised her head and identified her choice for a new alias." In the meridian of Pepsi's late 1970s career, she was netting close to a $1000 a day. One early morning at her center wheeling apartment, she was visited by an FBI agent. Pepsi's son had recently been nominated to the West Point Military Academy. The agent informed Pepsi that his mandatory background check disclosed his mother's occupation resulting in denial of his appointment. The agent went on to offer her a deal, whereby the revelation could be overlooked if she agreed to become an informant for the agency. Big Ray said that Pepsi agreed and her son went in to graduate West Point. Pepsi, equipped with the weaponry to conquer man's frailty, also went on to serve her country. She relocated to Washington D.C., wired and bubbly servicing congressman, senators and diplomats. Big Ray claimed, "J. Edgar Hoover never drank another Coke."

FIFTY-SEVEN

RICH AS ROCKEFELLER

Old Greek residual power conferred upon by "Big Bill" was on the wane in the city. Paul "No Legs" Hankish, a paraplegic, suffering from epilepsy, hearing loss, missing fingers and confined to a wheel chair, was dictating to public officials, policemen, business owners and his boosters, arsonists, drug smugglers and contract killers. Hankish was now in full command and ruled a boundless, nation wide criminal empire with absolute power for the next twenty years.

However, the second generation of young and aspiring "Turks" shed their white aprons and abandoned their father's "greasy spoon" kitchens. Most were now wearing business suits instead of aprons, thriving in main stream America and carrying college diplomas instead of dishes. A case in point was my good friend Parry Petroplus, who was fortunate enough to be the son of a successful first generation Greek-American bank realtor. The "Greek Tribal Rule" in Wheeling was displaced by Middle Eastern influence, leaving the Greeks, Italians and Irish with a few innocuous enclaves. Parry, still a Linsly Institute Cadet, was working part-time as a bell hop at the McLure Hotel, now jointly owned by Lias' brother-in-law, Greg Manos. The McLure Hotel was a Wheeling icon with legendary significance leading back to the Civil War. It was built in 1852 and was once considered the finest hotel in the state. The majestic McLure was host to numerous national figures, among them the less notable, Senator Joseph McCarthy who delivered his infamous "Communist infiltration" speech before the Wheeling Women's Club. Many question the veracity of the story that he summoned a Wheeling prostitute to his room and before engaging her asked, "Are you now or have you ever been a member of the Communist party?"

Parry tells the following story:

I was an enterprising young man, unaware of one of the more dubious bell-hopping duties I would be forced to encumber. Some obligatory tasks became absolute unsavory challenges. This undisclosed obligation included shadowing "ladies of the day and night" from the lobby to their destination on one of the seven floors of the 300 room hotel. Of course I unexpectedly realized a substantial reward for my navigation, discretion and/or silence. My most generous contribution came from a ranking member of the Wheeling Chamber of Commerce who received my commitment and assurance that his modified lunch break would remain confidential.

One morning, I was summoned to the manager's office and informed that West Virginia Governor, John D. Rockefeller IV and the first lady would be arriving soon after the dinner hour. I was told to wait outside the front door and prepare for the limousine to arrive. I grabbed a luggage cart and immediately assumed my post. I was excited to meet the Governor and the first lady. When the limo pulled up to the curb, a plain-clothed state trooper rushed to open the door for the first lady. She stood at the curb and awaited her husband who lumbered to his feet, and I led them to the elevator. Leaving their suite, I rushed back to the limo where a uniformed state trooper was loading their luggage onto the cart. He accompanied me back to the Governor's suite where I assisted in disposing the luggage. The Governor was shoeless, sitting on the edge of the bed. Without raising his head or hand, he thanked me, and I left with "Tipota" (nothing). The manager asked me if everything went okay and asked if me I was willing to share my gratuity with him. I told him that I would give him half of the fish hooks the Governor had in his pockets.

Parry went on in life to become an extraordinary success in the business world. He became involved in state and national politics, recognized as a powerful influence and contributor. Once during his attendance at a Washington, D.C. fundraiser for Senator Rockefeller, he seized upon the opportunity to remind the Senator of his faux pas. He said the Senator apologetically responded, "Parry, I probably thought my wife tipped you." To which Parry quickly replied, "Well just give me a hundred now, and I'll call it even."

FIFTY-EIGHT

HEART OF MOLD

Much to his alarm, months following his release from Lewisburg Prison, Paul Hankish was observed by the FBI in a photograph taken at the infamous Gold Coast restaurant in Miami. The photo was displayed on national television during the Sons of Scarface production hosted by Geraldo Rivera, announcing: "Leaders of organized crime having dinner at the Miami restaurant." The photo was taken during one of Hankish's many trips to his new condominium he purchased at 2049 South Ocean Drive in Hallandale. The live documentary probed the history of organized crime, and how prevalent it had become. Many of Hankish's friends and associates were provided complimentary use of his condo, and FBI surveillance provided photographic surveillance of public officials and prominent Wheeling community leaders visiting and occupying the unit. Guests at the condo ranged from a county sheriff to Hollywood celebrities.

Paul's ingenuity and temerity were boundless. A few local businessmen who had a close relationship with Hankish were called upon by the Wheeling Society for Crippled Children to hold a special fund raising activity for the organization. Without the knowledge of the organization, they approached Hankish for assistance. They decided to hold a "Night at the Casino" event at the Esquire Supper Club and sought Paul's expertise and assistance. Hankish agreed to have one of his men privately oversee the operation and provide them with the personnel and equipment to operate a blackjack and crap game. The event was a tremendous success with over two hundred local businessmen, their wives, girlfriends and employees joining them. What the contributing patrons and sponsors were unaware of was that the dice were loaded, and the blackjack dealer, recruited from New Jersey, was cheating, dealing seconds "out of the Shoe," (a glass box holding multiple decks of cards to reduce the dealer's opportunity to cheat) filled with marked cards. The games went on until early morning. Many players lost thousands. When the count was complete, the Wheeling Crippled Children Society received an enormous amount from the event. It was estimated to be nearly $25,000. What remained a closely held, unaccountable fact was that Paul Hankish left that morning with nearly as much cash. Hankish shared his infrequent public evening hours between the Esquire Club and the Eagle Inn. He was always accompanied by "muscle" and female followers. The Eagle was one of the most popular cabaret junctions in the tri-state area during the reign of the "disco seventies." The Inn was owned by a respected insurance executive and Vietnam veteran G. Michael Fahey. Mike often joked that he was responsible for keeping FBI agents and mobsters under the same roof.

I owned a flower shop in the McLure hotel in downtown Wheeling (Faraday Florist). Gregory Manos had just purchased part ownership in the hotel and was working as the manager. It was during the numerous lunches with Greg in the Colonnade Dining Room of the McLure that we had lengthy and detailed discussions about his brother-in-law, William G. Lias.

One mid-afternoon I received a phone call from "Big Bill's" widow, Alice Lias. She said, "Yiorgios, this is Alice, did you hear that 'Candy Kitchen' Mike died?" I told her that I did, and she asked me if I was getting many orders for funeral baskets of flowers. When I told her that she was my first call, she said, "Send a fifty dollar cross of red carnations with a stream of white roses down the center and on the card, I want it to read, with deepest sympathy, Alice Lias. Now you stay by the phone until I call you again, don't leave until you hear from me." The phone rang for the next three hours. A typical caller would say, "I want to send a basket of flowers to 'Candy Kitchen' Mike. I already ordered flowers from another florist, but Alice told me to call you." Hours later, Alice telephoned "Yiorgios, talk slow and tell me everybody that has called you to order flowers for Mike." After reading her the names and the amounts, she said, "Okay, that's good, *Kaleeni'ct*a." (Good night).

At Greek Easter, the members of St. John the Divine Greek Orthodox church gave special attention to floral decorations inside the church and particularly the Icon that was paraded during Mass. Traditionally, the previous florist decorated the Icon with white carnations. That was about to change. As the biggest church donor, Matriarch Alice called the shots. She advised church council members that Faraday Florist would be decorating the church, and she thought something special should be done. I nearly ran out of Easter Lilies and special ordered expensive Phalaenopsis Orchids for the Icon. She continued to be a devoted customer and great friend to me for her entire life. She would often call me on Saturday mornings, and I would take her to the matinee performance at Wheeling Downs Greyhound racetrack. She liked to wager quinellas and would box the 4-6-8.

Of course, I walked the tightrope. I worried that Paul Hankish, also a valuable customer, would be offended by my relationship with Alice, but somehow I avoided the conflict. Hankish was not only a coveted customer, but he encouraged his out of town associates and friends to order from my shop when sending flowers to his family or friends. I had Mafia family members as common customers from Godfathers to Capos from New York to Florida: Nicasia, Bruno, Ippolito, Valeneti, Naples, Covello and Mannerino. Some ordered arrangements that cost as much as a used car. There were many occasions when the cost of the flower order justified delivery from Wheeling to the Youngstown area and parts of western Pennsylvania. Nevertheless, I was always instructed not to transfer any order by Floral Telegraph Delivery or directly to another out of town florist. This, of course, would leave record and divulge the sender and receiver.

FIFTY-NINE

FRIENDS IN HIGH PLACES

One of Hankish's close New York mob affiliates was Joey Ippolito. He was, among other things, a national speedboat racer and major drug dealer who often visited Hankish in Wheeling and joined with his friends for dinner at the Esquire Club. Hankish often joined Ippolito and other members of the Gambino family at Leona Helmsley's St. Moritz Hotel in New York City. "Joey Ippolito was a second generation Mafia member. He had power from Philadelphia to Florida into Southern California. "A former champion offshore power boat racer, Ippolito relocated to California following discharge from his four year prison sentence for marijuana smuggling," this according to Donald Freed and Raymond P. Briggs in their book *Killing Time*. They also claimed O.J. Simpson's close buddy Al Cowlings was an occasional body guard for Ippolito. Joey Ippolito owned a fashionable Italian restaurant in Malibu and was alleged to distribute cocaine in Santa Monica and Brentwood. He also allegedly maintained a relationship with O.J. Simpson and James Caan, both of whom he introduced to Hankish. According to a convicted cocaine dealing associate of Hankish, Caan and Simpson were occasional customers of Hankish, meeting at his Miami Condominium. Ippolito inherited his father's connection to the New Jersey Cavalcante family.

Hankish enjoyed the company of a variety of celebrities even while serving his initial, 1 to 10 years prison time at the State Penitentiary in Moundsville. He had among his many controversial visitors, Al Zied, a close companion and notorious contract killer, who was accompanied by the former world light-heavyweight boxing champion and hall of famer, Billy Conn. The warden, Otto C. Boles, was questioned by local news reporters regarding his visitation policy, and the warden gave his assurance that the ex-convict Abraham aka Al Ross-Zeid would not again be afforded visitation rights at the institution. However, he said there would be no restriction in the case of Billy Conn, explaining, "After all, Jack Dempsey visited here before too."

Only a few years later, Abraham Zeid's decomposed body was found in a pond on a farm in Donegal Township, Washington County, Pennsylvania on June 25, 1965. The property was owned by a Pennsylvania attorney with close ties to mafia members. This same site was on the list of possible locations for the burial of Jimmy Hoffa's remains. Hankish was indicted for the murder, which allegedly came about following Zeid's arrest and threatening proclamation, "I will never do time; I know too much." Hankish and an accomplice are said to have committed the murder of Zeid at the request of the Pittsburgh Genovese family who feared Zeid was seeking to turn state's evidence for a plea bargain deal. No arrest resulted from the indictment nor was there further investigation of the Zeid matter.

SIXTY

Winter Winds

On February 20, 1972, I was vacationing with a friend in Miami, celebrating my 29th birthday. We were guests at the Fontainebleau hotel. That Friday evening, Ann Margaret was appearing in the Show Room. We were outside enjoying the moon over Miami and watching the crowd roll in and found a stone seat near Dustin Hoffman and his agent. I introduced myself to the surprisingly congenial Hoffman, and we discussed seating for the Ann Margaret Show. He then asked if we would like to be his guest for Dion Warwick who was appearing next door at the Eden Roc the next day. Of course, we were only too happy to accept his offer. That next evening, we wandered next door to the Eden Roc Hotel and secured our guest tickets from the Maître d'. Our seats were great and among the celebrities seated near us was Jimmy Hoffa, who had received his Presidential Pardon just two months earlier on January 23, 1971. He was introduced during the show and brought the crowd to their feet. Hoffa stood up waving his arms at the cheering crowd, many of them repeatedly cheering; "Jimmy." Little did he realize that his popularity remained much greater among the general public than among his former cohorts, who were allegedly responsible for his disappearance three years later.

SIXTY-ONE

RED LIGHTS OUT

In the early 1970s, the high tide of Urban Renewal eliminated the entire whore house district of Center Wheeling. The renewal project condemned and demolished a three block square area of mostly dilapidated commercial and residential structures. The few remaining prostitutes, left with no other choice, moved outside the city limits, and business began flourishing at truck stops and outposts along Interstate 70 near the Pennsylvania border. The social consciousness was changing. Disco and Go Go were replacing poker and prostitution in the Friendly City of Wheeling, but its economic woes had just begun. Wheeling remained light years from the coveted "All-American Cities Award." Local merchants choked on their greed and lack of vision and succeeded in keeping a mall from being developed in downtown Wheeling. They rendered the default of a once robust city, and many of these same anti-mall, retail merchants soon abandoned the city they helped doom, relocating to the newly developed mall in neighboring St. Clairsville, Ohio, leaving downtown Wheeling barren, with flocks of pigeons atop vacant buildings and empty parking lots.

The patron attraction of downtown Wheeling became Paul Hankish's Coffee Shop. When Hankish closed the infamous Academy Billiards, he partnered with William "Pee Wee" George, one of six eastern Ohio brothers who were extremely successful in the vending and gambling business. Hankish and George opened the Regal Coffee Shop on 14th and Market

Street and, for a brief time, remained partners in a cross-country bookmaking operation. Following Hankish's discharge from Lewisburg penitentiary, he and George terminated all of their partnerships with the exception of their "Lazy Shadow" real estate holdings. Hankish is said to have exercised his cunning brilliance to dissolve the book making relationship with his long-time partner, "Pee Wee" George. He knew "Pee Wee" disliked chasing money and took losses like anyone else.

Thus without his knowledge, Hankish allegedly schemed to purposely mislead George. He began taking bets on football games with intentional bad betting lines (odds) that Hankish produced, and worse, he had confidants place bets with him on fixed games, resulting in weeks of superficial losses, costing thousands of dollars for their partnership. Of course, these were paper losses to Hankish, but real losses to George. "Pee Wee's" reaction was predictable; he wanted out.

Hankish then took sole possession and relocated his bookmaking operation next to the former Rogers Hotel on 14th Street and assigned "Butch" Floria as his front man. This location was used essentially for "walk ins" and local "cinch" bookies who laid off wagers they felt were too large or too much of a risk to handle alone. Florio operated for ten years, untouched and unedited. The majority of Hankish's major wagering activities were restricted to pay phones throughout the tri-state area. One of his associates told me, "Every weekend, I carried around as much as $500 dollars in quarters. We used pay phones in three states, on the street, hotel lobbies, restaurants libraries and hospitals."

Paul Hankish was convicted in 1971 on federal charges of beer hijacking and served 32 months at Lewisburg federal penitentiary. An associate shared the following: "When Paul was doing time in Lewisburg for this rap, he was intrigued by the ongoing success of a number of his fellow inmates, some of whom had trouble reading the newspaper. They were visited without limitations by gorgeous women arriving in Mercedes Benz automobiles, dressed to the nines and covered with gold and diamonds. They routinely dropped off rubber banded rolls of hundred dollar bills for their husbands and lovers, a large part of which was used to bribe prison officials. When he finally realized these guys were dealing in drugs and he discovered the magnitude of the illegal drug profit, he made up his mind that when he left prison, he would get in the drug trade."

The *Pittsburgh Press* reported the government allegation that Hankish operated a drug ring that began in 1981 which supplied half the cocaine and marijuana sold in the Wheeling area alone. His drug sales and gambling operation netted nearly $6 million in seven states.

More than a decade had passed since Hankish was literally blown to pieces in a failed assassination attempt. He continued to battle serious health problems unrelated to the explosion along with the lingering affects resulting from the dynamite blast. There was seldom a day that he escaped the pain and anxiety of having to remove pieces of shrapnel constantly surfacing from his wounds. He continued to suffer from petit-mal epilepsy, diabetes and high blood pressure. The bombing left him with no legs beneath his knees, missing fingers and hearing loss. His years of crime and haunting torment from the media and law enforcement, progressive health problems and prison time morphed him into a contemptuous, intractable monster. However, his public persona was quite the opposite; he was quiet, well-mannered and smiling. When his cocaine trafficking converted to self-addiction, he became careless, imprudent and paved the road to his demise. Through it all, Hankish struggled to act fiercely independent, obsessed with his personal grooming and dignity. He endeavored to walk with the aid of forearm crutches, often ignoring the need and dependency of a wheel chair. He wanted the public to see a strong and self-determined figure.

SIXTY-TWO

CHECK PLEASE

On September 29, 1989 Paul Hankish was named in 89 of a 218 count indictment involving eleven co-defendants. A superseding indictment was filed on April 12, 1990, which contained 221 counts. Among the charges against Hankish were 23 separate counts of engaging in criminal enterprise to distribute cocaine, a RICO conspiracy charge, each of which carried a prison term of 20 years and millions of dollars in fines. Nearly one half of these counts alleged cocaine distribution within 1000 feet of a school, each count carrying a 40 year prison term. Hankish was tied to several murders, including the contract killing of a Pennsylvania bookie and another racketeer.

An article in The *Charleston Gazette* cited Hankish's contacts in Lebanon. FBI records established his international criminal contacts from Beirut to South America. The Northern District U.S. Attorney, William Kolibash, called the indictment, "The largest racketeering organization we've had. I was surprised by its extensive operations in Texas, Missouri, Rhode Island and Florida." According to the indictment, Hankish answered to the Gambino family in planning his murders. On July 17, 1990, Hankish's trial began in Wheeling, and on July 24, 1990, he entered into a plea agreement with the government. A portion of the plea agreement provided that the government would agree that in view of the nature of the particular charges and Hankish's admission, the sentence in the matter would be imposed under the pre-sentencing guideline law. Another provision of the agreement provided that all but three counts of the indictment would be dismissed against his wife, Patricia A. Hankish. Moreover, in the event she was convicted, the United States would recommend probation.

A *Pittsburgh Press* synopsis of Mrs. Hankish's attorney's courtroom summation concluded that her only sin was meeting Paul Hankish and becoming his wife. "She was 19 when she met and fell in love with Hankish, then 29 who already was married. The relationship began before 1964 when he lost his legs in a car bombing only four months after being released from prison. 'This did not change her feelings toward him and she continued to see him,' the attorney said, noting that the Hankishes married January 21, 1970 after he and his first wife were divorced. While Hankish had no job, the new Mrs. Hankish knew he 'played cards and shot dice' and as a gambler, was away from home almost every evening. Government attorneys contend that she often would take delivery of stolen property, make payments for it and even state where the items she would like to have stolen could be found. The prosecution also said that Hankish and his wife evaded taxes by preparing fraudulent papers for state authorities that said they traded in an older Mercedes toward a newer model."

Mrs. Hankish's lame defense attorney vowed she never had any connection with her husband's business dealings. "Although Mrs. Hankish knew her husband had a fascination for crystal, she did not know it had been stolen. If indeed it was," he said. "Mrs. Hankish is not a gambler. She would not know a straight from a flush or snake eyes from box cars." As for mail fraud, he said, "The only knowledge Mrs. Hankish had was that Paul Hankish had purchased an automobile, and she was told to have it registered in her name, which she did."

Her attorney also pooh-poohed the firearms charges, noting that they stemmed from a search of her home. "One of the agents idly picked up a cane that was leaning against the wall at the corner of the fireplace and, while idly twirling the cane in his hands, discovered it to be a cane gun. This was the first knowledge by Mrs. Hankish that the cane was, in fact, a gun.

Obviously the cane did not belong to Mrs. Hankish, since she had no use for it."

Patty Hankish was charged with nine counts: RICO Conspiracy, conspiracy to defraud the government, engaging in illegal gambling business, mail fraud, social security fraud and two counts of possessing unregistered firearms. The provisions to dismiss all but three counts against Mrs. Hankish were in addition to the provision which set forth the specific charges that Hankish would plead guilty to the maximum term of imprisonment for each charge, which totaled 77 years and a fine for each count.

In opening arguments, prosecutors said Hankish ruthlessly carved out a gambling empire in Northern West Virginia and Southwestern Pennsylvania, he took millions of dollars from high rollers like former Pittsburgh Steelers owner, Art Rooney Sr., who he code-named No. 42. But the prosecutor did not detail the relationship between Hankish and Rooney. It is alleged that Rooney founded the Steelers with $5000 he won betting on horses. In the1930s, he supposedly won $250,000 during a day at the track. A source involved and very close to Hankish and his wagering operation was adamant on denunciation of the prosecution's assertion that some form of relationship existed between Hankish and Rooney. He stated further, "Why would a guy like Art Rooney mess with Paul. He could get down on the square in Vegas for millions."

Hankish was charged with the murder of Melvin Pike, a reputed racketeer from Uniontown, Pennsylvania, who was slain outside the gymnasium while waiting for his ten year old daughter to finish her gymnastic lessons. During Hankish's trial, rumors spread that he put out a contract to kill the U.S. Attorney. A better bet would have been that he was planning to assassinate the Pope. Although the U.S. Attorney's Office played a major role in his conviction, the long line of plea bargaining of former Hankish associates resulted in his rapid conviction and became the main focus of his ire.

Preceding Hankish's arrest on these charges, the FBI raided his residence. Evidence confiscated and later used at trial was a vast amount of expensive stolen jewelry and Waterford Crystal. Sources revealed that the contractor who had recently built Hankish's home turned informant to avoid prosecution and, at the FBI's request, assisted in installing hidden surveillance equipment throughout the home. The cameras revealed kilos of cocaine concealed in the custom designed hinged, wooden baseboards. During the raid, agents were unable to locate the cocaine, and federal authorities speculated that Hankish may have been provided advance warning of the raid by an appointed, ranking officer of then Governor Moore's West Virginia State Police.

For years, Hankish's organization remained near faultless and free from worthy prosecution. Former Assistant U.S. Attorney David Jividen, who played a prominent role in the overall conviction of Hankish and his family of murderers, extortionists, arsonists, drug dealers and shoplifters, explained "If the FBI with the assistance of the DEA had failed to get a break with the arrest and cooperation of a local drug dealer, Hankish's organization may have survived for another decade."

It was Donald R. Clark[12], a drug dealer who said he began buying and selling narcotics in high school and graduated to selling a kilogram of cocaine to an FBI agent, who identified Paul "No Legs" Hankish as one his major suppliers. Clark said he paid Hankish $2000 an ounce for the cocaine he received from him. He was apprehended with a kilo of the purest form of cocaine ever found on the east coast of the United States. Clark pled to 10 counts, including drug charges, extortion and loan sharking. He testified that he initially turned to Hankish's chief lieutenant, Charles "Buddy" Jacovetty, to get financing to buy drugs from another supplier. He said he received $12,000 from Jacovetty for his first purchase and $15,000 to $40,000 each time thereafter. (*Pittsburgh Press*, 7/21/90). The FBI and DEA used Clark and began trailing Hankish and his associates, particularly Jacovetty, who was involved in extortion, loan sharking, bookmaking, cocaine, and stolen food stamps.

Another critical informant offered Witness Protection by the DEA was the owner of the Odessy Club, a popular

---

12   Robert Stuart, *Pittsburgh Press.*

Wheeling hangout for drug culture enthusiasts. The proprietor, AKA "Moon Man," provided key evidence to the Drug Enforcement Agent against Hankish. Former Special Assistant U.S. Attorney Dave Jividen praised DEA agents for their exemplary performance and results in executing the Title III Wiretapping of "Moon Man's" operation that solidified the case against Hankish. The federal wiretap referred to as Title III was adopted in 1968 and later revised to cover modern day electrical communication. It requires court approval and establishes authorization covering real-time surveillance of e-mail, fax, and the internet. The following information was taken from the Administrative Office of the U.S. Courts on behalf of the Federal Judiciary. Between the years 2002 and 2012, state and federal judges across the United States received 23,925 applications for wiretap, with all but 7 granted. In 2012 alone, that number jumped to 3,395. During the year of the Hankish investigation and arrest, only 738 applications for wiretap were submitted. Also during this period, the FBI was not permitted to investigate drug cases. According to federal sources, only the DEA was directly involved in his drug trafficking investigation and ultimate prosecution of the Hankish organization.

Paul Hankish's dominant drug operation stretched across the United States. His solid rock, South American, uncut pure cocaine made him the attraction of Hollywood millionaires. Hankish's association and suspected alliance with Bebe Rebozo, the millionaire and close personal friend of former President Richard Nixon, brought them both under intense scrutiny from the CIA and FBI. Justice department officials have confirmed that government files include an astonishing photo of Nixon, Rebozo and Hankish.

The prosecution presented a wide range of witnesses in Hankish's trial. One of the more hell bound revelations was captured by Roger Stuart of the *Pittsburgh Press*: "A convicted killer due for a parole hearing tomorrow on an Ohio prison sentence testified today that he undertook two murders-one unsuccessful-at the behest of reputed mobster Paul N. "No Legs" Hankish."

SIXTY-THREE

The Devil Made Him Do It

Ron Asher, 50, a prizefighter, said Hankish arranged for him to go to New Jersey in 1967 or 1968 for a hit, arising from Black Muslims "moving in on our territory." He said he was furnished with a handgun and silencer when he arrived in New Jersey, but added, he could never find the guy, who had gone underground. He stayed there for about three weeks and was compensated for his time. Asher said his second contract slaying assignment occurred in Canton, Ohio in 1974 when he helped another man, identified as Ron Bris, kill a woman. "How did you do it?"asked Assistant U.S. Attorney, John Reed. "Broke her neck," said Asher. Asher said that Bris wasn't sure she was dead, and she was stabbed with a 6 to 8 inch knife. Asher said the assignment was made by Hankish when he visited Hankish at Lewisburg federal penitentiary. Asher estimated that he got $2,000 to $3,000 for the failed assignment, and he was supposed to get $10,000 for killing the woman in Ohio. Asher testified that he shoplifted $2 million in merchandise and fenced it with Hankish during a ten year period in the mid 1960's. He also testified that he participated in armed robberies, including one that netted more than $200,000 in a Las Vegas casino.

Asher committed his crime of murder in Stark County, Ohio, and following his admission of the crime in federal court, the Canton, Ohio Prosecutor affirmed that he would press murder charges against Asher even though he was granted immunity to testify by the West Virginia U.S. Attorney. Prosecutor Robert Horowitz was quoted, "The immunity grant in federal court doesn't bind the state of Ohio, and I know we can prosecute him. What I don't know is whether or not we can use his testimony in that court because the testimony was given under the promise of immunity. The victim was Carla Aldina Dellebra." Victim Carla Aldina Dellebra, AKA "Canton Mary," was the madam for alleged Wheeling Island whorehouse operator Aggie Toomer. Dellebra was, prior to her murder, cooperating with FBI and Internal Revenue authorities.

In an August 31, 1990 article, the *Cleveland Plain Dealer* revealed "[t]he late Gus Shaheen, who was Stark County Coroner in 1974, didn't perform an autopsy on Dellerba's body, which he examined at the funeral home. He ruled her death a suicide." Following his testimony in Wheeling federal court, Asher completed his 2 years of a 17 year sentence for killing a man during a robbery in Martins Ferry, Ohio. He walked out of Chillicothe Correctional Institute a free man.

SIXTY-FOUR

SHOW ME THE MONEY

With two world champs;
Joe Louis & "Pete"

One of my dearest friends happened to be a long-time and close personal friend of Paul Hankish. With the exception of life styles, they shared a great deal in common. They were both of Lebanese extraction, brilliant and loved sports. My friend, who I will identify as "Pete," was a successful businessman with the loyal heart of a lion. He was held in high esteem throughout the community for his charity and positive values. His family devotion and business success was parallel to his philanthropy. The following story, however, is meant to illustrate the wide ranging reputation and influence of his friend, Paul Nathaniel Hankish.

I was once again Pete's guest on a trip to Las Vegas in the mid1970s. He and I traveled together to every Pittsburgh Steeler Super Bowl of the 1970s and over our twenty five years of friendship, hit every major racetrack, casino and golf course up and down the East coast. This venture was one of several gambling junkets promoted by one of Youngstown, Ohio's favorites, Johnny Adornetta. The casino host was the Hilton International, which at this time was one of the premiere venues in Vegas. The flight out of Pittsburgh was filled with guest players from eastern Ohio, western Pennsylvania and the two of us from Wheeling. Among the notable junket guests aboard the flight was Chester Stupak, the reigning king of Pittsburgh's south side gambling racketeers. Among Chester's floating gaming interests was his recently acquired outlet atop the Alamo nightclub in Bridgeport, Ohio, just across the Ohio River from Wheeling. Chester and his assembled crew were running a high stakes crap game that drew players from Youngstown to Pittsburgh. Chester was always quick to announce his important wagering rule before the first role of the dice, "Your first bet is your last," which meant you could not wager more on any toss of the dice that exceeded your first wager. Seated next to Chester was his son, Bobby, who would become the greatest huckster Las Vegas had ever seen. Two of the most notorious gamblers on the face of the planet remained in their seats for most of the flight, downing cocktails and peanuts. During the entire flight, these two eccentric millionaires remained gentle, polite and quieter than a rat pissin' on cotton.

Bobby Stupak became a legend in Las Vegas, and one of his major accomplishments was building the legendary Stratosphere Hotel and Casino. A fascinating article written by Geoff Schumacher and published in the Las Vegas Sun talks about the rise and fall of the "Polish Prince" Bobby Stupak. In his article, Schumacher quotes Las Vegas Review columnist John Smith: "If P.T. Barnum had a hedonistic twin, Bobby Stupak might be the guy. He is one of the great Vegas wild men." Smith's chapters chronicling the life and crimes of Bobby's father are noteworthy. "Chester was a major player in Pittsburgh's gambling rackets from the beginning of World War II until his death in 1991. He was a man of stature in Pittsburgh's backroom inner circles. He was to illegal numbers and cards what Carnegie was to steel." In Chester's early days, he would travel with a picnic basket full of cash, covered with a cloth towel. He would take his crap game to steel mill and rail yards. He attracted players by paying 30 to 1 on two sixes, and if you bet $100 and took down $3,000, he would let you bet the $3,000 back and pay you $90,000 for a win. He was unmatched in his skill and courage.

The cost for our Las Vegas Hilton Junket was $2,500 up front that you could draw down from the cage or sign a marker from the table of your choice. The Hilton paid for your flight and hotel expense and provided you with a Gold Players card that entitled you to unlimited meals and the beverage of your choice during your entire stay. My first morning in Vegas found me accompanying Pete to an ultramodern Racing & Sports book parlor at the Stardust Casino. Upon arriving, Pete went directly to the cashier's window, who summoned a green-visored supervisor. Pete made some introductory remarks, handed him a bulging envelope and departed. When we got back in the car, I asked if he had made a bet. He said, "No, 'Henry' [pseudonym for Paul Hankish] had a package for that guy and asked me to drop it off." At the time, I had no idea or interest in who "that guy" was, but it was clear that a large payment had been made for a new or old wager. Much later, I became aware that the Sports Book Parlor was owned by Las Vegas Kingpin, Frank "Lefty" Rosenthal, portrayed by Robert Di Niro as Sam "Ace" Rothstein in the movie Casino.

The following day, we learned that Sammy Davis Jr. was appearing in the main showroom of our hotel. The evening show would open with the appearance of Lola Falana, who was soon dubbed the Queen of Las Vegas and the highest paid entertainer in town. That evening we decided to take in the show. Without reservations, we arrived pompously at the showroom door just minutes before show time. Convinced that healthy gratuities got you most of what you wanted in Vegas, Pete was holding a fifty dollar bill by its ear and swaggered up to the tuxedoed Maître d'. The Maître d' reacted quickly, waving us off like a white gloved policeman, exclaiming, "Hey, sorry pal, we've been booked since this morning." Undaunted, Pete pulled out another fifty. The Maître d' responded with increased frustration and regret, "Pal, that's more than I made in the last three hours. I'd love to take your cash, but I couldn't find you standing room for a grand." Pete reattached his fifties to his rubber banned roll and instructed me, "Stay right here, I'll be right back." He walked away with brisk confidence, moving swiftly across the room to a wall of house phones from which I later learned he placed a call to Paul Hankish. Upon his quick return he said, "I think I got things worked out." Meanwhile, the Maître d' was preoccupied and, between repetitive denials to hopeful attendees glanced over toward us, shrugging his shoulders in apology. Within minutes his phone rang. We watched as he reacted to the caller with a raised but servile tone. Hanging up the phone, he politely summoned us with a gentle wave, then addressing Pete with respectful wonderment, "Mr. P., please follow me."

Before entering the showroom, the Maître d' paused, put his arm on Pete's shoulder and said, "I don't know who you are, or where you get your juice, but I had to turn the Mayor of the city down about four hours ago." As we were escorted down the aisle, we saw a packed house without a visible empty seat. The show was about to begin. The lights were dimmed and the crowd silenced by tantalizing, pulsating music chilling the room. Loud applause erupted as spotlights followed the emcee walking out on stage. We arrived at center stage, front row and waited while the Maître d' apologized to the foursome who were being led from their seats by the table captain. We were then surrounded by the wine steward, waitresses, water boy and a photographer. We sat comfortably, and Pete gently slapped the back of my head and pronounced, "Its show time boy!"

Among our notable experiences, Pete and I were in New Orleans for the 1985, XX Chicago Bears/New England Super Bowl. The Saturday before the game we made reservations for the glass enclosed clubhouse at the Fair Grounds Racetrack. We paid for preferred seating and were placed at a dinner table adjoining Jimmy "The Greek" Snyder (born Dimetrios Georgios Synodinos, in Steubenville, Ohio), a famous TV sports commentator and Las Vegas bookmaker who was accompanied by Wade "Bum" Philipps, who at the time was head Coach of the New Orleans Saints. We ordered lunch as we waited for the races to begin and observed "The Greek" head down, pen in hand scrupulously handicapping the races from the Morning Telegraph Racing Form. Following the second race, Pete commented that Jimmy "The Greek" was betting at the $50 dollar window and sending it hard with his and Bum Phillips' money. He asked me to follow the "Greek" to the window and try listening to duplicate his bets. I anxiously awaited for the "Greek" to rise and head to the window to make his wager on the third race. Instead, he handed his cash to Bum Phillips who strode to the window. I followed Phillips and stood behind him. His six foot two inch frame, elevated to 6' 4" with his cowboy boots, made it impossible to steal his bets. I could barely see above his elbows, let alone his shoulder to try and see or hear his wager. When I got to the window, the clerk, obviously aware of my dilemma, smiled and said, "They bet $50 across on the 4 horse." I thanked him, tipped him a sawbuck and placed the same wager. Pete and I duplicated the wager of the allegedly best sports handicapper in the United States for each of the remaining races and never cashed a ticket. As Phillips and Jimmy "The Greek" were leaving, I made eye contact with Jimmy, and he stopped, patted me on the shoulder and said, "Sorry fellows, did my best."

Pete and I hit the Meadows Harness racetrack in Washington County, Pennsylvania routinely on Saturday evenings. We enjoyed dinner in the clubhouse and betting on the trotters until the last race. Art Rooney Sr. was in the clubhouse sitting with a friend having dinner. Our pals, Bill and Whitey, were at the high-end wagering mutual windows. Both these "All-American" charismatic figures were full-time school teachers, working part-time at the racetrack. I wanted very much to meet Art Rooney and followed him to the wagering window. After he had placed his bet with Whitey, I apologetically introduced myself, and he gracefully acknowledged. He swaggered unpretentiously to his table holding an unlit cigar in his left hand. Whitey was smiling as I approached the window, "George, I

saw you talking to 'the man'; did you ask to borrow a million?"
"No Whitey. I told him I was a field goal kicker from Turkey,
and if the Steelers got in a pinch for a substitute kicker, he could
find me in Wheeling." Whitey and Bill roared. Then I asked,
"What did he bet?" Whitey summoned me closer, "The 'Chief'
sends a guy downstairs to make his big plays. He knows he's
always being watched. He plays exotics up here, and if I ratted
him out to anyone, I'd be on the other side of this window."

SIXTY-FIVE

ORGY PORGY OF CORRUPTION

Prior to his arrest and conviction, Hankish was alleged to have several million dollars in valuable real estate placed in the hands of nominees to escape detection by the Internal Revenue Service. According to a Justice Department source, among those obscure nominees were a local attorney, a local businessman whose allegiance to Hankish was forged by his girlfriend's cocaine addiction. The third nominee was a bank president. This same source divulged that these nominees took full possession and either sold or developed properties and other tangible assets partially or fully owned by Hankish while imprisoned, leaving him, of course, without his entitled benefits. From his prison cell, Hankish attempted to secure a contract killing for two of the subjects. The information was intercepted by federal authorities who interrogated the assigned "hit man," and the kill order was stopped. It was also alleged that Hankish partnered with one of his out of town attorneys who held custody of several hundred thousands of dollars in oil and gas commodity futures. These investments were allegedly derived from their joint heroin profits.

While Hankish was serving time in prison, his son, Christopher, is said to have stolen in excess of two hundred thousand dollars in jewelry, most of the returned Waterford

Crystal and other valuables from the home of his step mother Patricia Hankish. The bulk of the Baccarat crystal, Georg Jensen bowls, pendants and Waterford crystal was boosted from various locations, much from a Neiman Marcus store in Dallas, Texas.

SIXTY-SIX

A LIFE WITHOUT MERCY

Robert "Skinner" Dorn

While on the subject of shoplifting, one of Hankish's most skilled, sordid and productive boosters was Robert "Skinner" Dorn. During trial, Skinner gave everything up but his underwear. A Wheeling native and Linsly attendee, Skinner ran a skilled and professional team of cross country shoplifters. They targeted upscale department and jewelry stores from coast to coast. Many of the heists were fingered by drug addicted, disgruntled or complicit store employees, eager to share a portion of the take or profit. Hankish would get calls and information from sources across the country who found willing participants employed at targeted businesses. Hankish would summon and immediately dispatch Skinner and his crew. Hankish paid the crew 30 points (30%) for each item of the total haul. He lamented, "I don't know how he did it, but Paul fixed games every week; some Forty-Niner games were supposed to be fixed. Paul and old man DeBartolo were friends. He told me he laundered a lot of money for Bartolo. He claimed he was one of the guys responsible for getting DeBartolo started.

Paul gave me eight basketball games once; I bet them all, and they all won."

Having spent much of his adult life in prison, Skinner combined his prison smarts with his rather remarkable intrinsic intelligence to boost his felony success and pose a major menace to society. He spent prison time in San Diego, Detroit, Moundsville, Huttonsville Medium Security in Randolph County, West Virginia and the Federal Penitentiary in Morgantown, West Virginia. His innate business acumen drove his scheme-driven aspirations, which were exceeded only by his perverse mentality. To give you an example of his institutionalized manifestations, he once expressed to me his former girlfriend's regret that they were unable to foster a child during their relationship. He seriously lamented, "Hell, if I knew she wanted a kid, I would have gone to Walmart or somewhere and stole one."

At the time of my interview, he was 42 years of age and had only recently finished a flat ten year sentence on cocaine distribution charges. The sentence was reduced resulting from his cooperation with federal prosecutors seeking evidence in their indictment of Paul Hankish. He had now spent nearly one half of his life in prison. He said:

Prison puts a hole in your heart. Holidays were the toughest times in the joint. Naturally Christmas was brutal, but New Year's Eve may have been the worst for me. In the Dorm, we watched the ball drop and thousands of people singing 'Old Lang Side' [sic]. Guys and broads huggin' and kissin' and wishin' everybody a happy new year. Most of us knew almost half of the guys in here would never see a new year, let alone a happy one. I knew how to operate in the joint. If you had money, you were on top. There wasn't a joint in the country where you couldn't find a guard on the take. The guards sold us everything, candy bars, cigarettes, dope. When I did time in Moundsville, the crooked warden stole my savings account.

I hated my last lockup. It was that minimum security federal prison in Morgantown. I figured Paul was going to have me killed. I didn't expect to leave that place alive. I didn't know how he was going to do it, but he had contract killers everywhere. He had a contract killer in New Orleans that lived in the swamp. That guy would kill you and take you back to the swamp and feed you to the alligators. He had another guy in Columbus who owned a restaurant. He would cut your head off and put it on his fireplace mantle. [John Dillon, a psychopathic, contract killer who owned the Top Hat restaurant in Columbus] I was in the guy's house, and he had four skulls on his mantle. After I ratted Paul out to the feds, I figured it was over. If I didn't get it in prison, I knew he'd get me on the street. I just hoped he wouldn't give the job to the guy from New Orleans.

I thought he would use the Muslims to kill me. They were the worst. They controlled the kitchen and took care of their own. I paid a guy to taste my food for the first six months. If you wanted extra food, you had to pay or trade. I became head of the laundry, and the Muslims always wanted clean underwear. We were only issued five pairs of underwear a week, and the Muslim tradition was to wear clean underwear every day. I traded them clean underwear for food. I hated those fuckin' Muslims; the D.C. Muslims were the worst. They washed their feet in the sink and saved empty honey bottles that they would fill with warm water and squirt up their ass to keep it clean and keep shit stains off their underwear. This past New Year, I traded the Muslims for ten pound of ground beef and loaves of bread. We stayed up all night cooking hamburgers with an iron. About a year ago, I got to be friends with this Jew guy, and he helped me convert to become a Jew. He knew what I was up to, but we were friends. The Jews, like the Muslims, were allowed to have a special diet, and I liked that Matzo ball soup and chopped liver. The bastards made Catholics eat pork chops on Good Friday.

SIXTY-SEVEN

LAST OF THE OMERTA

Sam "The Plumber" DeCavalcante was called to testify in the Hankish trial. In his late sixties, he entered the courtroom impeccably attired with a star quality appearance. He convincingly denied ever knowing Paul Hankish, saying only that he saw him around once or twice in Florida at a restaurant. Sam died a short time later, and the *Miami Herald* carried the following obituary:

To the valets at the Collins avenue luxury condo who parked his two gray Cadillacs, the elderly wavy-haired gentleman was known only as Mr. D. He kept an address and a low profile at 5601 Collins for many years and was "always a gentleman." He had a bit of a sweet tooth apparently-his friends were often seen arriving with boxes of pastry. When the valets heard that "Mr. D" had died Friday, they were surprised and saddened. They were even more surprised to hear that he was Simone "Sam the Plumber" DeCavalcante, once a major don and model for Mario Puzo's, The Godfather. Decavalcante moved to South Florida in the mid 1970s after heading what the government called New Jersey's only home-grown mafia family, which ran bookmaking, loan sharking, pornography, forgery, extortion and labor racketeering operations. Accordingly to Doug Haas, the former head of the Multi-Agency Organized Crime and

Intelligence Unit for South Florida, perhaps the most important consigliore work DeCavalcante did was in 1986 when he stopped Nicky Scarfo, a Cosa Nostra leader from the Philadelphia area from starting a mafia family in Florida. "One of the leaders consulted Sam, and we had a source close to Scarfo and we were told that Sam had opposed putting a family here because it would lead to trouble."

SIXTY-EIGHT

GOLDEN FOOLS

Authorities and victims were misled into believing
DeCavalcante should have been credited in 1988 for his sincerity
in saving the lives of marijuana smugglers, William Sundell
and Victor Lubijewski of Rhode Island, who had gone afoul
of mobsters there and were under sentence of death. Sundell
later said he paid Paul Hankish $200,000 to have Decavalcante
remove the hit.

What actually happened was offered in court testimony and
captured by Roger Stuart of the *Pittsburgh Press*:

A Rhode Island marijuana smuggler testified today
that alleged crime boss Paul "no legs" Hankish once
used his influence with the Gambino crime family
in New Jersey to have a mob "hit" cancelled against
one of the smuggler's associates. William Sundel,
federal prisoner, testified in Hankish's racketeering
trial that Hankish brokered a deal in late 1983 through
"Sam the Plumber" DeCavalcante by arranging for
the intended victim to pay $200,000 for infringing on
the Gambino family territory. Sundel and an associate
had brought a shipload of marijuana to Atlantic City
and then shipped it to Michigan. Sundel also testified
he was savagely beaten in his Portsmith R.I., office by
two of Hankish's musclemen when he fell behind in
paying Hankish for sports betting losses. Sundel said he

was told by Gambino family member Joey Ippolito to contact Hankish regarding death threats against Victor Lubiejewski.

Ippolito who was serving a federal prison sentence at the time, arranged for Sundel to later meet with Hankish at a New York hotel. Hankish told Sundel at that meeting to see Ippolito in prison and get him to say that the load of marijuana in dispute was his. Sundel said he made the visit to see Ippolito in prison and after getting that confirmation, Hankish traveled to broker the deal thru DeCalvalcante. Lubjiejewski had testified earlier that Sundel told him the protection would cost $400,000 and that Sundel would contribute $200,000. However, Sundel testified that in actuality, it cost only $200,000, all supplied by Lubiejewski and that he gave it to Hankish. "So you lied to him (Lubiejewski)" U.S. District Judge Robert Merhige asked Sundel. "Yes sir," Sundel said. Sundel also testified that "Mr. Hankish was an avid sports fan and so was I. I started betting with Mr. Hankish, I was just a sports bettor." Sundel estimated that he bet between $350,000 and $400,000 a month with Hankish, adding, we would settle up when one owed the other $50,000. He said that Hankish paid him once in 1984; he had to pay Hankish between seven and nine times. He also said that when he fell behind on his payments, Hankish had "two gentlemen" come after him to collect in his Portsmith Office. Sundel identified one of the men as Jesse Anderson, who was previously identified as a driver for Hankish. Sundel did not identify the other man.

This was, in fact, a minor league shakedown of two vulnerable jerks who were encroaching on Joey Ippolito's territory. Hankish developed the plan for Ippolito with DeCavalcante's approval. They convinced Sundell and Lubijewski that they were going to be killed for stealing mob business, and that the contract was being enforced by Sam "The Plumber." Hankish went to Rhode Island accompanied by Jesse Anderson, and Jimmy G. Anderson is said to have beaten a resistant Lubijewski to near death to prove how serious they were. The smugglers turned over $200,000 in cash, which Hankish delivered to his friend "Demus," who in turn handed the cash to DeCavalcante.

SIXTY-NINE

Duke of Hallandale

Joseph "Demus" Covello was a powerful mob figure. Among his few arrests was one that occurred in 1984 when he was charged with 17 counts of bookmaking from his operation based in Hallandale, Florida. News reports claimed his operation cleared nearly one million dollars a month. The operation was run by Demus and his partner Anthony "Skippy" Salerno. I was a guest at Demus' Charlie Brown's nightclub in Hallandale, during a trip to the Steeler's Super Bowl in 1975. Charlie Brown's was an exclusive and upscale club that remained open all-night and catered to mobsters, celebrities and South Florida's elite. It was a modern day Copacabana and, like the Copa, enjoyed a degree of notoriety from its famous guests.

Demus was known as the bookmaker's bookmaker, revered and respected with a national constituency and a reputation as one of the biggest and best in the business. Among the many prominent bookmakers across the country that laid off bets to Demus were bookies from Pittsburgh, Youngstown and Cleveland. During our table conversation, he disclosed why he and his Godfather, Sam "The Plumber," quickly abandoned their home field to relocate to Florida in the 1970s. "Me and a ton of other guys, including the Governor of New Jersey were facing federal indictments. When I got tipped off, me and Sam jumped in my car and outraced all of them to Washington, D.C.

Within a few hours, we were sitting in Edward Bennett Williams Law office[13] before the Governor left his mansion.

Florida newspaper accounts cite detectives in Demus' trial as testifying that he took in $500,000 a day at the height of the football season. I recall a story from a Charleston, West Virginia bookmaker: "The Steelers were playing the Bengals and giving them 9 ½. I was holding a ton on the Bengals. I needed to lay off at least ten dimes (thousand) and couldn't get anyone to take it. I called Paul, and he gave me Demus' number. I never met the man, but told him Paul would okay me and asked him if he could take ten grand on the Bengals getting 9 ½. There was silence and a long pause. I thought we had a bad connection, or he was just thinking about taking the bet. I said, is that okay Mr. Demus? He calmly replied, 'Is that all you want?' I thanked him and sent the money to Hankish."

---

13   Among a few of Edward Bennett Williams' high profile clients were Frank Sinatra, Hugh Hefner, Frank Costello, Jimmy Hoffa, John Hinkley Jr, and Senator Joseph McCarthy. Williams was a graduate of Holy Cross and Georgetown Law School. His debating team partner at Holy Cross was Robert Maheau, Howard Hughes' right hand man for many years.

SEVENTY

IT AIN'T HAY

Jesse Anderson, who the FBI originally identified as Paul Hankish's chauffeur, was shot to death in Meigs County, Ohio on January 22, 1987. Word spread that Hankish ordered the killing upon discovering that Anderson had turned federal informant. One source I interviewed described the killing as follows: "Jesse was dealing coke to 'red necks' and then started squeezing them so they set him up. Paul had plenty of reasons to whack him, but had too much heat on him at the time." A related report to the director of the FBI dated September 4, 1987 reads as follows:

"Common information available to all above investigative agencies has determined through intelligence sources and debriefing of additional subjects in the tri-state area that Hankish and his associates are involved in large scale cocaine activity, extortionate credit transactions, interstate transportation of stolen property, illegal gambling, interstate prostitution and contract murder. Pittsburgh division has conducted subscriber identification and background determination on numerous individuals developed as a result of the initial Pen Register activity conducted from January through March 1987.

Numerous individuals have been determined to be involved in gambling. Anderson was on his own with this extortion spree that cost him his life."

SEVENTY-ONE

JOHNNY CAME MARCHIN' HOME

Among the Lias/Hankish organization's intriguing characters interviewed for this book was Johnny Mathews. On March 11, 1999, I drove north of Wheeling to Warwood, West Virginia, a quiet and well-kept suburb. He was standing in front of his house awaiting my arrival. An elderly pristine groomed gentleman, now approaching his 80th birthday, Johnny and his two brothers enjoyed years of success with their underworld connections and activities. They were employed as chauffeurs, burglars, slot machine mechanics and on call for any venture. Johnny chose our lunch venue; he said, "I like the buffet at the Big Boy's in Martins Ferry, Ohio." I spent the next two hours at the Big Boy's with Johnny, while he voluntarily disclosed much of his relationships and experiences as an associate of Lias and Hankish. He began, "I had a good life and made a lot of money with those guys, but I stayed away from drugs, whores and alcohol."

I opened my pointed line of questioning asking him about doing time in the West Virginia State Penitentiary at Moundsville in the late 1940s where he was serving time for armed robbery of Mike's Spaghetti House in Center Wheeling. He paused, scowled and began:

"It takes the heart out of you. I went in on my son's birthday. My wife told him that I was going back to the Army. You know I spent combat time in World War II, frozen, injured and a decorated veteran, but it was like eatin' pie compared to servin' time in that shit hole. I worried about my wife and kid every day. I was broke, and she had to find work. What cash I left her would only hold her for a few months, and I was starin' at ten years. There was no welfare, food stamps or Medicaid available, none of that shit; you were on your own. If you didn't have friends or relatives, you were shit out of luck. I knew it would be tough for her to wait for me and I hated it, but no sense in ruinin' more lives. I wanted things to go right for my kid. I didn't give her much when I was on the outside, and I found her in a bar and figured I'd lose her in a bar."

I ordered from the menu, and Johnny walked back from the buffet carrying two plates from the salad bar. One was a dish of macaroni salad, and the other was a large plate of beans that he had drained from the soup bowl. Finishing, he lifted his butter knife and began skillfully eating his beans off the knife. It must have been a prison eating ritual. He quickly cleaned his plates and pushed them aside. I asked him if that was all he was going to eat? He said, "Kid, I'm like a Volkswagen, it doesn't take much to fill me up." He then continued talking about his imprisonment.

The corruption inside was the worst I had ever seen in my life. The blacks were mistreated at every turn. Their cells were the worst, food was seconds and only a few of them were given jobs. Hell, we had a one hundred acre farm, we made license plates, mattresses; there was plenty of work. There were about 600 black guys and 70 black and white females housed in Moundsville. The women were housed in segregation, but the majority of them were forced into prostitution with the inmates who had cash, and the guards screwed them like dogs. The Warden was the Madam. He always kept most of the money and a few girls for himself.

One of the inmates was a former dental technician and made good money in the joint. He paid a guard to give him a key to one of the storage rooms, and he took a female inmate in there and boned her. When the

Warden found out he went crazy, and he shot and killed the poor bastard. The Warden told his parents that he died from tuberculosis. He told them he had him buried to save them the expense. When they asked where there son was buried, he told them that he had no memory or record of the number on the grave site marker.

Johnny said he went to work for Lias soon after he left prison:

Me and my brother repaired his slot machines and collected the cash at a few locations for him. Bill was good to work for, but I nearly screwed up big time and his wife, Alice saved my life. She tipped me off that Bill got word that I was stealing from him, and I was. Alice told me that he was setting me up and had already made arrangements to do me in. I backed off and lived to tell about it.

I played second trumpet in the penitentiary band and was the only white member. The highlight of my musical career was one September when we took a bus to perform at Wheeling Park. I saw my wife and kid in the crowd but wasn't permitted near them. It was tough seeing your kid twenty feet away from you and you couldn't hug him.

They put me in the 'hole' (punitive segregation) a couple of times. For weeks they only gave you a slice of bread to eat each day. The guard would step on the bread and then throw it in the cell. The only drinking water available was from a black rubber toilet in my cell.

I asked Johnny what he did to get placed in the "hole?" He said:

"I was feeding unused bread to the birds during winter. I would throw it outside my cell window. The guard who's 'cut' was in my area said that the grass didn't grow where I had fed the birds. He struck me across the face with his club, and I fell to the ground right away hoping he would stop. Then the son of a bitch put me in the hole. When I first busted out (released from prison) I was broke and used to go down to 'Hobo Park.' It was located near the old Wharf Parking Garage near the river on 12th Street. 'Bay Rummers' slept there. Bay Rum was a hair tonic that most of them drank. You could buy two bottles for a quarter at Murphy's 5 & 10 store."

When I questioned him about Lias' partner George Seibert, he indicated that Seibert was unlike Bill. "He was powerful and tough in different ways. He had juice with the straight people, strong family and big political connections. He could show you white blackbirds. He had the restaurant and bowling alley in Elm Grove. Slots, dice, blackjack, he did it all, and they never touched him. The mayor of Pittsburgh and his wife would come down to Wheeling Downs, and after the races, they would go to Seibert's to gamble and booze. The mayor would stay drunk for days, and Rusty, the black bartender, would drive the mayor's wife back to Pittsburgh and stay with her while the mayor was in Wheeling."

I asked Johnny where and how he made most of his money, and he said, "Kid, I made scores everywhere. It was a lot easier in the fifties and sixties. Me and my brother Jimmy made thousands robbing businessmen. Back then, automobile dealerships had master keys for all General Motors, Ford and Chrysler products. Jimmy made the deal with guys who worked there, and we copied the master keys. We robbed guys who kept cash in their glove compartments, hidden under the seat or in the trunk of their cars. We grabbed "Esquire" Ernie for six grand."

I asked him who he feared most, Hankish or Lias. Shaking a pointed finger, he said, "Bill would kill you for an orange, but Paul would put poison in a milk bottle and kill your kids." He ended our discussion with a comment about leaving prison; "Another thing I will never forget, when I got discharged and was on parole, the parole officer used to set up meetings at the Windsor Hotel on Main Street. He always expected a bribe, and I had to spend what few bucks I had to buy that son of a bitch a bottle of whiskey. He was always drunk and mistreated the black guys. He always found fault with them and made them kiss his shoes before they left. About a year later he came up missing."

His identifiable remains were discovered on the bank of the Ohio River. Authorities found his nude body, and nearby, his shoes with his feet still inside them.

SEVENTY-TWO

Hang on to Your Religion

A publication titled West Virginia Penitentiary Official Report and Souvenir, provided an analysis of the penitentiary demographics and conditions about the time Johnny Mathews was an inmate at the institution. "Among the inmate population were 691 Baptists, 349 Methodists, 171 Catholics, 2 Jews, a Mennonite, one Pilgrim and a Mohammedan. There were 1,950 inmates and 840 cells." The managing editor for the *Charleston Daily Mail* wrote: "County Sheriff's handled Capital Punishment duties in West Virginia until 1899, when hanging began at the pen. At a given signal, the trap door is sprung causing the body to fall through to a depth of slightly over that of its height to instantaneous death. By 1936, 60 killers and six rapists had gotten the noose. Half were black and half were white."

Abuse and malfeasance was not confined to penal institutions in the West Virginia. The mental Asylum in Weston was a condoned and ignored concentration warehouse of horror, operating for nearly a century. An article written by Scott Finn appeared in the *Charleston Gazette* in 1986 quoting Charles Armentrout describing what he called the "shocking and pitiful" condition of the state's mental hospitals. In particular, he illustrates the depth and scope of the wretched and deplorable conditions at the Weston Asylum. He described mentally retarded children shackled all day to chairs, sitting naked in their own filth. Children and psychotic adults mingled freely. He called Weston State Hospital a fire trap. A corner of the cafeteria ceiling had collapsed-several two-by-fours kept the second floor toilets from crashing down. The hospital had two or three times as many residents as they were built for, so crowded that he saw seas of beds, in many rooms so close together that a hand couldn't be run between them. Workers toiled for pennies an hour, 12 hours a day, six days a week. And the stench of human waste was everywhere. "Comparatively speaking the cows at Weston have better care and better food than many of the state's mentally deficient patients," Armentrout wrote. In 1980, the former superintendent of the Weston State Hospital told Gazette reporter Sandy Wells of an even darker side of the mental hospital. Between 1949 and 1957, at least 775 patients were lobotomized in the state's mental institution, according to Dr. Thomas Knapp. "Surgeons either drilled through the skull or entered through the eye socket. They severed connections between the frontal lobe and the rest of the brain. After the surgeries, some patients were blinded or paralyzed. Others became virtual zombies."

In 1937, an Ohio County State Senator introduced legislation to return the funeral cost wrongfully incurred by a Benwood resident. Mrs. Amanda Kurl of Benwood, had paid $237.50 for a funeral involving a wrongfully identified former Weston Asylum inmate. The surviving family of George Marzic, a former Benwood resident, was notified of his death at the Weston Asylum five years earlier, in 1932. His remains were then returned to Benwood for funeral rites and burial. Mrs. Kurl paid for the burial which the Marzic family was unable to afford. Five years later, an inmate supposedly recovering from treatment, identified himself as George Marzic, the wrongfully identified deceased. His aggrieved family was immediately notified of the tragic error. Weston officials then correctly identified the deceased as Samuel Karson, explaining to the Marzic family that the identity of the two had been confused for some time.

Relief finally arrived under the Enlightenment Era of West Virginia Governor Gaston Caperton's infusion of honest and effective government. In the mid-1990s, Weston was closed and replaced as an adult psychiatric facility with a modernized 150 bed hospital affiliated with the West Virginia University School of Medicine and Nursing. Caperton also closed the West Virginia State Penitentiary in compliance with an order to close from the West Virginia Supreme Court who deemed the institution unfit, providing cruel and unusual punishment. This State Penitentiary during the early 1950s housed 2156 of the worst inmates. The Crime Castle was a six acre enclosure on a ten acre tract of land in the middle of the city. The inmates were surrounded by a solid wall of hand-cut sandstone, measuring 675 x 395 feet, and seven feet wide at its base, tapering to twenty eight inches. At the top, a stone walkway was 42 inches wide. In 1964 the inmate population shrunk to 1300, with 140 inmates housed at Camp Fairchance, a trustee farm location near the institution. These select 140 were employed in farming, mining and sawmill operations. Inside the main prison, inmates were employed in industry, producing paint, tobacco, soap, clothing, license plates, mattresses and printing.

SEVENTY-THREE

CORRUPTION INSIDE THE WALLS

Up until the Caperton administration, with the exception of Jay Rockefeller's term in office, incompetence and rampant corruption prevailed throughout the West Virginia penal system. The previous Governor, Arch A. Moore, allegedly sold paroles and clemency like candy bars. His weakness also blinded him to the depravity of his appointees in charge of the prison system. I vividly recall, only days after the inauguration of Gaston Caperton, FBI agents sweeping the governor's office, seizing computer hardware used by former Governor Arch Moore's staff. They were attempting to establish coordinates between paroles, pardons and clemency awards with Moore's campaign contributions and bank deposits.

Arch Moore passed away at the age of 91. By Rivard of the *Charleston Daily Mail* wrote of his passing:

"Arch Moore, West Virginia's only three term governor and six-term congressman, died at the age of 91, just a day after his daughter, Shelley Capito Moore took office as West Virginia's newest Senator. During his second term in 1975, Moore and his campaign manager were indicted on charges of extortion making Moore the first sitting Governor in the state to be charged with a crime. During the same period, Moore brokered a still controversial deal with Pittston Coal Company after its dam broke on Buffalo Creek in Logan County killing 125 people and costing 4,000 homes. The state sued the company for $100 million but Moore negotiated a $1 million dollar settlement. The state ended up paying the federal government $9.5 million in clean-up costs and interest. He was eventually convicted of mail fraud, extortion and income tax violations. He was sentenced to 5 years and 10 months in federal prison." (*Charleston Daily Mail*)

The penitentiary warden held absolute and intoxicating power within the walls of the prison. Many initiated and participated in unrelenting schemes of bribery, fraud and extortion. They added further protection to their evil by providing free goods and services to equally corrupt state legislators and other public figures in the form of automotive repair and painting, manufacturing and refinishing of furniture and any other conceivable measure of service or free goods that would satisfy their need. Moore did not hold exclusive rights on corruption. During Paul Hankish's brief incarceration under governor W.W. Baron, Hankish was permitted exclusive entitlement to eat his meals in the privacy of the guard's dinning hall. He was also granted unlimited conjugal visits. Most if not all of his evening cell mates were prostitutes furnished by his pal and Wheeling Whore House King, "Big Red" Richardson.

I have interviewed Wheeling meat and produce vendors who explained the bribery, diversion and theft of food by wardens and administrators. They schemed by overpaying for goods by thousands of dollars, misstating inventory by demanding fraudulent invoices. They demanded inflated invoices that would generate excess cash for kickbacks and theft of steaks and ribs described as baloney and pork, which was the basic staple fed to the inmates. One vendor, Dominick Orlando, said, "The delivery truck's first stop was the warden's house and then to the penitentiary; if you didn't play ball with the warden, you didn't get in the game."

SEVENTY-FOUR

Pray For Coal in Your Stocking

Back near Christmas of 1949, it was announced that another "Execution Change" at the West Virginia State Penitentiary was nearing completion and would be ready for use by Christmas. In fact, the *Wheeling Intelligencer* headline read; "ELECTRIC CHAIR WILL BE INSTALLED BY CHRISTMAS." The story went on: "The Warden stated that most of the necessary equipment had arrived and they were simply awaiting a few more parts before General Electric Engineers would arrive to oversee the installation. Mercifully, during the 1949 session of the state legislature, a bill was passed to change the way the state would carry out the death penalty. Electric wiring for the chair has already been completed and the chair will be located in front of the prison gallows, which will not be dismantled because of the possibility it might be used again. Under this special action of the legislature, all persons found guilty and sentenced to death before the 'Execution Change' bill was passed, would not receive the benefit of electrocution, but would suffer death the old fashioned way and hung in the gallows."

SEVENTY-FIVE

ARTIC FISH

One of Paul Hankish's vicious and most reliable underworld assassins was described by the Pittsburgh Post Gazette as Robert "Codfish" Bricker, a notorious contract killer. Bricker was a frequent patron of the Esquire Club in Wheeling and often in the company of his latest female attraction. On this night, he was in the company of another of Hankish's most proficient and feared enforcers; Irish Jimmy Griff, a handsome, smooth and fearless ex-marine whose loyalty was treasured by those he befriended. Jesse Anderson once told me, "I have had to do business with big city Muslim gang leaders, Black Panthers and New York guys, some of the toughest in the game, but no one scares me more than Jimmy G." On this occasion, Bricker was summoned to the Esquire Club to await the arrival of a Saturday night regular who happened to be an employee of one of Hankish's local adversaries. This particular individual's persistent public insults drew Hankish's rage. He failed to heed the warnings he received, mistakenly believing his friendship with his employer, a local gaming machine operator, would provide him some form of protection. Hankish called on the psychotic killer, whose face and reputation was virtually unknown in the Wheeling area and perfect for the task. He told Bricker, "I want you to make his big mouth tighter than his asshole and let him know who sent you." Jimmy G. identified the target as he arrived, and he and Bricker sat unassumingly at the bar until the subject entered the restroom. Bricker said he walked up behind the target, now straddling the urinal. He grasped him by his head of hair, gently slid a razor across his throat, calmly explaining, "The next time Paul sends me down here, I'm takin your head back home in a shopping bag." Bricker, later asked Jimmy G., "Will you tell Paul he owes me a pair of socks and a shoe shine? This jackoff couldn't stop cryin' or pissin'."

The Gazette revealed that Bricker, who had just died in prison, was serving a life sentence. He had twice escaped the death penalty when the Pennsylvania Supreme Court overturned his conviction for another murder. He was suspected of being involved in seven murders. His first murder became known as the "Wedding Day Murder." While he was on parole, Bricker got married and needed money for the honeymoon. He telephoned a local car dealer who was an old acquaintance. When they met, he took $500 from him, then shot him twice, kicked him out of the car, ran over him and dragged him for 300 yards. He pleaded guilty to this murder, but then Governor Milton Shapp commuted his sentence to life in prison. Bricker was released after serving ten years. The Pardon Board issued the following statement: "If this man is released, he will become a useful member of society." The same year he was paroled, he allegedly killed a man and buried him in a shallow grave. The body was discovered almost six years later after two federal informants implicated Bricker and told the investigators where to look for the body.

Beginning in 1978, Bricker was allegedly involved in 5 murders in eighteen months. The first was the killing of Melvin Pike, a 63 year old Uniontown racketeer and mob enforcer who was muscling the gambling empire of Paul "No Legs" Hankish. Informants testified that the name "Codfish" was based on Bricker's reputation as a cold-blooded killer.

SEVENTY-SIX

THE ROOT OF ALL EVIL

Hankish relished acts of revenge, particularly when they were profitable. All of his venomous reprisals were calculated, and this particular one offered gratification beyond profit. A bon vivant named "Bootsie" Rubella brought Hankish to Fairmont, West Virginia in 1952. Bootsie introduced him to Joe "Dolly" Seriani, the charismatic owner of Dolly's Bird Land, a popular all-night club on the east side of town. Paul became friends with Dolly and the owner of the Army-Navy Club, "Champ" DeBlasio, another popular figure among Fairmont night club owners and book makers. Sources indicate that DeBlasio fingered the Community Market burglary which led to Hankish's first felony arrest and conviction.

One of Hankish's accomplices was Fairmont native, Johnny "peek a boo" Bruno. In the mid 1960s Hankish was convicted for masterminding the hijacking of a trailer truck load of 1456 cases of Stroh's beer stolen from an interstate carrier, thereby constituting a federal crime. One of the co-defendants was John Bruno, who turned state's evidence and testified against Hankish resulting in his conviction and incarceration at Lewisburg Penitentiary. Naturally, Bruno expected retaliation for his cooperation with federal authorities, but prayed that time would mitigate his doom. Soon after Hankish's release from prison, Bruno got word that a contract had been put out on his life. Hankish knew Bruno was broke, but put together one of his classic ploys to invoke fear, suffering and resulting profit. He understood the feds were watching him closely and would never consider the commission of any predictable act that would result in another conviction. Hankish then sent two of his associates; Leo Colandris, a southern West Virginian who owned a number of night clubs, slots and vending operations in Mason County, and his personal enforcer, Jesse Anderson, to Fairmont to meet with "Dolly" Seriani. Anderson said that Paul sent "one long" (a thousand) for Dolly to put the word out in and around Fairmont that they were in town looking for Bruno. For the next six weeks, Bruno stayed at his sister's home, never leaving at night and sleeping in the closet with a shotgun. Bruno, not only broke, but suffering poor health, blind in one eye, was now waiting to be murdered. A few weeks later, Hankish then instructed Dolly to put the word on the street that if Bruno came up with $10,000 he would call off the hit. Hankish knew that Bruno had a number of friends and sympathizers in the city of Fairmont and hoped they would raise the money. During my interview with Dolly, he said, "The best they could raise was about $7500. I took it to Paul, and he just laughed and said, 'Now tell that rat, coward pile of shit that he bought some time, and if I don't get the rest in 3 months, I'll send Jesse back down there with a shovel and bury him alive." John Bruno died of natural causes three weeks later.

Joe "Dolly" Seriani was a magnetic force. Fresh out of the military, in 1948 he opened a nightclub in his hometown of Fairmont, West Virginia. He told me that he didn't have a lock on the front door. "From the day I opened, we ran 24 hours a day seven days a week. It was like robbin' a bank every day. I sold hijacked liquor, draft beer, meatball sandwiches and rolls of 8mm porno films. We had a pool table, two rubber machines and a wall of pin balls and slots. Our poker game started on Friday, and we quit on Sunday in time for church. The Mayor would always meet me after church, and I always made sure that his envelope was bigger than the one I put in the basket at church."

Not all of Paul's compelling acts went smoothly. In one incident he sent two of his enforcers to collect a past due football gambling debt. The debtor was relatively wealthy, living on a country estate and owned a few thoroughbred horses. When the enforcers arrived and parked in his driveway, Roger told Curt to stay in the car and wait for him. He knew Curt had a short fuse and feared what might happen in the event the subject offered lame excuses or failed to pay. Roger knocked, and the subject, Rouhana Naim, immediately answered the door. Recognizing Roger, he immediately responded, "Roger, honest, I've been expecting you. I've got the money ($4000) on the kitchen table." Handing over the envelope, Rouhana boasted, "Look it has Paul's name on the envelope. Sit down, open it and count it." As Roger was counting the money, Rouhana blurted out, "I've got a favor to ask of your before you leave." Roger politely agreed and listened as Rouhana explained his dilemma. "You won't believe what a shitty month this has been for me. My daughter started screwin' around with this long-haired doper, the old lady is blaming me, and yesterday I took the boy's dog to the vets, and he said the dog had maybe a week to live, and I should put her down. It's gonna be tough to tell my boy, and I love that dog almost as much as he does. See that 22 rifle over there. I was just trying to get enough nerve to go down to the barn and do it. I gotta come up with a story and bury her before the boy gets home from school. I'm asking you Roger; she's tied up down there in the barn. If you'll put her down for me, it'll be a favor I won't forget." Roger agreed, picked up the rifle and began walking toward the barn. When Curt saw Roger marching toward the barn with rifle in hand, he jumped out of the car and yelled, "What the hell's going on? Did he come up with the script?" Roger decided to play with him, "No, I took the bastard's rifle and I'm headed for the barn to shoot his dog." Curt followed Roger to the barn. Roger fired two shots from the rifle killing the dog. He then heard shots coming from the nearby stables. Roger quickly ran to the area and shouted, "Curt, what the hell did you do?" Curt responded, "I shot one of his fuckn' horses to let him know how serious we are."

SEVENTY-SEVEN

SHAKESPEARE BEHIND BARS

Hankish was not only tormented by his confinement in the penitentiary, but suffered incessant anguish over the betrayal, perceived and otherwise, from those he once relied upon and many that remained indebted to him. The majority of his co-defendants testified against him, and he believed that some who escaped indictment or arrest also turned informants. Equally bothersome, his former silent partners and nominees, holding confidential joint investments including valuable real estate, were now exclusively benefitting from his inability to defend his interests or retaliation. Among these were an attorney, a night club owner and the president of a Wheeling bank. On the list of those whom he despised was his son Christopher. While imprisoned, his father wrote the following letter to Christopher, dated September 26, 1995:

"Chris, I have not spoken to you for 3 years since you robbed Patty and Peter's house [his current wife and son] and I never intend to do so. Thus I am writing this letter and sending it to 15 people to contradict your comments about me. Especially about me telling you to pass out Parley cards and that I was interested in them. Nothing in any type of business with you interests me. You lied and stole from five friends of mine in Pittsburgh, you owe untold debts there, and thus Wheeling is your new hunting ground. Your comments that this person is an informer is comic at best since you patronize Pee Wee George at his bar and visit him at his home when you well know that he testified against me. It was quite humorous how he would not let Joe Nassif go to the Sportsman bar. Also it is quite evident who got you to borrow fifteen hundred over the phone from Martin at the Chinese restaurant. I feel badly for your mother since you contribute nothing to defray expenses at her home but still live there. Hey! Here's a thought, rob her house. Your sister is too wise and put her valuables in a safe deposit box."

Paul Hankish
02623-016 G-Unit
2680 Hwy 301 South
Jessup, Ga. 31599

Hankish continued his stream of literary denunciation, copies of which were mailed to various unaffiliated persons throughout the Ohio Valley. Among the diatribe, he illustrated his vile contempt for an otherwise distinguished Wheeling attorney who represented Hankish and his wife for a number of years. This letter was under date of March 10, 1995 and addressed to "Gummer" Yahn. It read in part:

He refers to Mr. Ogden Nutting (Publisher of the *Wheeling News Register*) as Ogden Nothing; he did this to Mr. Nutting untold times. When you paid my first wife the final $25,000 you owed her, you told her you wouldn't pay the $3500 interest. You admitted owing it but simply were not going to pay it until somehow you found out you were being taken before the West Virginia Ethics Commission over it. Then your kind heart encouraged you to mail her check in Pittsburgh. After telling my second wife her fee would be capped at $50,000, you blatantly took $10,000 out of her money for yourself, knowing full well you could not represent her because of a conflict of interest. When you visited me while I was under house arrest, to return my $5000 you were holding, you admitted you were in error. James Byrum warned me 10 times what type of human being you were, using Arch Riley and his office to further your gains. Yes, after you owing me money for 25 years and loaning you money for your kid's education, I admit I was a fool for trusting you. About your cancer of the kidney, I laugh and hope you suffer like the dog you are. Did you care when you raped my second wife financially, knowing she was suffering from Leukemia and was looking to you for guidance? Do you care that I have hepatitis C, diabetes and advanced cirrhosis of the liver? You remind me of General Bull Moose; "What's good for Gummer is good for the country." When Arch [Riley] was in the Prosecutor's office, you went to Rita's Truck Stop, Cece Hendricks at the Windmill and met Red Richardson and collected from them and Charlie Maroon for protecting whore houses, all the time poor Arch knew nothing about your actions and was the greatest victim till me. I hope you suffer a horrible death. 'Feature of things to come.' Can you imagine Henry Jepson, Stan Turk, Bob Levenson [prominent Wheeling business owners] along with pinballs, pre-signed IRS returns, arson and a long letter to each member of your family?

Copies of the letter were sent to all of the alleged victims and various others.

Hankish was brutal, but effective in his revenge. He understood the power and ramifications of the information he publicized and used it indiscriminately. He knew every prominent individual in the area who was the victim or corroborator of undisclosed crime and corruption. He kept a long list of cocaine addicted attorneys and physicians, as well as prominent Wheeling officials that he corrupted, along with Wheeling area businessmen and their wives. Hankish also had reels of video tape retrieved from hidden cameras placed in one of the local whore houses that catered to select Wheeling officials and businessmen. He mastered and exploited the power of information, spoke privately about his subject's financial woes, gender preference and any other weakness or disparaging events in their lives. He was the master of the "dry snitch," distancing and concealing himself as the purveyor of false innuendo. Recovering from his drug addiction, while paralyzed with hate and anger, it became obvious that mass mailings replete with vile and invective accusations fed his emotional rage and offered him some form of demonic comfort.

SEVENTY-EIGHT

CRIMINAL FICTION

Hankish refused to let facts interfere with his pursuit of a bitter revenge. He was, in fact, the ghost writer of the following fictionalized report titled: INVESTIGATION OF FEDERAL AUTHORITIES IN THE NORTHERN DISTRICT OF WEST VIRGINIA. This twenty page fabrication was distributed throughout the state of West Virginia in September 1992. It was circulated discriminately, but anonymously, to newspaper offices, businesses and homes of prominent individuals. Paul Hankish was the engineer, with endorsements from sycophants, disgruntled law enforcement officers and an alleged deranged sheriff. The report provides no evidence, false and unrelated facts, lacks documentation and is replete with grammatical slaughter and folly. It was a failed retaliatory effort by Hankish, with the support of a few misguided outcasts who were overcome with hate and envy. Hankish's goal was an attempt to embarrass those who he somehow believed deceived him or were, in fact, responsible for his conviction. His disdain drove him to attempt to tarnish the reputation of the man who led the charge that ultimately destroyed his organization and put him behind bars for what became the rest of his life.

SEVENTY-NINE

INVESTIGATION OF FEDERAL AUTHORITIES IN THE NORTHERN DISTRICT OF WEST VIRGINIA

Although West Virginia politics as a whole is notorious, two governors and several state politicians, judges and law enforcement officers have been sent to prison on a variety of corruption charges in recent years, this report will concentrate on the counties of Marshall, Ohio and Hancock. A brief history of the area as it relates to crime is needed in order to provide the reader with an understanding as to why and how these areas have been infested with organized crime. Wheeling is by far the largest and most populous of all the county seats. Benwood, West Virginia, which is situated in Marshall County, by most standards, would be considered a suburb of Wheeling.

Wheeling, West Virginia has always had a notorious reputation. It was considered a wide open town for gambling and prostitution up until the1960s. Walter Winchell referred to Wheeling as "Little Chicago" in a column about gambling, gangsters and prostitution. When Lias retired on 1960, Paul Hankish stepped in to run organized crime. Joe Dobkin and his sons, Jack and Benny, began enlarging their "Amusement" machine business. They entered into an agreement with Hankish and were allowed to open bars and furnish bars run by Hankish with "Amusement" machines. These machines were not only used for amusement, but for gambling. Under this arrangement, the Dobkin business flourished while others remained somewhat stagnant. During 1987, the government began an intense investigation of the Hankish operation. That investigation culminated in the arrests of several of his business partners and the seizure of their businesses and property. The Dobkin family was not bothered by these raids. In 1990, the last of the Hankish group was prosecuted under the RICO statutes. Hankish pled guilty during the trial to all RICO counts. Hankish is currently in federal prison serving a life sentence.

In the wake of the Hankish arrest, the Dobkin family expanded and took control of the gambling machines in the Wheeling area.

Estimates by federal authorities were given in 1991 that the Dobkin family made several millions from illegal activities in the late 1980s. According to local law enforcement, the bookmaking went to Benwood at the time of Hankish's arrest and is controlled by Sparachane. In December 1991, the Dobkin organization was indicted by Kolibash. Their businesses and property was seized. Because of the seizure and closing of the businesses over four hundred locations were now available for gaming machines in the Wheeling area.

According to law enforcement, Sparachane moved quickly to fill the vacancies. According to Chief of Detectives Davis, other law enforcement officials and independent witnesses, Sparachane now controls all vice operations in the Wheeling area. (The truth is, Dobkins continued their successful electronic slot machine operation, but were gradually overtaken by Undo's youngest son, Herk Sparachane. Herk went on to lead the State organization of Limited Video Lottery Operators. The Sparachane/Dobkin separation resulted from a contractual dispute that led to a brawl between sixty year old Undo and his twenty year junior Jack Dobkin. Witnesses claim that Dobkin returned soon thereafter to retrieve his abandoned machines from the sidewalk. The transition of power had little to do with politics or patronage. It was more about business acumen and the popularity and fearless demeanor of Herk Sparachane, currently managing one of the top Limited Video Lottery operations on the East Coast of the United States.) According to a federal task force officer, Sparachane may have paid for Kolibash's education at the West Virginia University and at Brown University in Providence, Rhode Island. Sparachane and Kolibash are seen together in public often. Long time Sparachane associate, George Sidiropolis was appointed by Governor Caperton as Commissioner of the West Virginia Department of Motor Vehicles. He has since been appointed Assistant Director of Highways and responsible for prioritizing all state building projects. Sidiropolis is the man whom a witness said, "If I ever need to get rid of someone, I just tell Sidiropolis and that person will never be seen again." The witness said his friend was given a job by Sidiropolis in the state government. Nick Sparachane, Undo's son sat on the board of directors of Project Best, a business set up to manage the pension funds of several unions.

All complaints made to federal authorities have fallen on deaf ears. An example of the protection was given by one witness. Chuck Little, an Internal Revenue Service Investigator attached to Kolibash, was interviewing the witness in a bribery case. When Little asked about a check to Sidiropolis, the witness explained that Sidiropolis was an associate of Sparachane. Upon hearing this Little looked at the witness, closed his notebook and said, "Well that ends that." The fallacy continued, but to the deserving dismay of the author and his contributors it was dismissed by the initiated eye of responsible journalists and ridiculed by legal authorities.

This "Report" was mailed throughout the state of West Virginia and was circulated among various state agencies and institutions for years following its original distribution. It was used by various inmates seeking parole during the time in which I served as a member of the parole board. On several occasions, the Governor's office or the Corrections Commissioner was compelled to respond to an inmate's complaint, citing the "Report" and accusing me of being unqualified to conduct a fair parole hearing. Two illustrations of these complaints are excerpts from letters written by inmates prior to their scheduled hearings: "Dear Governor Underwood, As Chief Executive of this state, are you aware that one of your parole board members is not only unqualified, but is a notorious mobster as well? I'm referring to George Sidiropolis. His being on your parole board does nothing to improve the image of this state and reflects badly on your administration." "Dear Chairman Carter: I respectfully request that George Sidiropolis not be present at my parole hearing because of his influence with your boss, the Governor, as well as his alleged ties to Wheeling's mafia." The third complaint came from a violent sex offending kidnapping, rapist, child murdering escapist, who was for some unknown reason sentenced to life with mercy, making him parole eligible.

I recall that all of the complainants were serving time for first and second degree murder, with the exception of the *Charleston Gazette* newspaper editor Don Marsh, who irresponsibly, editorialized that I was illegally appointed to the Parole Board by the Governor. He neglected to note that prior to my appointment, the recidivism rate among parolees was at seventy five percent. Female inmates were being routinely sexually assaulted by prison employees and work-release supervisors. The dormitories were racially segregated. Correctional officers were selling drugs to inmates at an alarming rate, and convicted, fixated child sexual predators were being treated and released with the same intensity as third time DUI offenders. The member I replaced was an avid proponent of rehabilitation for sexual offenders, who the Gazette lauded for establishing sexual offender treatment programs at the institutions and a leading educator in the successful treatment of pedophiles. What they failed to mention was that in the previous six years, the recidivism for sexual offenders of West Virginia parolees may well have reached an all-time high.

Denmar Correctional Center, a medium security institution, is buried in the hills of Pocahontas County, West Virginia. During my term on the parole board, nearly sixty five percent of the inmates were either involved or had instant convictions of sex offenses. The sex offender treatment program at Denmar was praised by officials and Charleston newspapers. I recall the parole interview of a young man serving one to ten years for statutory rape. He had been denied following his first parole interview. He had an excellent work record, no rule infractions, an acceptable home and work plan. I was outvoted by the two remaining board members who denied his parole for the second time. They denied him parole because he failed to complete the sex-offender program. When he was told the reason for his denial, he said, "Can I ask you one question?" Granted permission, he said, "You know that guy you granted parole to earlier today, the guy who raped that little boy in Parkersburg, well he's been our group leader in the sex offender classes for the past two years. In fact, he hands out certificates to graduates of the class. Well, just before I came down here, he was in another guy's cell poking him up the ass."

The distinguished Gazette Editor (who may have suffered a moment of selfish ambition) conveniently chose to remain silent during my full term of service, during which time I not only served as an exemplary member and acting/temporary Chairman, but was chosen by the Governor to clean the five year backlog and prepare all reviews and recommendations for Pardons and Clemency applications. I was also designated to write Special Reports for the Cabinet Secretary of the Department of Military Affairs & Public Safety for presentation and review by the Legislature. Following my retirement, at least two subsequent appointees to the Parole Board lacked comparable, qualifying experience or a college degree. Neither factor was mentioned in the Gazette's announcement, now apparently forsaking what they believed to be their ongoing responsibility to protect public interest.

EIGHTY

The Real Cleveland Indian

At the age of 20, I became the youngest Executive Director of Public Housing in the nation. I think my record still stands today. In 1965, President Lyndon B. Johnson created an additional cabinet level agency; the Department of Housing & Urban Development. President Johnon's Great Society of the Sixties was nearing its peak and funding for new urban renewal, public housing and a myriad of social programs was almost limitless. Beginning in 1967, I oversaw the construction and ultimate completion of two major public housing projects for the cities that employed me. They were among the first "Turnkey" projects in the nation. The developer for the projects was Tec-Chem Research & Development Corporation, a newly formed development company based in Youngstown, Ohio. The principles of this corporation found immediate success resulting from their political connections in Washington, D.C. This influence provided them a tremendous advantage in accelerating funding and approval for project awards up and down the Atlantic Coast region. It is safe to assume that others like myself had no idea that this organization was connected to the Cleveland Mafia. It was from this encounter that I decided to embark on my journey to narrate my experience and began collecting information for this book.

In 1967, I was introduced to Dominick Bartone. Bartone assumed the role of a sub-contractor under whomever Tec-

Chem chose as the general contractor for their projects. It was discovered later that Bartone's role was the front man for the Cleveland Mob, who secretly shared in the company's profits. Bartone aggressively expressed interest in grant writing policy and procedure that was required by HUD for all federal grant programs. I spent a great deal of time advising him of the protocol and inner-workings for securing federal grants for municipalities. His coarse style and villainous demeanor was not uncommon to me. I was growing up in a valley dominated by thugs and mobsters. Bartone was a personality cast from modern day mob movies, years before they were scripted. He wore monogrammed, white on white, cuffed sleeved dress shirts, open to his chest that revealed a gold-linked chain necklace supporting a crucifix. He wore a gold Patek Philippe watch and customary diamond ring on his pinky finger. He represented the quintessential, narcissistic big city mobster, the type who went to the funeral and wanted to be treated like the corpse.

The stealth controller/CEO of Tec-Chem Research and Development Corporation was an unusually charming and charismatic gentleman. He found the majority of his success with his intellect and style. He was the legitimate front man for the company. He often boasted of his relationship with Bobby Baker[14], a D.C. lobbyist, and Spiro Agnew, who at the time was Governor of Maryland. In fact, I was present during a meeting at the Shoreham Hotel in D.C., when Bill Alvarez and others were discussing the pending success of a fraudulent million dollar electrical change order for the construction of the Rayburn House Office Building that was under completion.

Dominick and I got along well. I spoke conversational Italian, and we shared the Southern Italian dialect, which he enjoyed using, particularly during his emotional rages and disparaging characterizations of his adversaries. Dominick convinced me to visit him in his hometown of Cleveland. He said, "You've gotta

---

14   Bobby Baker was an aide to once U.S. Senator Lyndon Johnson. He was involved in scandal with prominent mob bosses. In 1962, Baker got with mobster Sam Giancana and Meyer Lansky helping to build casinos in the Dominican Republic. He was found guilty of theft, fraud and tax evasion and forced to resign his post as Secretary to the Senate.

come to Cleveland and spend a couple days with me. We'll go to the races and hit some hot spots." When I arrived near Cleveland, I checked into the Blue Star Motor Lodge, which was near Northfield racetrack. That evening, we hit every night spot on Euclid Avenue and the outskirts of Cleveland. The next day Dominick picked me up for lunch. We went to the Mayfield Italian-American Club. The only thing American about this club was the apple pie I ate for desert. They were hosting their customary guest luncheon, and at one table, there were guys wearing tool belts and Cleveland Indian baseball caps, eating like they were going to the electric chair. Seated near them was a table of four well-dressed "pencil necked" businessmen, gently wiping red sauce from their upper chin between cautious bites of sauce drenched spaghetti & meatballs.

A short while later, I was informed that this was the exclusive enclave of the Cleveland Mafia. The business-suited "stiffs" (as Dominick referred to them) were mostly local elected officials. As we traveled around Mayfield Heights and up and down Euclid Avenue, Dominick would introduce me to his friends as, "This is my pal George; he's half Greek, but he's got an Italian heart." He was also generous in offering his opinion of many whom I met, describing them: "He's a jackoff," "They named a street in Cleveland after that prick, One Way." Those he liked he praised as, "Good people, solid, and stand up." Too often I had to experience his Sicilian temper. Fearless to a fault, he would often impulsively react with senseless rage. He victimized gas station attendants, waitresses and pedestrians.

A month later I was back home, sitting in my office when the secretary came in and said, "There's a man here that wants to see you." I said, "A man, what man? Does he have a name?" She told me it was an FBI agent. I walked out of the office, and there he stood, black wing tipped shoes, trench coat, blonde hair and blue eyes. He had an all American look that we pejoratively referred to as a "Snuffer." I extended my hand with a simultaneous introduction, and he held it as he asked if we could step back into my office. As I sat in my chair, he closed the door and remained standing. He reached into his jacket and presented his badge holder and identification. My eyes fixed on his gold badge, and I heard him say, "George, I've made a special trip down here this morning from Pittsburgh to see you. I'm assigned to a task force on organized crime. I'm here to offer a young man some advice that will keep you out of trouble if you obey it. I did a quick background on you, and I'm convinced that you're an honest, aspiring young man with great promise. I want to help you keep it that way. First, I want you to know what danger you face by associating with Dominick Bartone. We have had Mr. Bartone under constant watch prior to his release from federal prison years ago. I want to assume you know little, if any of his criminal past. My purpose here today is to inform you of how dangerous of a man he is. Dominick went to prison on a number of charges, and one of them was gun running to Fidel Castro. He acted as an ambassador, a go-between for the Mafia to win over Castro's friendship during and after the Cuban Revolution. He burglarized the Dayton, Ohio U.S. Armory and stole airplanes, rifles, machine guns and ammunition to sell to Castro. He is an international crime figure with ties to organized crime figures across the United States and around the world."

He leaned forward and asked, "Who introduced you to Mr. Bartone?" I told him that I was unsure, but that it was either a gentleman named Bill Alvarez or Vic Cullota. I explained that Alvarez headed the development company that built the housing projects, and that Vic was the "punch list" contractor. He stood up, "Look I've got to get back to the office and if I haven't yet convinced you, I'll leave you with this; Dominick Bartone is considered among the most ruthless mobsters in the United States. His Youngstown and Cleveland Mafia associates are only interested in using you to help them expand their operation, and when their done with you, they will have ruined your future." Leaving my office he turned and said, "I've done my good deed for the day, now it's up to you."

The Agent was so right. Dominick was also tied closely to the Western Pennsylvania, Mannerino family located in New Kensington, PA. Subsequent revelations about Bartone's mob involvement were absolutely astounding. Bartone and his associates were no strangers to West Virginia. He and Alvarez developed a close working relationship with the future Attorney General, Chauncey Browning, who once served as Commissioner of Institutions for the State of West Virginia and awarded a "sweetheart" contract to Alvarez for remodeling of the West Virginia State Penitentiary in Moundsville. On October 3, 1978, Vanderbilt University Television Archives published an abstract from NBC News' David Brinkley disclosing the Mafia interest in the West Virginia coal industry which was prevalent in the 1960s and 1970s. Dominick Bartone and Meyer Lansky were involved with Big Creek Mining in West Virginia. He and Meyer Lansky visited the State Capitol in Charleston to meet with Browning and coal company executives. The article quotes a Securities Commission Investigator, Thomas Krebs, "Coal is money, is the new gold rush, that's why the mob wants in."

Throughout my entire adult life, I have kept contemporaneous notes of my most notable experiences, realizing that someday they would serve my book writing aspiration. My indigenous roots, private business experience and high-level appointed positions to public office afforded me unique opportunity, trust and influence with a broad range of people, from Mafia soldiers to federal prosecutors. I have enjoyed a very diverse and interesting journey, living among the very best and meeting extraordinary characters up and down the East coast and beyond. However, notwithstanding any murky socialization, my closest brush with the law has been a traffic ticket.

I called Dominick to tell him we needed to talk and should meet as soon as possible. He arrived in Wheeling the following day, and we had dinner at the Bella Via restaurant in Elm Grove. As soon as he got in the car, he asked, "So what's so important that we couldn't discuss on the phone?" I told him about the visit I had from the FBI and what they had to say about him. He was furious, "Okay, now you tell me, what have we done so far that's illegal? I'll tell you what, zero, *niente*, nothing, and that's the way it will always be. Those guys are like used car salesmen; they work on commission. If they don't make up some story about someone or make an arrest they worry about not getting paid or promoted. I shook my head in agreement hoping his rage would subside. We arrived at the restaurant, both ordered spaghetti and meatballs, and as our dinner arrived, Paul Hankish struggled past our table with his bodyguard. He spoke to me while looking directly at Dominick, who did not raise his head and ignored him.

As we began eating our dinner, Dominick commented, "I know you get along with that guy, and you should. He knows who I am, and he knows that it was my friend who gave the Greek the okay to whack him. But that's their business." When I asked Dominick if the guys that tried to kill him were surprised that he survived he replied, "I know these brothers that set that whole thing up, and it wasn't their first rodeo. They handle dynamite like Willie Mays catches fly balls. When I tell you that guy was lucky, I mean not one out of a million could have survived that blast."

In his book, *Ultimate Sacrifice*, Lamar Waldron connects Bartone's criminal involvement that spreads from the Mafia/CIA plot to assassinate Castro to Jack Ruby and the assassination of former President John Fitzgerald Kennedy. He writes, "Ruby's partner in the Hoffa plane deal was Dominick Bartone, according to Congressional testimony. Hoffa's dealings with Castro, which also involved Jack Ruby and his partner Bartone, gave Hoffa's mob allies the perfect cover for their plot to assassinate Castro in conjunction with a CIA backed coup. At the time, Ruby and Bartone were dealing with two Cuban leaders who were going to lead the CIA coup against Castro." One journalist stated that Dominick was a Cleveland gangster dating back to the days of Al Capone. Bartone worked with Ruby in smuggling arms to Castro between 1957 and 1959. Dominick's smuggling operations were not confined to Cuba. According to former Hoffa prosecutor Walter Sheridan, "On May 22, 1959, Customs agents arrested Bartone and his co-conspirators," seizing a "plane and its cargo just prior to its scheduled departure" for Trujillo's Dominican Republic. Waldron continues, "The arms and planes deal involving Jimmy Hoffa, Jack Ruby and

Dominick Bartone was very complex, which was one reason the Kennedy's Senate Crime Committee was so important." CIA documents showed evidence of extensive deals between Bartone and Jimmy Hoffa of the Teamsters Union. During his term as United States Attorney General, Bobby Kennedy uncovered much evidence showing Bartone's involvement with Hoffa to assist the CIA in their plot to assassinate Fidel Castro.

Waldron describes the involvement of who he described as "Two Western Pennsylvania mob leaders, Gabriel Kelly Mannerino and John LaRocca engaged in the Cuban gun running operations with Jimmy Hoffa." Mannerino and LaRocca were later rewarded by the CIA for their help in the 1959 CIA-Mafia plots and for keeping them quiet. He goes on to state, "Noted journalist Robert Sam Anson writes that in 1971, Mannerino and LaRocca were acquitted on Teamster kickback charges when one of the 'star witnesses' for the defense turned out to be the local head of the CIA."

Bartone was the subject of the 1978 U.S. House of Representatives John F. Kennedy Sub-Committee on Assassinations, as well as other federal investigations into the assassination of President Kennedy. Russ Tarby wrote the following in the *Syracuse New Times*: "The Warren Commission ignored witnesses who testified Ruby was connected to organized crime and involved in gun-running, narcotics and gambling. In 1979, the House Committee on Assassination presented that evidence. Ruby was tied directly to organized crime figures such as Santo Trafficante in Havana, Nofia Pecora in New Orleans and Dominick Bartone in Cleveland and Miami. One of Bartone's partners on the gun running deal was Ruby. Bartone's pal, Jack Ruby also shared an interest in the Teamsters. The United States House Committee on Assassinations concluded: "The Committee believes on the basis of the evidence available to it that the national syndicate or organized crime as a group, was not directly involved in the assassination of Kennedy, but the available evidence DOES NOT PRECLUDE THE POSSIBILITY THAT INDIVIDUAL MEMBERS MAY HAVE BEEN INVOLVED." They also tried selling Pesos for Meyer Lansky after Castro prohibited the circulation of Cuban Pesos of $100 denomination or more. Following Castro's nationalization of casinos and his outlaw of gambling, likely millions of dollars in $100 denomination remained from Lansky's casino operation and would quickly become worthless.

EIGHTY-ONE

GREED TOO STRONG FOR PRINCIPLE

Following dinner, framing it in an off-handed, casual manner I asked, "Dominick, I know Kennedy double crossed the outfit, but do you think they had anything at all to do with his assassination?" He scoffed, "I'm gonna pretend you didn't ask me that question and because I like you, I'm just gonna tell you this much and if you ever repeat it, I mean if you even tell your mother, I'll deny it and we're finished, okay?" He offered the following measured response:

Meyer Lansky born Meier Suchowlanski. Major organized crime figure known as "Mob's Accountant" (Getty Images)

"The only thing I know is that a guy named Lansky, a Jewish guy—his brain wouldn't fit in your trunk, and it would take you two months to burn his bankroll—might have gotten permission to make the call. He's a world power who owned Cuba before Castro got there, and he was supposed to have made a deal with certain people and the Cubans to let this go down. A lot of strong, legitimate people were pissed at Kennedy, and his brother cost people a lot of money. I guess all this made it easier for them to make a move. Maybe it was a trade off? Kennedy goes, Lansky gets to operate in Cuba again, and he and his pals get their casinos back. Now I don't know what happened after that. All I know is that maybe Castro double crossed them. Why, I don't know, maybe it was the heat, maybe it was the Russians, maybe people got cold feet? I don't know what happened. Maybe it was all bullshit."

Then he abruptly asked, "You want some dessert?"

Years passed until I heard from Dominick again. Although I understood the potential peril of my friendship with Dominick, I was pleasantly surprised to receive a phone call from him in the spring of 1971. He said he was just released from federal prison on "some chicken shit" federal income tax evasion charges. "I just opened a concrete business and wanted to give you my phone number, so call me if you find anything that could be thrown my way." I told him that I would call him if I heard anything. We talked about old times and acquaintances, but never spoke again.

EIGHTY-TWO

DYING WITHOUT A SWORD

Paul Hankish died handcuffed to a hospital bed on May 11, 1998. He was transferred there from a federal penitentiary in Virginia. His personal physician, Angelo Georges, driven by his professional loyalty and compassion, arrived at the hospital from Wheeling, heeding the family's request. Dr. Georges indicated that he was "shocked to see a dying patient on life support and under guard by two armed federal correctional officers." Hankish was a paraplegic suffering from diabetes, hepatitis C, cirrhosis of the liver and a ruptured belly button. Dr. Georges, Hankish's son Peter, and his first wife Patty were at his side when he passed away. In his final moments, he removed his oxygen mask, motioned for Angelo to come closer and said, "Why is it that every time I'm near death, I look up and there is some Greek doctor in the room."

EIGHTY-THREE

PARADOX LOST

Now following generations of raging vice and corruption, the city of Wheeling has transformed into a cruel anomaly. Like too many "Rust Belt" cities across America, Wheeling suffers the effects of an aging and declining population and is stricken with an immobilized economy and social dormancy. The absurdity of course is a 21st century city, now free of organized crime and raw political corruption, which has by a desperate act of the West Virginia Legislature, once again become a gambling mecca. Wheeling now boasts a state lottery, thousands of slot machines in bars and coffee shops, a full blown casino offering thousands more slot machines, crap tables, blackjack, poker and roulette.

Paradoxically, this contemporary revenue stream and power vacuum is now shared between legalized gambling casinos, limited video lottery vendors, and state and municipal government. This once repugnant, illegal behavior is now sanctioned, praised and overseen by trustworthy prosecutors, incorruptible judges and honorable law enforcement. It demonstrates the antithesis of the outrage over moral values and political corruption during the vested vice years under Lias. Wheeling, now free of uncontrollable debauchery finds its leaders struggling to control and improve a distressed and sorrowfully less populated downtown. The inner city streets, once heralded as the busiest in the state are plagued by deteriorating infrastructure and a league of abandoned buildings.

Risk neighborhoods are less prominent resulting from flight, demolition and an overall progressively languid population. Nevertheless, Wheeling remains the proverbial example of the "one eyed" man providing a relatively superior advantage for his kingdom. Wheeling remains relatively dominant among most cities throughout the colonized state of West Virginia, a state struggling to outlive a bleak history of shameful economic and social repression, which has resulted in leading the nation in drug overdose deaths, childhood poverty, infant mortality, teen pregnancy and reduced life expectancy. West Virginia also remains at the bottom ranking of states for the well-being for the thirteenth consecutive year. It remains nonetheless, a state inhabited by generations of abundant tormented, but unwavering patriots with righteous manners and sacred beliefs. Perhaps their history of suffering cannot be adequately explained, however, their hopes and success has been undeniably thwarted by the relentless greed and indifference of their failed leadership and barons of commerce and industry. For too long, they have enabled the barons of commerce and industry to write and control legislation that would have otherwise protected and advanced their interest and served the greater good.

Wheeling continues to offer some recognizable progress, while it attempts to promote waterfront revival, inner-city housing and historic preservation. Without question, the city harbors two exceptional medical centers offering quality and affordable care with advanced medical technology. We have excellent public and private schools and universities, a world class park and recreation system, a reputable symphony orchestra, and a precious variety of artistic and cultural events and activities. We have seasoned media outlets, even though the ultra-conservative media sources hold possession of arbitrary power and often desire not to publish ideas and positions contrary to their own. Wheeling has the good fortune of being rewarded by its proximity to Pittsburgh, Pennsylvania, just a one-hour, interstate drive north of the city. Pittsburgh provides nationally recognized medical facilities, vast cultural and entertainment venues and robust economic opportunity.

As Wheeling strives to compete and recover its once charitable splendor and quality standing, it persists to some degree to be a covetous isolated bedroom community for the few surviving "ne plus ultra." We, thus, remain an appealing, but disengaged community, struggling to avoid the insular poverty that plagues much of the state. We are losing our educated young, while exercising a seemingly futile attempt to discover replacement for surrender of the core retail and manufacturing base of the past and recovery from economic obsolescence. However, like many others, I continue to love Wheeling for some of what it is, much of what it once was, and hope that it will someday soon reclaim its deserving prominence.

BIBLIOGRAPHY

Author's Interviews:
Sheffield T. Abood, Fort Pierce, Florida
Jesse Anderson, Wheeling, WV
Dominick Bartone, Cleveland, Ohio
Frank "Sonny" Blake, Wheeling, WV
Chauncey Browning, Esq., Charleston, WV
James Byrum, Esq., Wheeling, WV
Lou "The Mailman" Calagis, Matthews, NC
Leo Calandros, Point Pleasant, WV
George Caravsious, Esq., Wheeling, WV
Tom Cerra, Wheeling, WV
State Senator John Chernenko, Wellsburg, WV
Charles Comas, Wheeling, WV
Joseph Covello, Hallandale, Florida
Vic Cullota, Youngstown, Ohio
Dr. Angelo Daniels, Wheeling, WV
Don Daniels, Wheeling, WV
Pete Demus, Steubenville, Ohio
Robert Dorn, Wheeling, WV
Rich Heslop, Columbus, Ohio
Fritz Falcone, Wheeling, WV
Bernard Folio, Clarksburg, WV
Dominick "Mink" Gaudio, Follansbee, WV
Curt Griffith, Wheeling, WV
Jimmy Griffith, Wheeling, WV
Dr. Angelos Georges, Wheeling, WV
James Guida, Weirton, WV
Dewey Guida, Weirton, WV
Charles "Jocko" Jacovetty, Wheeling, WV
David Jividen, Esq., Wheeling, WV
Edward "Catfish" Joseph, Wheeling, WV
Johnny Joseph, Wheeling, WV
Joe Knoll, Wheeling, WV
Gus "Nitro" Kougenakis, Wheeling, WV
Alice Lias, Wheeling, WV
Gregory Manos, Wheeling, WV
Johnny Mathews, Wheeling, WV
Tommy Mathews, Wheeling, WV

Bob McDade, Wheeling, WV
Robbie "Little Flash" McKee, Wheeling, WV
G. Michael Fahey, Wheeling, WV
Joseph Mucheck, Benwood, WV
Joseph "Chinky" Nassif, Wheeling, WV
Ernie Nemeth, Lorraine, Ohio
Domenick Orlando, Wheeling, WV
Dr. John Palmer, Wheeling, WV
William G. Petroplus, Esq., Wheeling, WV
Parry Petroplus, Morgantown, WV
Dr. Richard Hawkey, Bradenton, Florida
Morey Rivlin, Wheeling, WV
Joseph "Dolly" Seriani, Fairmont, WV
Freddy Shia, Wheeling, WV
Anthony "Herk" Sparachane, Benwood, WV
Ray Thalman, Cambridge, Ohio
John "Sheriff" Tiano, Clarksburg, WV
Mike Vasilou, Wheeling, WV
Peter Vogler, Lexington, Kentucky
Andy Zaleski, Wheeling, WV
Anthony Zambito, Wheeling, WV

Magazines, Journals and Newspapers quoted:
Pittsburgh Press
Wheeling News Register
Wheeling Intelligencer
Miami Herald
Charleston Gazette
Charleston Daily Mail
Cleveland Plain Dealer
Detroit News
Syracuse New Times
Time Magazine
Life Magazine
Coronet Magazine
Greektown
San Diego Reader
WV Penitentiary Official Report
Detroit News Rearview Mirror
Harry Hamm 1964 Investigation

Unpublished Material:
Brief History of the Northern Panhandle; anonymous; undated, circa 1992.

Letters:
Letter, Paul Hankish to "Gummer" Yahn, March 10, 1995
Letter, Paul Hankish to Christopher Hankish, September 26, 1995

Books cited:
Ultimate Sacrifice, Russell Tarby
The Fall and Rise of Jimmy Hoffa, Walter Sheridan
The Prince, Machiavelli
The Other America, Michael Harrington
The Rich and the Super Rich, Ferdinand Lundberg
Killing Time, Donald Freed & Raymond Briggs

State, County and Local Agency Reports cited:
Criminal Identification Bureau, WV Dept. of Public Safety
California Commission on Crime, March 1949
West Virginia Board of Probation and Parole
District #6, Pre-Parole Report, James Frame
Criminal Court of Marion County
WV Probation and Parole Officer's Field Report

Archives:
Cuban Information Archives, Lefty Clark
Archive.com/ctrl/@listserv.aol.comty
Vanderbilt University Television Archives

Studies:
Dr. Fredrick Hoffman

Radio Columnists:
Drew Pearson, January 1952, *Wheeling News Register* by Shar Southall

Federal Government Agency Reports:

- Drew Pearson, January 1952, *Wheeling News Register* by Shar Southall
- FBI Memo to J. Edgar Hoover, Report PGD 92-231; Gladys Bradley Murder
- FBI FOIA, May 23, 1955
- FBI Pittsburgh Field Office, October 23, 1990
- U.S. Internal Revenue Agent report to FBI re; Lias "numbers" game
- Dept. of Justice Bureau of Investigation, U.S. Penitentiary, Atlanta GA.
- U.S. Dept. of Corrections, 1931 & 1932
- U.S. Immigration & Naturalization Service 1932
- IRS/FBI 1948 File 73-402w
- FBI Memo May 23, 1955
- FBI Memo December 12, 1956, Tolson to Congressman Dante B. Fascell, Fla.
- FBI Memo to J. Edgar Hoover, August 14, 1947
- Department of Justice Report 1962
- FBI Report File PG 231 1959
- FBI Report File PG 231 1960, Lias declared U.S. citizen
- FBI Report Anti-Racketeering, File 62-9, September 22, 1960
- FBI Report File 92- 3217, November 24, 1961
- FBI Report February 16, 1964 Issue of *Wheeling News Register*
- FBI Hankish Surveillance Report, 1967
- FBI Report File 62-227 August 31, 1967
- House Committee on Assassinations 1979
- Wheeling Workshop of the Central West 1930

INDEX

A

Academy Billiards 184, 199, 231
Aggie's 217
air traffic controller 23
Alabama Invisible Empire, Knights
    of the Ku Klux Klan 63
Albert Anastasia 193
Albert Berry 46
Al Capone 60, 61, 291
Al Cowlings 228
Alderson, West Virginia 51
Alice 85, 86, 100, 105, 116, 122,
    134, 145, 168, 201, 202, 225,
    226, 262, 300
Alice Lias 85, 116, 122, 134, 202,
    225, 226, 300
Allen's Coffee Shop 184
Alley C 42
Al "Mags" Magrini 179
Alma's Red Barn 150, 217
Al Molnar 179
Almost Heaven, West Virginia 219
Al Ross 144, 157, 171, 174, 229
Amanda Kurl 266
American Bayer Corporation 108
American Social Hygiene Associa-
    tion 128
American war veteran 37
AMVETS Post 171
Andy Malchano 31
Annie's Dream 87
Ann Margaret 230
Anthony "six toes" Baio 57
Anthony "Skippy" Salerno 257
Antoinette Kokoliades 40
Antonio "Undo" Sparachane 149
Appalachian coal fields 44
Aqueduct 139, 140
Archbishop of Ireland 46
Arch Riley 81, 168, 277
Army-Navy Club 273
around the world is fifty 218

Art Rooney Sr. 236, 245
Assistant Director of Highways 283
Assistant U.S. Attorney David
    Jividen 237
Assistant U.S. Attorney, John Reed
    239
Atlanta Constitution 62
Atlanta penitentiary 61
Atlantic City 254
Atlantic Coast region 286
Attorney General of the United
    States 195
August Petroplus 70
Austin V. Wood 33, 73, 81
Automatic Cigarette Company 90
Auto Ranch Incorporated 176
Avellino Christmas tree 28
Avellino extended family 13

B

Baby Ruth 31
Baccarat crystal 248
Badge of Military Merit 39
baked cod fish 28
baked lamb 122
Baltimore Lunch 34, 35
Baltimore & Ohio 41
bank chairman 105
Baptists 265
Barbara 29, 213
BARB'S BONGO 217
Barbuit at Billy's 150
Barbuit table 147, 149
Bartender, Ft. Henry Billiards 183
Baseball Tickers 184
Basil 6, 40, 41, 42, 43
bathtub gin 47, 58
Baton Rouge 172, 173
Battaglia/Trotta family 125
Battista 196
Bayer Aspirin 108
Bay Rum 263

Bay Rummers 263
beer hijacking 198, 232
beer license 168
Beirut, Lebanon 191
Bella Via restaurant 215, 290
Bellview, Kentucky 178
Belmont County, Ohio 185
below the bridge 216
Bengals 258
Benny Phillips 160
Benwood 11, 17, 20, 21, 23, 24, 31,
32, 39, 40, 67, 149, 150, 172,
266, 281, 282, 301
Bernard Folio 159, 300
Big Bill 6, 9, 43, 46, 48, 52, 61, 62,
67, 70, 76, 78, 86, 87, 88, 91,
94, 100, 103, 105, 107, 108,
110, 112, 122, 129, 132, 133,
134, 136, 142, 144, 147, 149,
154, 161, 167, 168, 201, 221,
225
Big Creek Mining 290
Big Red 176, 189, 217, 218, 269
Bill Alvarez 287, 289
Billy Conn 229
Billy's 144, 147, 148, 150, 157, 163,
165, 168, 169, 217
Birmingham 64
blackjack dealer 225
blackjack table 214
Black Muslims 239
Black Panthers 271
Blue Laws 113
blushing boys 127
Boat Rides 90
Bobby Baker 287
Bobby Lane 214
Bobby Stupak 242
Bob Levenson 278
B&O "Bulls." 33
B&O hospital 36
bookmakers 11, 90, 91, 257
bootlegger 48, 132, 134
Boston 141

box men 148
Boy Scouts 102
Brentwood 228
Bridgeport, Ohio 192, 242
Brooklyn 52, 88, 165
brother-in-law, Greg 221
Brown University 283
Bruno 211, 226, 273, 274
Bugsy Siegel 160
Building Service Employees Union
138
bullpen girls 54
Bull's nightstick 34
Bureau of Immigration & Natural-
ization 117

C

Cabinet Secretary 285
Cadillac Square 144
California 113, 228, 302
Camp Fairchance 267
Camus 31
Canada 49, 72, 115, 213
Canadian Club 214
Canadian government bonds 196
Canadian liquors 48
Canton, Ohio 57, 239
Capone mob associate 57
Carla Aldina Dellebra 240
Carl G. Bachman 73
Carlos Marcello 137
Carnegie 43, 242
CAROUSEL 217
casino owners 148
Castro's revolution 196
cathedral on Eoff Street 121
Catherine McNicol Stock 59
Catholics 251, 265
Catoris Candy Store 196
Cedar Bar 217
Center for Disease Control 146
Center School 117

Center Wheeling 42, 43, 67, 70, 96, 98, 103, 114, 118, 142, 152, 183, 203, 231, 260
Center Wheeling Outdoor Market 43
Center Wheeling Savings Bank 70
Central Park West 45
CEO of Chrysler/Dodge 100
Chairman Carter 284
Chamber of Commerce 103, 222
Charles "Buddy" Jacovetty 237
Charles Callaway 201
Charles Street 125
Charleston 80, 183, 184, 219, 234, 258, 265, 268, 269, 284, 285, 290, 300, 301
Charleston Daily Mail 265, 268, 269, 301
Charleston Gazette 234, 265, 284, 301
Charles Wasserman 122, 123, 124, 136
Charlie Brown's 257
Charlie Jr. 215
Charlie Kupchak 152
Charlie Maroon 278
Charter House 185
Chauncey Browning 290, 300
Checkers 32
Chester Stupak 242
Chester, West Virginia 140, 156, 157
Chicago 46, 59, 61, 74, 114, 216, 244, 281
Chief of Detectives Davis 282
Chief of Police 96, 118, 128, 151, 176, 178, 186, 190
chopped liver 251
Christmas 27, 28, 30, 36, 38, 49, 98, 105, 250, 270
Christmas Eve 28, 38
Christmas Eve culinary exhibit 28
Christopher Paul 191
Chrysler Imperial 178

Chrysler products 263
Chuck-a-Luck 67
Chuck Colson 195
Chuck Comas 110, 111
Chuck Little 283
CIA coup 291
CIA-Mafia plots 292
Ciero brothers 139
Circuit Judge for Kanawha County 219
City County building 189
City Emperor 219
city manager 53, 73, 78, 93, 219
City Officials 80
Clarksburg 68, 159, 168, 300, 301
Cleveland 7, 48, 73, 82, 94, 105, 113, 139, 161, 165, 172, 174, 177, 201, 215, 240, 257, 286, 287, 288, 289, 291, 292, 300, 301
Cleveland Indian baseball caps 288
Cliff McWilliams 127, 184
Cloverdale milk 29
coal room 35
Coast to Coast 149, 150
cocaine trafficking 233
coke bottle glasses 153
College basketball 212
Collins Avenue 168
Colonel's Sausage 145
Colonnade Dining Room 225
Columbus 166, 251, 300
Comas brothers 111
Community Market 273
Congress 116, 121, 129
Connecticut College 59
contract killers 204, 221, 251
Convertible Club 172
Cook-Waite Laboratories 108
Copacabana 257
cornstalk fiddles 20
Coroner 11, 204, 240
coroner's jury 94
Coronet Magazine 133

Corrections Commissioner 283
Cosa Nostra 156, 160, 194, 197, 253
cosmopolitan whorehouse 53
Counsel for Hazel Park 138
Country Club 103, 173, 174
county sheriff 224
Cowboy Willis 24
Crime Castle 267
Croatian and Serbian songs 20
Cuba 158, 193, 291, 294, 295
Cuban gun running 292
Cuban Information Archives 193, 302
Cuban leaders 291
Cuban Revolution 289
Curt 275, 300
Curtis Trent 188
Customs agents 291
Czechoslovakians 35

D

daily double 94, 139
Dallas, Texas 186, 248
Dan McKee 67
Darkies 63
David Brinkley 290
David Stern 14
Davy the Jew 14
D.C. lobbyist 287
D.C. Muslims 251
DD-214 38
DEA 237, 238
Deane and David Heller 133
Dean Martin 60, 158
Deborah Ramirez 193
DeCavalcante family 192
Delaware 132, 134
Delaware's watchdog 132
Delegate 82
Demas 146
Democratic victory 170
Denmar Correctional Center 284
dental technician 261
deportation battle 120

depot office 23
Detective Noll 176
Detroit 7, 48, 49, 52, 74, 100, 106, 115, 137, 166, 172, 174, 250, 301
Detroit Mafia 7, 137
Detroit News 49, 301
Detroit River 49
Dick Bowden 128
Dick Wright 162
Different Cities 111
Dion Warwick 230
director of the FBI 259
Disco and Go Go 231
District Judge C. McGarrahy 119
Dobkin family 282
Dodge City 145
Dodge Estate 100, 106
dog tags 37, 38
Dollar Savings Bank 104, 109
Dolly's Bird Land 273
Dominican Republic 287, 291
Dominick Bartone 286, 289, 290, 291, 292, 300
Dominick Orlando 269
Donald R. Clark 237
Donegal Township 229
Don Marsh 284
Dormas 146
Doug Haas 252
Douglas MacArthur 82
Downtown Wheeling 27, 216
Dr. Forrest Kirkpatrick 167
Dr. Randolph J. Hersey 118
Dr. Thomas Knapp 266
dry snitch 204, 279
DUCK INN 217
Dun & Bradstreet 154

E

east coast syndicate 90, 93
Eastern Conference 214
Eastern establishment 44
Easter outfits 21

Easter Parade 21
East Liverpool 60
East Wheeling 9, 73, 109
Echard "Whitey" Brown 191
Eddy Cantor 59
Eden Roc Hotel 230
Ed Sullivan 121
Ed Tolbert 176, 188
Edward Bennett Williams 160, 258
Edward J. DeBartolo 212
Ed Weith 128
Eisenhower 31, 32, 82, 123, 125
Elby's Big Boy 212
ELECTRIC CHAIR 270
Elkins, West Virginia 68, 107
Ellis Island 41
Elm Grove 57, 178, 191, 263, 290
Elsa Russell 73
E.L. Steinbecker 67
Emil George 175
Eoff Street 106, 121
Espionage Act of 1917 45
Esquire Supper Club 224
Eucharist 161
Euclid Avenue 288
Eugene Giampolo 22
Eugene Meacham 74
Execution Change 270
extortion 237, 238, 252, 259, 268, 269

F

Fairgrounds 84
Fairmont, West Virginia 66, 173, 273, 274
Far East restaurant 191

FBI 8, 51, 54, 57, 62, 66, 68, 76, 79, 80, 81, 83, 89, 91, 92, 101, 103, 104, 106, 116, 118, 125, 131, 133, 134, 137, 144, 147, 155, 156, 157, 158, 159, 161, 163, 165, 167, 168, 172, 177, 192, 194, 197, 198, 199, 200, 220, 224, 225, 234, 237, 238, 240, 259, 268, 288, 290, 303
FBI agents 116, 157, 165, 168, 194, 225, 268
FBI files 62, 66, 76, 80, 144, 147
FBI memorandum 81, 118
FBI report 89, 106
Federal authorities 162
federal building 197
Federal Bureau of Investigation 8, 65, 125, 176
federal district court 119
Federal Housing Program 85
federal judge 107, 109, 136
Federal Judge Harry Watkins 133
Federal Road Camp 51
Ferdinand Lundberg 302
Fidel Castro 158, 289, 292
Firestone Building 106
Flamingo Grill 21, 149
Flamingo in Vegas 160
Florida 87, 133, 168, 170, 193, 226, 228, 234, 252, 253, 257, 258, 300, 301
FOIA 66, 156, 303
Follansbee 60, 300
Fort Henry Club 103, 111
Fourth Circuit Court of Appeals 108
Fourth of July parade 103
France 46, 168
Frank Castiglia 113
Frank Costello 45, 90, 113, 119, 258
Frank "Lefty" Rosenthal 243
Franklin Delano Roosevelt 29
Frank Slemaki 35
fraternal organizations 103

fried zucchini 28

Friendly City 61, 95, 103, 110, 128, 136, 144, 231

Fritz Falcone 218, 300

G

Gabriel "Kelly" Mannerino 193, 201, 211

Gambino Family 192, 193

gas rationing coupons 121

Gazette 234, 265, 266, 271, 272, 284, 285, 301

General Dwight D. Eisenhower 31

General Electric 66, 270

General Manager 88, 131, 132, 133, 158

General Motors 66, 263

Geoff Schumacher 242

George and Antoinette 83

George Boury 212

George Caravasious 136

George F. Mellott 180

George Kellas 165

George Marzic 266

George Retos 88

George Seibert 49, 52, 62, 69, 72, 74, 136, 149, 263

George Sidiropolis 283, 284

George W. Oldham 71, 73

Georg Jensen bowls 248

Geraldo Rivera 224

German Bank building 41

Gladys Bradley 52, 152, 303

Globe Amusement Company 78

Goldberg brothers 66, 152

Gold Coast 193, 194, 224

Gold Players card 243

Good Friday 251

gorilla 200

Governor Arch A. Moore 159

Governor Caperton 283

Governor Milton Shapp 272

Governor Moore 204, 237

Governor Neely 80

Governor of New Jersey 257

Governor of North Dakota 59

Governor's Mansion 204

Grace Kelly 137

Grandma Avellino 28

Grand Opera House 41

greasy spoon 221

Great Depression 9, 13, 16, 52, 121, 153

Greatest Generation 16, 24

Great Hall 41

Greece 117, 118, 119, 137, 168

Greek-Americans 70, 145

Greek-American veterinarian 88

Greek coffee houses 145

Greek Czar 52

Greek dice game 147

Greek Easter 226

Greek heritage 88, 167

Greek-Italian-American 27

Greek-Italian Catholic 13

Greek Orthodox Church 122, 163

Green Lantern 217

Gregory Manos 84, 116, 165, 168, 201, 225, 300

Greyhound racetrack 60, 226

Gus Petrakis 152

Gus Shaheen 240

gypsies 112

Gythion, Greece 117

H

half and half 218

Half Dollar Bank 130, 199

Hallandale 224, 257, 300

Hancock County 159, 162

handcuffed druggist 219

Harlem 45

Harmony Hill 20

Harry Clouse 91, 92

Harry Hamm 157, 170, 171, 179, 197, 301

Harry Richardson 187

Harry Wiedetz 91, 92

Hart, Schaffner and Marx 153
Harvard University 136
Harvard, Yale & Princeton Club
	136
Havana 158, 160, 193, 196, 292
Havana Casinos 160
Hazel Park 137, 138, 140, 141
Hazlett Avenue 199
H.C. Ogden 81
Heinz baked bean 39
Henry Jepson 278
Henry Robinson Luce 125
Herbert Hoover 9, 102
Herk Sparachane 282
High Street 11, 17, 18, 19, 21, 24,
	30, 31, 39
High Street boys 19, 24, 30, 31, 39
Hilton International 242
hired muscle 218
hit man 247
Hollywood celebrities 158, 224
Hollywood setting 85
Holy Communion 161
Holy Cross 258
horse book 78, 81, 90, 91, 92, 93,
	152, 154
hospital administrators 204
Hot Baller 21
Hot Springs 139
house of prostitution 97, 157, 186,
	187, 204
Howard Allen 171, 184
Howard Hughes 258
Hugh Hefner 258
Huntington, West Virginia 140

I

I.D. tags 37
Immigration and Naturalization
	Service 115, 119
Immigration Board of Appeals 119
indentured servants 218
Internal Revenue Commissioner
	134

Internal Revenue Service 8, 9, 68,
	130, 132, 133, 145, 199, 247,
	283
INVESTIGATION OF FEDERAL
	AUTHORITIES 280
Ippolito 226, 228, 255
Irish Jimmy Griff 271
Irving Slobtkin 197
Island of Sicily 17
Italian restaurant 228
Italians 17, 155, 169, 221

J

Jack Dempsey 149, 229
Jack Kelly 137
Jack Ruby 291, 292
James Byrum 182, 277, 300
James Caan 228
James Couzens 129
James E. Mathews 177
James T. "Blackie" Licavoli 48
James V. Bellanca 138
Janet's 217, 218
Jay Mathews 141
Jay Rockefeller's term in office 268
J. Edgar Hoover 54, 81, 103, 131,
	220, 303
Jesse Anderson 199, 200, 201, 204,
	255, 256, 259, 271, 274, 300
Jesse James 29
Jesus 29
Jew 13, 14, 15, 251
Jewish girl 52, 154
JFK political coordinator 162
Jim Edwards 140, 141
Jimmy G. 256, 271, 272
Jimmy Tripodi 160, 161
Jim Scott 175
Joe Adonis 90, 123
Joe Colangelo 183
Joe Dayten 71
Joe Nighten 71
Joe Trupo 168
Joe "Whitey" Dice 65

Joey Naples 192, 212
John Bruno 273, 274
John Crock 118
John D. Rockefeller IV 222
John F. Kennedy 125, 292
Johnny Adornetta 242
Johnny Joseph 148, 300
Johnny Lee 186
Johnny Mathews 53, 54, 260, 265,
    300
John Smith 242
John Snyder 172
Jo Jo Pecora 155, 156, 157, 159
Jolly Bar 172, 213, 214
Joseph Arrington 174
Joseph "Demus" Covello 192, 257
Joseph H. Hannon 125
Josephine 6, 13, 27, 28, 29
Josephine Avellino Gianopolis 13
Judge Alexander Holtzoff 124, 125
Judge Clarence P. Lemire 131
Judge Watkins 131, 137, 138
Justice Department 192, 247

K

Katherine Lias Caravasious 136
Kennedy appointee 162
Kennedy forces 162
Kennedy guy 163
Kennedy's father 162
Kennedy's Senate Crime Commit-
    tee 292
Keno Board 178
Kentucky bookmaker 212
Kentucky Derby 87
King of the Road 217, 220
knockout joints 145
Kokoliades family 41
Korean War 16
Krizaneks 24
Kroger 191

L

Laconia building 105, 109
Laconia Inc. 109
La Cosa Nostra 160
Las Vegas Hilton 243
Las Vegas Sun 242
Laurel & Hardy 213
LCN members 197
Leaders of organized crime 224
Lebanese 199, 212, 241
Lebanese extraction 241
Lefty Clark 193, 302
Lenny Strollo 192
Leo Colandris 274
Leona Helmsley 228
Lewisburg Prison 224
Lexington 87, 301
Lias/Seibert 71
Lid Man 21
Lieutenant C. G. West 180
Lieutenant Fred Risovich 179
Lieutenant William J. Thomas 176
Lilian Levin 154
Limited Video Lottery Operators
    282
Linsly Institute 221
Listerine 126
Little Chicago 46, 114, 216, 281
loan sharking 237, 238, 252
Looch & Helen's 217
Louis' bread wagon 42
Louis George 171, 174
Louis Goldberg 73
Louis Hat Shop 144
Louis Kartsimas 78
Louis M. Kulpa 176
low hanging fruit 139, 153
Lucky Luciano 137
Lyndon Johnson 159, 287

M

Machiavelli's doctrine 7
Macy's 98

Madam Lias 53
madams 96, 128
mafia 48, 159, 161, 162, 192, 211, 229, 252, 253, 284
Mafia chieftain 45
Mafia figures 170
Mafioso 161
mail fraud 235, 236, 269
Main Street 117, 118, 142, 263
Maître d' 230, 243, 244
majestic McLure 221
Malibu 228
Mamie 31, 32
managing editor 265
Mannerino family 289
mano il nero 28
marijuana smuggling 228
Marine war stories 31
Mario Puzo's 252
Market Street 78, 81, 92, 106, 126, 130, 174, 184, 197, 199, 200, 213, 216, 231
Marshall County 281
Marshall county courthouse 25
Marshall Plan 88
Marsh Wheeling stogies 21, 61
Martin at the Chinese restaurant 277
Martins Ferry, Ohio 172, 178, 240, 260
Mary Harris 44
Mary Pappas 105
Mary "The Peddler" 17
Marzic family 266
Matriarch 202, 226
Matzo ball soup 251
Maximum and Medium state penitentiaries 181
Mayfield Heights 288
Mayfield Italian-American Club 288
mayor of Pittsburgh 263
McCarran-Walter Act 115
McDonough 162

McLure Hotel 221
McMechen 14, 25, 67
Meatless Mondays 102
Meatless Tuesday 102
Medicaid 261
Meigs County 259
Melvin Pike 236, 272
Mercedes Benz 232
Mercurochrome 39
Methodists 265
Mexican 196
Meyer Lansky 90, 287, 290, 293, 294
Miami Condominium 228
Miami Herald 192, 252, 301
Miami restaurant 224
Michael Harrington 10, 302
Middle Eastern influence 221
Mike Gallo 138
Mike Kitchen 30, 35, 38, 39
Mike Moses 178
Mike Russell 54, 71, 72, 152
Mike Z. Kotellos 178
Mildred Klienedler 19
Miller's funeral 144
Ministerial Association 80
Mink Gaudio 87, 138
Missouri 38, 234
Mohammedan 265
Monster 205
Mora 22
Morey Rivlin 153, 154, 301
Morgan's Halfway house 156
Morgantown 250, 251, 301
Mother Jones 44
Mother Josephine 27
Moundsville 45, 180, 229, 250, 260, 261, 290
Mountain State 46
Moustache Pete 161
Mt. DeChantal Visitation Academy 144
Multi-Agency Organized Crime and Intelligence Unit 252

Murder Inc. 193
Murphy's 5 & 10 263
Muslims 239, 251
My Club 203

N

National AMVETS 171
national anthem 122
National Prohibition Act 46, 49, 61
Naturalization courtroom 118
Negro 33, 173, 199
Neiman Marcus 248
Nero Claudius Caesar 127
Net Worth Expenditures Method 130
Nevada 38, 39, 158, 172
Nevada Jones 38, 39
Newark, New Jersey Police Department 177
New England 141, 244
New Jersey 172, 176, 177, 192, 197, 225, 228, 239, 252, 254, 257
New Kensington, Pennsylvania 155, 171, 193
New Mexico 45
New Orleans 139, 172, 173, 216, 244, 245, 251, 292
News Register reporter 67, 174, 175
News Register staff writer 201
New Year 28, 250, 251
New Year's Eve 250
New York 9, 33, 41, 45, 54, 65, 68, 87, 88, 113, 137, 139, 161, 162, 165, 170, 177, 192, 193, 213, 226, 228, 255, 271
New York City 33, 41, 65, 68, 228
New York Costello family 113
New York families 161, 162
New York Families 193
New York, Gambino Family 192
New York guys 271
New York hotel 255
New York Police Department 177
Nicasia 226

Nick Frank 152
Nick Vosvick Miller 142
Nicky Scarfo 253
Night at the Casino 224
Norman Farber 173
Norman MacEwan 180, 188
Norteman 74
North American 64, 66
North American Newspaper Alliance Inc. 64
North Central West Virginia 159
Northern District U.S. Attorney 234
Northern Panhandle 76, 156, 162, 204, 302
northern West Virginia 162
Northern West Virginia 236
North Wheeling Hospital 177
NOSEY'S 217
numbers racket 76, 172
Nut 203

O

Oakland 191
Office of Price Administration 121
Ogden Corporation 141
Ogden Nothing 277
Ohio 9, 11, 12, 19, 23, 32, 41, 49, 54, 57, 60, 67, 73, 76, 81, 83, 84, 90, 91, 93, 94, 97, 104, 121, 132, 134, 143, 144, 146, 156, 157, 160, 161, 162, 167, 168, 170, 172, 173, 174, 177, 178, 180, 182, 183, 185, 186, 188, 191, 192, 201, 203, 214, 215, 231, 238, 239, 240, 242, 244, 259, 260, 264, 266, 277, 281, 286, 289, 300, 301
Ohio County Courthouse 12, 84
Ohio County Intermediate Court 173
Ohio County Prosecutor 54, 67, 168
Ohio County Sheriff 67, 91, 172

Ohio Democrat leaders 132
Ohio penitentiaries 143
Ohio River 19, 132, 157, 242, 264
Ohio State University 144
Ohio Valley General Hospital 11,
    97, 167, 201
Ohio Valley officials 67
O.J. Simpson 228
Old Lang Side 250
old man DeBartolo 249
old school 161, 213
Oldsmobile 164, 174
Ontario 49
Otto C. Boles 229
Outlaws 218
out of the Shoe 225
Owl's Lounge 82

P

Panas 72
pancreatic cancer 191
Pandelos 146
Pappas 105, 146
Pardon Board 272
Parkersburg 285
Parma, Ohio 174
parole board 52, 176, 179, 182, 185,
    187, 189, 283, 284
Parole Officer 180, 181, 184, 302
Parry Petroplus 221, 301
Past Posting 93
Patrias 40
Patricia Hankish 248
Patricia Rose Hankish 191
Patricia Worsham 178
Patty and Peter's house 276
Patty Bonovich 73
Paul Hankish 7, 11, 157, 164, 166,
    168, 173, 175, 180, 182, 183,
    188, 189, 190, 191, 199, 224,
    225, 226, 231, 232, 234, 235,
    241, 243, 244, 250, 252, 254,
    259, 269, 271, 277, 280, 281,
    291, 296, 302

Paul Nathaniel Hankish 6, 7, 144,
    164, 175, 182, 241
Pavlovian 24
Pearl Harbor 92
Pee Wee George 185, 276
Pee Wee Herman 138
pencil necked 288
Pennsylvania 54, 76, 91, 106, 124,
    138, 143, 155, 156, 157, 159,
    161, 162, 171, 192, 193, 196,
    197, 201, 227, 229, 231, 234,
    236, 242, 245, 272, 289, 292,
    298
Pennsylvania attorney 124, 229
Pennsylvania Crime Commission
    156
Pennsylvania Supreme Court 272
Pen Register 259
Pete 157, 161, 167, 241, 243, 244,
    245, 300
Peter Killi Hankish 191
petit-mal epilepsy 233
Phalaenopsis Orchids 226
Philadelphia, Pennsylvania 197
Phil Mattuci 60
Pilgrim 265
pimps 54, 128, 152, 218
PINK ELEPHANT 217
Pirate Café 142, 143, 144
pit boss 148
Pittsburgh 51, 54, 57, 65, 82, 103,
    105, 106, 118, 122, 125, 136,
    137, 144, 156, 157, 162, 167,
    172, 173, 178, 192, 214, 229,
    233, 235, 236, 237, 238, 241,
    242, 254, 257, 259, 263, 271,
    276, 277, 289, 298, 301, 303
Pittsburgh family 156
Pittsburgh Field Office 57, 303
Pittsburgh Genovese family 192,
    229
Pittsburgh mafia chieftain 192
Pittsburgh, Pennsylvania 106, 157,
    298

314

Pittsburgh Post Gazette 271
Pittsburgh Press 233, 235, 237, 238,
    254, 301
Pittsburgh Steelers 214, 236
Planning Division 179
played cards and shot dice 235
playoff bowl 214
Plymouth 200
pneumonia 58
police chief 53, 93, 128, 219
polio vaccine 16
Polish Prince 242
Poor Farm Cemetery 38
Portsmith R.I. 254
postmaster 73
Potista 117
Presidential candidate 45
Presidential Pardon 230
President Kennedy 162, 196, 292
President Nixon 33, 195
president of a Wheeling bank 276
President Roosevelt 63, 102, 121
President's Food Committee 102
President Truman 116
Prime Minister 113
Princeton 46, 136
prizefighter 239
Professional odds makers 212
Progressive "Bull Moose" 45
Prohibition 46, 47, 48, 49, 52, 61, 91
Project Best 283
Prosecutor's office 168, 278
prostitution 53, 97, 124, 127, 128,
    157, 170, 176, 178, 186, 187,
    204, 217, 219, 231, 259, 261,
    281
provolone cheese 28
P.T. Barnum 242
public health menace 96, 98
Publisher of the *Wheeling News
    Register* 277
punitive segregation 262
Purple Gang 48, 137
Purple Heart 39

Q

Queen of Las Vegas 243

R

Racing & Sports book parlor 243
racket czar 134
Raleigh County 181
Randolph County 250
Raven 128, 217
Raven's Roundhouse 217
Ray "Boots" Highland 57
Rayburn House Office Building 287
Raymond P. Briggs 228
Red Dog 156, 157
Regal Coffee Shop 197, 231
Republican Senator 129
Republican Williams 132
reputed racketeer 236
Revenue Agent 65, 303
Reverend Charles Aurand 191
Rhode Island 234, 254, 256, 283
Richard M. Nixon 31, 32
RICO conspiracy 234
RICO statutes 282
Ringer Brothers 152
R.L. Bonar 179
Robert "Codfish" Bricker 271
Robert Dean 180
Robert Di Niro 243
Robert E. Lee 63
Robert Maheau 258
Robert Sam Anson 292
Robert "Skinner" Lee 249
Rogers Hotel 232
Roger Stuart 238, 254
Ron Asher 239
Rose Bowl Café 191
Rosemarie Hankish 192
Rosie 24, 25
Rosie Willis 25
Rouhana Naim 275
Round the World 128
route 30 156

Roy Hundley 57
Russell brothers 62
Russell Morman 173
Russ Tarby 292

S

Sacrament of Penance 161
Saddle Oyster Bar 171
safecracking gang 174
Safecracking tools 174
salami 211
salmon 82
Salvation Army 27
Sam "Ace" Rothstein 243
Sammy Bettini 214
Sammy Davis Jr. 243
Sam "The Plumber" DeCavalcante 252
Samuel Karson 266
San Diego 250, 301
Sands Point, Long Island 45
Sandy Wells 266
San Francisco 43, 212
Sans Souci Hotel and Casino 193
Santa Claus 34, 195
Santa Monica 228
Santo Trafficante 292
Saporitos 24
Scarnecchias 24
school teacher 219
Scoreboard Billiards 171
Scullys 24
Sears & Roebuck catalogues 62
second class whores 53
second degree murder 284
Secretary of the Treasury 129
Securities Commission Investigator 290
Sedition Act 45
Senate Crime Investigation Committee 171
Senator Estes Kefauver 132, 170, 171
Senator Joseph McCarthy 222, 258

Senator Kefauver 171
Senator Mathew Neely 131
Senator Rockefeller 223
Senator Taft 82
Sergeant K.J. Neely 175
Sheriff Warren Pugh 172
Shoot the Banker 59
Shorty Fragale 152
Sicilian 28, 57, 288
Simone "Sam the Plumber" DeCavalcante 252
Sinclair gas station 121
Sinclair Oil franchisee 122
singeing 111
slot machine mogul 134
Slovakian 20
Smitty 110, 111, 112
Social Security Administration 197
social security fraud 236
Social ticket 45
sodomy 46
Sons of Scarface 224
Soup List 67
Soup Money 72
South America 6, 234
South Benwood 21
Southern California 228
Southern Italian dialect 287
Southern Italians 17
southern West Virginia 44
South Florida's elite 257
South Ocean Drive 224
Sparachane 149, 282, 283, 301
Spartan 40, 100, 115
Spiro Agnew 287
Star Clothing 14
Stardust Casino 243
State Capitol in Charleston 290
State Maximum Security Penitentiary 180
State of West Virginia 133, 175, 186, 290
State Penitentiary 38, 45, 229, 260, 267, 270, 290

state senator 162, 163
St. Clairsville, Ohio 231
steakhouse/casino 81
Steeler's Super Bowl 257
steelworker 103, 191
Stella and Stanley Lewandowski 21
Sterling Drug 108
Steubenville, Ohio 60, 157, 160,
    214, 244, 300
St. John the Divine 122, 226
St. Louis, Missouri 38
Stockholm syndrome candidates
    218
stolen food stamps 238
Stone & Thomas 27
Storeroom Building 106
straight lay 218
Studebaker 25
stuffed grape leaves 27, 211
Subversive Activities Control Board
    115
Summit County 175
Sunday Blue Laws 113
Sunday Mass 161
Sunday paper 149
Sunset Club 191
Super Bowl 241, 244, 257
Switzerland 168
synagogue 154
Syrian 199, 200
Syrian extraction 199

T

Taft 45, 82, 160
tamburas 20
Tampa, Florida 193
Tannenbaum 28
task force on organized crime 289
tax court 130
tax stamps 145
Teamster's Presidency 195
Teamsters Union 138, 155, 193, 292
Tec-Chem Research and Develop-
    ment Corporation 287

Teddy Roosevelt 45
Tel-Autograph 85
Ten Commandments 154
Texas 166, 186, 234, 248
The Loop 217
The Menu 217
Theodore Russell 68, 75
The Rich & The Super Rich 170
The Torch 217
THIRD DEGREE 151
Thomas Krebs 290
Thomas Saad 182
Time magazine 125, 132
Tirre Shoe Company 109
Titanic 46
tobacco chewing johns 53
Tocca 138, 140, 141
Tom Duval 67
Tom Maren 141
Tommy Gianopolis 14, 23, 27
Tommy "Tomo" Tsoras 148
Tom Nagem 183
Tom O'Brien 183
Tom Padden 177, 183
Tony "Pro" Provenzano 211
Tony Z's brother 215
Top Hat restaurant 251
Trans-American Press Service 90
Trooper S.S. Satterfield 178
True Detective magazine 110
Turks 221
Turnkey 286
Two Western Pennsylvania mob
    leaders 292

U

Un-American 115
UNCIVIL SERVANT 132
Uncle Bill 72, 104, 136, 137, 165,
    168
Uncle Sam 103, 133
Uncle's bakery wagon 48
Uncle's horse-drawn bread wagon
    43

underboss 156
Undercover agents 159
Underworld characters 170
Undo 149, 150, 282, 283
Undo's youngest son 282
Union Grill 159
Uniontown, Pennsylvania 236
Uniontown racketeer 272
United States 5, 6, 8, 9, 16, 45, 50,
        59, 64, 71, 85, 90, 104, 109,
        116, 118, 119, 124, 125, 129,
        130, 131, 132, 133, 134, 155,
        158, 159, 162, 193, 195, 217,
        235, 237, 238, 245, 283, 289,
        292
United States government 45, 71
United States Government 132
United States senator 104
United States Supreme Court 16,
        116, 131
urban renewal 286
U.S. Army 88
U.S. Attorney 57, 71, 72, 74, 104,
        118, 155, 234, 236, 237, 238,
        239, 240
U.S. Attorney General Robert F.
        Kennedy 118, 155
U.S. Attorney Gibson 71, 74
U.S. Department of Justice 125
U.S. District Attorney Robert E.
        Maxwell 155
U.S. District Court 119, 124, 125,
        137
U.S. District Judge Robert Merhige
        255
U.S. Food Administration 102
U.S. House of Representatives 292
U.S. Immigration Service 122
U.S. Senate 8, 48, 63, 137, 171
U.S. Senator Jennings Randolph
        159
U.S. Senator John J. Williams 132
U.S. Senator Neely 80
U.S. Tax Court 130, 132

V

Vanderbilts 43
Vanderbilt University Television
        Archives 290, 302
Vegas wild men 242
venereal disease clinic 53, 97
Venezuela 141
Vermont Street 183
Vice-President Nixon 33
Vicky's Green Door 217
Victorian Era 216
Victorian splendor and values 46
Victor Lubijewski 254
vigilant Janet 217
Vincenzo Sciappa 28
Vito Genovese 193
Volkswagen 261
Volstead Act 49

W

Wailing Wall 18
Walgreen's Drug store 109
walk ins 232
Walter Gribben Jr. 108
Walter Sheridan 291, 302
Walter W. Dillon 180
wardens and administrators 269
War Production Board 121
Warren Commission 292
Warwood, West Virginia 164, 260
Washington Avenue 52
Washington County, Pennsylvania
        76, 229, 245
Washington, D.C. 115, 119, 124,
        125, 155, 223, 257, 286
water boy 244
Waterford Crystal 237, 247
Waterford Park 140, 141
Wedding Day Murder 272
Weidetz killing 94
Weirton 67, 162, 178, 179, 300
Weirton bank owner 162
Weirton Chief of Police 178

Weirton police department 179
Western civilization 44
western Pennsylvania 162, 196, 227, 242
Western Pennsylvania Mafia 54, 192
Western Union 90, 109
West Liberty State College 214
Weston Asylum 265, 266
Weston State Hospital 266
West Virginia Board of Probation and Parole 175, 302
West Virginia coal industry 290
West Virginia Ethics Commission 277
West Virginia Governor 155, 160, 188, 222, 266
West Virginia Governor Wally Barron 160
West Virginia Greek immigrants 42
West Virginia hoodlum 197
West Virginia House of Delegates 75
West Virginia Legislature 79, 297
West Virginia moonshine 132
West Virginia parolees 284
West Virginia-Pennsylvania state line 156
West Virginia Prohibition Act 46
West Virginia Racing Commission 79
West Virginia Report on Parolee 175
WEST VIRGINIA SNAKE'S CLUB 217
West Virginia State Fair Association 84
West Virginia State Police 67, 168, 175, 237
West Virginia State Troopers 86
West Virginia Supreme Court 203, 267
West Virginia University 267, 283

West Virginia University School of Medicine and Nursing 267
West Virginia U.S. Attorney 240
West Virginia voters 46
Wharf Parking Garage 263
Wheeling attorneys 124, 197
Wheeling Bank & Trust 106
Wheeling based U.S. Attorney 57
Wheeling Book Company 68
Wheeling businessman 138, 212, 213, 219
Wheeling business owners 278
Wheeling "Cat House" 127
Wheeling City Council 77
Wheeling city councilman 126
Wheeling city manager 219
Wheeling city officials 127
Wheeling community leaders 224
Wheeling Country Club 103, 173, 174
Wheeling doctors 118
Wheeling Downs 9, 11, 84, 85, 86, 87, 88, 106, 121, 131, 132, 133, 135, 139, 140, 141, 149, 166, 172, 226, 263
Wheeling Downs employees 140
Wheeling Downs Racetrack 9, 84, 86, 166
Wheeling eateries 146
Wheeling federal court 240
Wheeling German kids 169
Wheeling Intelligencer 63, 68, 71, 75, 109, 128, 270, 301
Wheeling Island 32, 84, 191, 240
Wheeling meat and produce vendors 269
Wheeling merchants 212
Wheeling native 146, 197, 249
Wheeling newspaper 44, 67, 73, 81, 83, 94, 127, 182, 184, 213
Wheeling newspaper reporter 83

Wheeling News Register 33, 46, 59, 67, 94, 104, 124, 126, 151, 164, 167, 170, 171, 175, 179, 197, 277, 301, 302, 303
Wheeling news reporter 94
Wheeling Park 262
Wheeling physicians 118, 212
Wheeling police 70, 94, 128, 165, 183
Wheeling Police Department 168, 176, 177
Wheeling Police officers 176, 178
Wheeling prostitution 53
Wheeling Public School system 117
Wheeling's elite 103, 218
Wheeling's elite businessmen 218
Wheeling's employable Greeks 88
Wheeling's mafia 284
Wheeling's numbers rackets 72
Wheeling Society for Crippled Children 224
Wheeling's Opera house 109
Wheeling's sanctimonious and sanctified citizens 8
Wheeling Steel Corporation 167
Wheeling stockbroker 120
Wheeling Symphony Orchestra 167
Wheeling syndicate 52, 53
Wheeling WASP 49
Wheeling, West Virginia 5, 40, 41, 105, 119, 134, 191, 197, 281
Wheeling Women's Club 222
White Front restaurant 92
wholesale jewelry company 197
Widow Russell 73
wild and wonderful Mountaineers 47
Wild and Wonderful West Virginia 159
Wilkinsburg, Pennsylvania 143
William E. Baker 70, 107, 108
William G. "Big Bill" Lias 6, 9, 43, 46, 70, 132, 201
William Hannig 102

William Kolibash 234
William Langer 59
William Sundell 254
Willie Mays 291
Windmill 278
Windsor Hotel 173, 263
wine steward 244
wooden matches 39
Woodrow Wilson 45
working girls 53, 54, 96, 98, 126, 127
WWII 11, 16, 213
WWII golden baby boomers 16